Understanding
Ancient Battle

Understanding Ancient Battle

Combat in the Classical World from the Unit Commander's Perspective

Hugh Elton

Pen & Sword
MILITARY

First published in Great Britain in 2023 by
Pen & Sword Military
An imprint of Pen & Sword Books Limited
Yorkshire – Philadelphia

ISBN 978 1 52675 397 7

A CIP catalogue record for this book is
available from the British Library

Typeset by Mac Style
Printed in the UK by CPI Group (UK) Ltd, Croydon, CR0 4YY.

Pen & Sword Books Limited incorporates the imprints of After
the Battle, Atlas, Archaeology, Aviation, Discovery, Family History,
Fiction, History, Maritime, Military, Military Classics, Politics,
Select, Transport, True Crime, Air World, Frontline Publishing, Leo
Cooper, Remember When, Seaforth Publishing, The Praetorian Press,
Wharncliffe Local History, Wharncliffe Transport, Wharncliffe True
Crime and White Owl.

For a complete list of Pen & Sword titles please contact

PEN & SWORD BOOKS LIMITED
47 Church Street, Barnsley, South Yorkshire, S70 2AS, England
E-mail: enquiries@pen-and-sword.co.uk
Website: www.pen-and-sword.co.uk
or
PEN AND SWORD BOOKS
1950 Lawrence Rd, Havertown, PA 19083, USA
E-mail: uspen-and-sword@casematepublishers.com
Website: www.penandswordbooks.com

Contents

Note on Units of Measurement, Names and Ancient Sources

Almost all distances discussed in this book that come from ancient sources are estimates, rather than measurements. The following equivalents are used here, and though not precise, are good enough for our purposes:

1 *plethron* = 30m
1 *stade* = 200m
1 Roman mile = 1.5km
1 bowshot = 300m (see discussion in Chapter 2.7)
1m = 1yd
1km = 0.6 modern mile
1kg = 2.2lbs

Latinate forms (Marcus) have been used throughout, rather than Greek forms (Markos) for personal and place names. Names from other cultures (Celtic, Persian, Punic, etc.) have also been given in Latin forms.

Greek words are *italicized*, with eta and omega marked by macrons, that is ē, ō. Latin words are underlined.

The military knowledge of both ancient writers and modern translators varies enormously. I've used the translations from the Loeb Classical Library for the most part, though all have been revised to a greater or lesser extent, most often to reflect the word order. For Vegetius I've used Milner's translation, for Mauricius' *Strategikon* the translation by Dennis. How consistently various technical terms were used by ancient authors remains a difficult topic, and the variety of terms for attack, engage, and push back often defies meaningful translation. The Greek word *ephodos* and the Latin word impetus are often translated as 'charge', but since the ancient words do not assume a running into combat I have used 'attack'.

Rather than using the traditional 'Persian Wars' and 'Punic Wars', these conflicts are here referred to as the Greco-Persian and Romano-Punic wars, respectively, to incorporate belligerents on both sides.

Note on Terminology

Light infantry (*psiloi*, *euzōnoi*, <u>velites</u>, <u>expediti</u>): Men lightly equipped, i.e. unarmoured, with no or small shields, usually intended to fight in loose formations with distance weapons such as javelins, bows, or slings. Typically deployed on the flanks of armies or as screens in front of the heavy infantry

Heavy infantry (*hoplitai*, *skutatoi*, <u>loricati</u>): Men fighting in the main line of battle, often armoured with large shields, intended to fight hand-to-hand.

Light cavalry: Men lightly equipped, i.e. unarmoured, with no or small shields, usually intended to fight in loose formations with distance weapons such as javelins or bows. Typically deployed on the flanks of armies.

Heavy cavalry: Cavalry with a focus on hand-to-hand combat, often armoured and deployed in close formations on the flank of armies.

List of Illustrations

Preface

O ver the past thirty years I've been fortunate to teach classes on ancient warfare at every university at which I've worked. Over this time, the content of these courses has changed greatly, and though students from the past few years will recognize much of the content of this book, those from earlier classes will see a great deal of change. My earlier focus on Roman structures and operations has now developed into a greater interest in the unit's battle across antiquity, but also in how ancient writers wrote about battle.

I've chosen to write boldly and with light referencing in this book. There is an enormous academic literature on ancient warfare, much of which is devoted to making an argument. Rather than engaging with this material directly, a process which would involve long footnotes and placing my detailed argumentation against that of others, I have chosen to write as much as possible from primary sources which are referenced in the text. In a wide-ranging work such as this there are inevitably going to be details that I've got wrong or overlooked, but I am confident that the overall argument is good.

I'm very grateful to Phil Sidnell for giving me the chance to discuss these topics, as well as for his patience in the time taken to provide a final manuscript and for his drawing the illustrations. I'm also very grateful to friends and colleagues who read draft chapters (Geoffrey Greatrex, Andrew McCoy, Simon Sharpe, and Conor Whately) though they bear no responsibility for the errors, to the students who helped develop many of my ideas, often by pointing out the problems with them, to audiences of various lectures and seminars over the years, and to scholars across the planet who have written articles and books, sent off-prints, and answered queries.

Location Map of the Battles

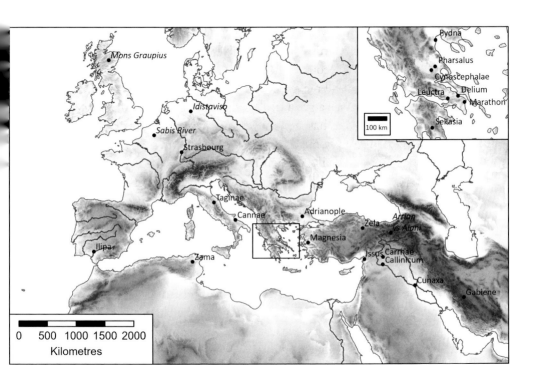

Chapter 1

Introduction

Understanding what happened when two armies met in an ancient battle was often ignored or passed over rapidly with few details by ancient writers. The fifth-century BCE Athenian Thucydides is justly praised as the first analytical historian, but he often said little about how ancient battle worked. Here is his description of a battle in 415 BCE between Syracuse and an allied force of Athenians and Argives.

> Coming to hand-to-hand fighting, for a long time they withstood each other. And there occurred meanwhile thunderclaps and some lightning and heavy rain. For those fighting in their first battle and least familiar with war, this contributed to their fear. But for those more experienced these events were thought to be from the time of year and their opponents not being defeated for so long provided their concern. The Argives first pushed back the left flank of the Syracusans, and after this the Athenians pushed back those opposite them. The rest of the army of the Syracusans began to break immediately and fell into flight (Thucydides 6.70.1–2).

This is descriptive, but not analytical, failing to tell us how the Argives and Athenians defeated their opponents. Such vagueness was not confined to Thucydides, but is a feature of primary sources for all periods of antiquity. Norman Whatley, in a seminal paper presented in 1920, wrote that 'the more I study the subject, the more sceptical I become about the possibility of reconstructing the details of these battles and campaigns with any certainty' (1964, 119). Despite Whatley's pessimism, however, from the late twentieth century something of a renaissance in ancient military studies has taken place, in many ways inspired by the publication of *The Face of Battle* by John Keegan in 1976.

The Face of Battle is a great book. Indeed, for many ancient historians, it is the only work about history outside the ancient world they have read, and perhaps the only work of military history they will ever read. It concentrates on the experiences of English or British troops in three major battles in northwestern Europe, at Agincourt in 1415, Waterloo in 1815, and the first day of the Somme offensive in 1916, taking a thematic approach so that battles are described in terms of men against men, men against horses, etc. For many historians, this focus on individual experience and the soldier's battle is a refreshing change from descriptions focussing on the general's battle. All too often, the approach taken by modern writers is that the Keegan approach is enough and that if we understand how men felt in ancient battles then our job is done. Examining individuals' experiences, however, is only one way to approach ancient battle. This book focusses above soldiers and below generals to focus on the regimental commander's battle.

1.1 Literary Sources

Any discussion of ancient battle must start with the literary sources, not all of which are of equal value. In antiquity history was a branch of literature, and so most historians writing in antiquity were interested in entertaining their audience and showing off their literary skills, as well as in presenting an accurate view of the past. In a serious fashion, the second-century BCE historian Polybius noted that:

> The point of History is first to get to know the words that were actually spoken, whatever they were, and second to learn the reason through which failure or success happened or was told. Although simply stating what happened beguiles us, it is of no benefit, but having added the cause, the use of history becomes fruitful (Polybius 12.25b.1–2).

By these standards, the description of the Battle of Syracuse quoted at the start of this chapter is lacking, even though Thucydides was an excellent political historian and stylist, and a well-informed contemporary who understood what he was writing about. In this, he differed from the Greek victim of a diatribe by the second-century CE writer Lucian in his satirical work *How to Write History*:

> Another, and this one is laughable, never having put his foot outside Corinth or gone as far as [its harbour] Cenchreae, never mind seeing Syria or Armenia, started thus, as I recall: 'Ears are less trustworthy than eyes, so I write what I have seen, not what I have heard'. And so accurately has he seen everything that he says about the dragons of the Parthians, although this is the standard for a host of them, and a dragon has a thousand men, I believe, that they are living dragons, enormous, he says, spawned in Persia just past Iberia. For a time they are tied to great poles and raised up high, bringing fear from afar as they advance; then,

when they get close, they are released and fall upon the enemy. Indeed, he said that many of our men were swallowed and others were wrapped round and then choked or broken; these were things that he saw himself, but in safety, however, making his observation from a tall tree. And it was well that he did this, not coming to the same place as the beasts, since we would not now have so amazing a writer (Lucian, *How to Write History* 29).

Many ancient battle accounts were highly formulaic, perhaps giving Lucian's victim confidence that he knew what he was doing. Lendon has recently discussed this (2017), noting a very common structure that begins with listing the troops engaged and how they were deployed, followed by speeches, a description, often very short, of the fighting and then an analysis of why the battle was won or lost. As Lendon points out, authors often described deployments in greater depth than actions and made little effort to relate the deployment and the battle description. Like most Hollywood movies, most ancient descriptions of battles are literary productions, so that we need to consider carefully how we use them in our analysis of battle. Our authors were not always eyewitnesses or participants, so if they were not describing their own experiences, we need to know what sources they used. And even when they were eyewitnesses, as Thucydides remarked of one action, 'it was not easy to learn from others in what way each thing happened. For by day events are more clear, but of those men doing all these things, each knows only about what is around them' (7.44.1).

1.2 Technical Military Writing

In addition to historians in antiquity writing about battles, there was an extensive field of technical military writing. Polybius suggested that there were three ways to learn generalship: from books, teaching, and experience (11.8.1). The earliest preserved theoretical writings come from the fourth century BCE, the *Cavalry Commander* by Xenophon and Aeneas Tacticus' *How to Survive Under Siege*. There was a wide range of genres, including technical handbooks (e.g. Hiero on artillery design and pseudo-Hyginus on the principles of camp layout), advice for generals (very generic in the case of Onasander, or lists of stratagems like those of Frontinus or Polyaenus), or books describing formations (Aelian, Arrian, Asclepiodotus, Urbicius). Sometimes these genres were combined in a single volume (e.g. Vegetius, Mauricius, Syrianus). Some authors show experience and technical knowledge, but others do not. The audience is often unclear, but is frequently emperors or philosophers, and

Mauricius' *Strategikon* is the only one written by and for soldiers. Arrian's *Order of Battle against the Alans* and Mauricius were original works, but others were highly derivative, and even Mauricius' work has some sections derived from Aelian. Thus, Urbicius' *Tacticon*, an early-sixth-century CE work, was an epitome of Arrian's *Tacticon* from the second century CE, but Arrian's work was, like that of his near contemporary Aelian and the first century BCE Asclepiodotus, derived from the lost *Tacticon* of Polybius via the philosopher Poseidonius. Similarities in all of these works thus reflect literary recycling, not unchanging practice. And though no one thought it strange for philosophers to write about battle, not everyone took their words seriously. Cicero told a story about Hannibal in exile. The Carthaginian general, having listened to a lecture on military matters from the philosopher Phormio, was asked what he thought. He replied said that 'he had seen many crazy old men on many occasions, but one crazier than Phormio he had never seen' (Cicero, *de Oratore* 2.75).

The institution of writing allowed best practices to be learned and passed on by literate societies, even if the works that we have are not always sure guides to Greek or Roman practice. This is very different from the way in which members of Celtic or Germanic tribes learned about warfare. The lists of stratagems as preserved by Frontinus and Polyaenus give a sense of what ancient writers thought was possible in battle, but we cannot use these to define what was normal. Polyaenus' chronological division of 900 stratagems is convenient for modern historians, but he is selective and, despite writing in the mid-second century CE, the majority of his examples come from the fifth to third centuries BCE. The chronological structure would make it hard to use as a reference tool for real generals, while the inclusion of stratagems used by the mythical Dionysus, Pan, and Heracles suggests an encyclopaedic approach rather than a practical one.

1.3 Material Evidence

Between the fifth century BCE and the sixth century CE, there were no important changes in the technology of hand-to-hand combat, though there were many changes in battlefield practice. Unlike most of the other elements discussed in this book, it is possible to model ancient equipment with confidence, and much good work has been done by reconstructors. The greatest value of this work is in understanding the equipment of individuals rather than its use in large formations in battle. The technology to produce ancient military equipment was available to all Iron Age societies, but the social organization and financial resources to produce equipment on a large scale was not. If individual elite warriors in fifth-century BCE Greece or first-century BCE Britain wished, they could have been equipped and fought in the same way as men in the armies of Alexander the Great or Scipio Africanus, but their societies could not have produced whole armies like this. Thus, the availability of armour, weapons and horses, and of training is important. Trying to understand the scale of issue helps us to avoid deterministic thinking and suggesting that victory was the result of equipment, and even when better equipment was available, it didn't automatically result in success on the battlefield.

1.4 Modern Historiography of Battle

Like an understanding of equipment, an understanding of how other societies approached warfare can often help in elucidating ancient warfare. Modern writers have much to say about how we write about war and warfare in general, and warfare in antiquity. Jeremy Black's 2004 volume *Rethinking Military History* is an excellent introduction to the field of military history as a whole, while Harry Sidebottom's 2004 *A Very Short introduction to Ancient Warfare* provides an excellent introduction to ancient military history. Many ideas from later periods can be usefully applied to the ancient world, although we should avoid the simplistic idea that because something was a later military practice, it must have happened in the same way in antiquity. However, the constraints of time, space, weather, and animal transport, are often better documented in other periods. The three-volume series edited by Millett and Murray on *Military Effectiveness* in the First World War, the interwar period, and the Second World War, has a very useful essay in its first volume on defining military effectiveness, showing the sorts of things that are often missing from our understanding of the ancient world. Their stress on the effectiveness of the armed forces in accessing state support for military activity is a modern conceptualization, but can be used as a tool to show the differences between the Roman Republic, where political and military success lay directly in the hands of those individuals supporting funding for a war, and either fourth-century BCE Athens or any Hellenistic kingdom, where the links were different. There are some very good books on later battle too, especially those by Rory Muir, Brent Nosworthy, and Paddy Griffith.

Modelling tools can also be used and, though not an approach taken here, they have been used very productively to examine ancient battle by Phil Sabin in his 2007 book *Lost Battles*. Such techniques are often useful in forcing attention to areas that might otherwise be missed, especially issues of time and space. One of the pioneering works in this respect is Trevor Dupuy's 1979 *Numbers, Predictions, and War* in which, despite an industrious and prolonged attempt to reduce every factor possible to a mathematical variable, his models are made to work by including a 'fudge factor' as a constant, thus drawing attention to the critical importance of the human factor.

1.5 This Book

This chapter has introduced some of the problems involved in writing about battle in antiquity. Like all of ancient history, battle is a complex business involving too many unknowns and great problems in handling source material. This book focuses almost as far as possible on the words of those who understood battle, not just those who wrote about it, with a preference for writers with military experience, especially Xenophon, Polybius, Caesar, and Mauricius. This focus on battle is very different from the (often unstated) desire of historians to reconcile the differences between all available sources. If all our sources were of equal value, e.g. eyewitness accounts, then this would be a good way to proceed, but we should not do this unless we believe our sources to be equally well-informed. I have thus focussed on case studies and then made some generalizations based on these rather than trying to generate a composite battle, taking evidence from a number of different events to gain an understanding of what actually happened in a 'typical battle'. However, no battle is typical, and such interpretations are shaped by events whose typicality we are often hard pressed to evaluate.

Our models of battle should have some relationship to the way in which ancient soldiers thought about battle. Thucydides in his description of the Battle of Syracuse that this chapter began with thus focused on the weather and experience of the troops, not on minutiae of tactics or equipment. This suggests that the lists of aphorisms contained in Onasander, Vegetius, and Mauricius are a good guide to what mattered to ancient generals, especially as they tend to fit the comments on best practice by Polybius and the descriptions of battle by Xenophon and Caesar.

A second point is that armies were combinations of many elements. Many modern historians have discussed the shortcoming of elements such as elephants, pike phalanxes, scythed chariots, cataphracts, or 'barbarized' late Roman infantry but less often confront the question of why contemporaries felt that these weapons were worth deploying. It seems more likely that the Seleucid king Antiochus III (223–187 BCE), one of the few men in antiquity to earn the title 'the Great', knew what he was about when he chose to field elephants or scythed chariots than some modern armchair historian like me, though whether Antiochus achieved what he wished to is a different matter. Thinking in these terms, rather than focusing only on results, may help us to assess the relative usefulness and weaknesses of these weapon systems. Although the tank is still one of the major weapon systems used by modern armies, it has many weaknesses: tanks are heavy (limiting their mobility in terms of long-distance transport as well as restricting them to certain bridges), very vulnerable when attacked from the side or rear, require infantry support in towns, and need to withdraw from the battlefield at night. Their crews' ability to see the battlefield is limited, unless their commanders exposes themselves. They also consume vast quantities of fuel and ammunition, are noisy, and break down often. Yet despite all these problems, tanks perform very well when used by generals who understand their limitations. Thus, unless we have well-informed contemporary evidence against it, we should accept that ancient generals usually knew what they were doing and used their weapons in the most effective way possible given the constraints of the time.

Finally, the concluding section of each chapter asks three questions:

- How was this period different from other periods?
- What could the regimental commander typically expect to do?
- How might a regimental commander affect the flow of the battle?

Chapter 2

Ancient Battle: An Overview

Most studies of ancient battle have focused on the soldier's battle or on the general's battle. This book focuses on the level between these two approaches, the regimental commander's battle and its concern with tactical matters. However, any rigid separation is artificial, and elements of all three levels of battle are occasionally incorporated into the discussion.

This chapter discusses ancient battle in general since many factors remained constant throughout antiquity. However, this does not mean that all battles were fought in the same way. By defining typical processes, we can think about which events were unusual and what was different about each period. Subsequent chapters focus on particular periods between the fifth century BCE and the sixth century CE.

2.1 Leadership, Friction and Luck

Battle involved many factors, some of which are hard to quantify. In the second century CE, Plutarch in his *Life of Pyrrhus* described a conversation between Scipio Africanus and Hannibal about who was the best general in history: 'Hannibal offered his opinion that of all generals the first in experience and ability was Pyrrhus, that Scipio was second, and he himself third' (*Pyrrhus* 8.2). Livy in the early-first century CE and Appian in the second century CE also told this story, though they made the order Alexander, Pyrrhus and Hannibal, and added Scipio's question to Hannibal about how he would have ranked them if he had been successful at Zama. The telling and retelling of the story suggests that generals were thought to be important to an army's success. But how?

One of the most important roles of a general was inspiring men. Alexander the Great was the best example of this, reviving a failing assault on the city of the Malli in 326 BCE by climbing a siege ladder and fighting hand-to-hand on the city wall before jumping down inside the city (Arrian 6.9–10). Many of his generals emulated his leadership, like Ptolemy defending a fort on the Nile against Perdiccas in 321 BCE, when he is said to have inspired his men by taking a sarissa and poking out the eyes of the lead elephant and wounding its mahout, then hurling other attackers back off their ladders (Diodorus 18.34.2).

And so did many generals in other periods, like Bessas, more than 70 years old, climbing a siege-ladder at Petra in Lazica in 550 CE (Procopius, *Wars* 8.11).

Leading like this was dangerous, and many generals were wounded or died in battle. This often led to defeat, as with Cyrus at Cunaxa in 401 BCE, Cleombrotus at Leuctra in 371 BCE, and Flaminius at Lake Trasimene in 218 BCE. Polybius was thus scathing towards Marcellus, killed in 208 BCE while scouting, and praised Hannibal for taking care of his own safety.

> For if the commander escapes unharmed, even if everything has collapsed, Fortune gives many starting points for recovery and minimizing reverses. But if he has fallen, just as the steersman of a ship, even if Fortune may give victory over the enemy to many, there is no benefit because all the hopes of each man depend on those leading (10. 33.3–5).

But generals could die and still win, as with Callimachus at Marathon in 490 BCE and Brasidas at Amphipolis in 422 BCE. Fewer generals died in battle in the Roman period.

Leadership was only one of many functions of generals, as shown by Onasander's handbook.

> A general should ride along the ranks, show himself to those in danger, praise the brave, threaten those who flinch, encourage those who hesitate, restore what is lacking, transfer a unit if necessary, assist the weary, and anticipate opportunity, the moment, the future (33.6).

This long list of tasks showed the need to constantly manage an army to reduce friction. Like leadership, friction is a nebulous concept, though well described by Clausewitz in the nineteenth century: 'everything in War is very simple, but the simplest thing is difficult'. Friction can be reduced with training and practice so that, for example, the time taken to change formation can be reduced, but it can never be eliminated. It increased with scale so that Vegetius cautioned that:

> a greater number is subject to more events. On marches because of its size it is always slower, a longer column is often ambushed even by a few men; in difficult country or at river crossings it is often caught in delays on account of the baggage. Moreover, fodder is collected with great labour for numerous animals and horses. Also difficulty with the grain supply, which should be avoided in every campaign, more quickly plagues larger armies (Vegetius 3.1).

Friction was predictable, but many unpredictable things happened in battle and could have significant consequences. Many ancient writers thus emphasized fate, chance, luck, fortune, and opportunity, very different from the way in which many modern historians analyse battles, even when they accept that they are non-linear dynamic systems. After some Pompeian successes at Dyrrachium in 48 BCE, Caesar thought the Pompeians had become too confident because 'they did not remember the common happenings of war, how often very small issues or false suspicion or sudden dread or religious scruples have caused great disasters.' (Caesar, *Civil War* 3.72.4). These sentiments were widely understood, so that even writers without military experience like Livy once noted that 'in war nothing is so trivial that it cannot sometimes be the cause of some great matter' (25.18.3).

For good reason then, many ancient generals were reluctant to enter battle. Plutarch's biography of Aemilius Paullus tells a story about the day before Pydna in 168 BCE:

Aemilius, when he united with Nasica, went out after deploying against the enemy. But when he saw their disposition and number, in admiration he stopped the advance, taking counsel with himself about this. The young officers, eager to fight, riding beside him, begged him not to delay, and of them all Nasica in particular, confident from his good luck on Olympus. But Aemilius smiling said: 'I would if I was your age, but many victories have taught me the failures of the defeated, and they prevent me from entering battle after a march against a phalanx already deployed and ready' (17.1–2).

In Plutarch's anecdote, Nasica's desire to engage reflected his youth, but Paullus was well aware of the common urge among soldiers to 'get on with it'. Thus, the Roman Emperor Julian's men before Strasbourg in 357 CE clamoured to be led into action now that they were finally face to face with the Alamanni, though like Paullus' men they too were weary after a long march. When to engage was a difficult decision for a general, and the difference between rushing into battle prematurely and seizing the initiative to catch the enemy off guard was often determined only by success.

Just as these unquantifiable concepts of leadership, friction, and luck should not be neglected in our attempts to understand ancient battle, we should not rely on them as explanations. It was foolhardy to rely on luck. In 409 BCE, an outnumbered Athenian army defeated the Spartans and their Megarian allies in a skirmish at the Horns. We have no details, but when news of their victory arrived, the Athenians 'became angry with the generals and were hostile to them, thinking that they took this risk hastily and gambled with the whole city' (*Hellenica Oxyrhynchia* 1.1–2). States, armies, and generals that prepared for battle tended to be more successful. As Mauricius said, 'it is not, as some inexperienced people believe, through courage and numbers of men that wars are won, but by the grace of God, tactics, and generalship' (Book 7, Introduction).

2.2 Training and Discipline

Armies are made up of groups of individuals acting together, with each of these levels having its own roles and skills. Individual skills, in fitness, weapons use, and riding, were often improved by formal and informal practice. Many cultures were praised in antiquity for having natural abilities, frequently in an exaggerated fashion. Polybius, Livy, Diodorus Siculus, and Strabo all told versions of a story that Balearic slingers were so effective because as children they were not allowed to eat until they had hit the target. Despite the repetition of the story, it is unlikely that Balearic slingers were significantly better than slingers from other parts of the ancient world, though we can neither prove nor disprove the assertion. State armies carried out more formal training, and Roman manuals give details of drills for marching and weapons. Training men as units required time away from other activities, so that it was mostly carried out by paid professionals. Training units to work together as an army was unusual, though it was sometimes practiced by state armies in lulls in the campaigning season. In general, the fighting skills of individual soldiers varied little over antiquity, but much greater attention was paid to unit training from the fourth century BCE onwards, especially by Roman armies, and to army training from the third century BCE, especially by the Romans.

Discipline was strongly related to training in terms of creating effective forces in battle. Going into battle was dangerous, and few humans or animals did this with comfort. For men to obey commands and to accept an unequal distribution of risk, affecting those at the front most, required a shared commitment to something. This commitment could be created by giving soldiers a group identity. Group identities could be formed by shared activities such as training, marching, fighting, and by rituals. Keeping men together for long periods of time also allowed these bonds to form while pride in one's city, tribe or people was another way to form group identity. Punishment was also required. If misdeeds of individuals were not punished then it was harder to keep men in the ranks, and it was general practice to put good men at both front and back of formations, as troops tended to slip away from the rear when battle started or began to go poorly.

2.3 Before the Battle

Before the day of battle, as armies neared each other, scouts were usually sent out to find out exactly where the enemy were. These scouts were usually cavalry, whose mobility would give them the best chance to return information in time for it to be acted on. With this information, a general might be able to choose a location for the battle that suited his purposes or even, if he were fortunate, to be able to ambush the enemy.

Finding the enemy was not always easy. Before Issus in 333 BCE, Alexander the Great had lost track of the Achaemenid Persians and allowed them to come between him and his supply lines back to Europe, forcing him to fight on ground chosen by the enemy, and in 378 CE Roman scouts near Adrianople wrongly believed that they had found an isolated part of the Gothic army that could be defeated in detail. The Roman Emperor Valens seized the opportunity, though as the battle began, it emerged that the Gothic force was larger than had been thought and that some of their cavalry had not been located. And fighting the Helvetii in 58 BCE, Caesar's subordinate Labienus had occupied a nearby hill with two legions. Caesar delayed battle because the commander of his scouts

> reported that the hill which Caesar wished to be occupied by Labienus was held by the enemy and that he had recognized them from their Gallic weapons and standards.... Much later in the day Caesar discovered from scouts both that the hill was held by his own men and that the Helvetii had moved camp and that Considius, terrified by his fear, had reported what he had not seen as seen by him (*Gallic War* 1.22).

Beyond giving information about enemy numbers, location, and perhaps intentions, good scouting might give a general more choices about how to engage than simply marching towards the enemy, perhaps allowing him to prepare an ambush, to detach a force for a flank attack, or to screen the main body of the army from enemy scouts. Demosthenes placed an ambush at Olpae in 426 BCE (Thucydides 3.107.3–108.1), Hannibal was able to install an ambush in a sunken stream bed before the Trebbia in 218 BCE (Livy 21.54), and the Roman Emperor Valentinian I sent out a flanking force at Solicinium in 368 CE to catch the Alamanni as they retreated (Ammianus 27.10. 915). In rare situations, generals were able to ambush the entire enemy army, as at the Teutoburger Wald in 9 CE when the Romans were ambushed by the German Arminius (Tacitus, *Annals* 1.50–51). Many such events were massacres, but sometimes the surprised troops were able to organize themselves sufficiently to fight a battle, even if they lost, as when the Romans were ambushed by Hannibal at Lake Trasimene in 217 BCE. On other occasions, ambushes were prepared but were detected, as in the manoeuvring before First Cremona in 69 CE and Strasbourg in 357 CE.

Sometimes scouts did not detect the enemy until the two armies were close together so that encounters grew into full-scale battles unplanned by either side. When the Roman and Macedonian armies met at Cynoscephalae in 197 BCE, they had previously lost touch with each other in hilly terrain and poor weather, resulting in a battle for which neither general was ready. Most battles, however, occurred between two armies that had spent an uncomfortable night preparing for confrontation. Once armies had located each other, they tended to camp close together. Battle did not always begin the next day and at numerous battles, including Plataea in 479 BCE, Ilipa in 206 BCE, Pydna in 168 BCE, and Pharsalus in 48 BCE, armies faced off for several days before the fighting began. Waiting to engage could sap soldiers' morale and during such periods of tension battles could begin from chance events as at Pydna in 168 BCE which developed out of a fight over an escaped baggage animal. Many other factors affected troops' mood before battle. Before the Trebia in December 218 BCE, the Roman army had to cross the river and many of these cold, wet men fought without having had breakfast (Polybius 3.72). Other battles were fought in the middle of the day, often after marching, as at Cunaxa in 401 BCE, Strasbourg in 357 CE, Adrianople in 378 CE, and Callinicum in 531 CE, with many of the men having had no food since breakfast.

2.4 Infantry and Cavalry Spacing

When armies deployed for battle, they formed long thin lines. In the late Roman period Vegetius assigned each Roman soldier a frontage of 3ft [approx. 1m] and 6ft [approx. 2m] between ranks. Thus, 'if you wish to draw up 6 [ranks] in line of battle, an army of 10,000 will take up 42ft in depth and a mile in length' (Vegetius 3.15). This is a depth-to-length ratio of 1:120, suggesting that most modern battle plans are very misleading. Polybius did similar calculations in his criticism of Callisthenes' description of Issus in 333 BCE, starting with the space taken up by a Hellenistic pike phalanx rather than numbers.

> A stade [200m] takes 1,600 men at marching intervals whenever they are 16 deep, each of the men having 6ft. It is clear that 10 stades will take 16,000 and 20 stades twice as many (12.19.7–8).

When Polybius described this formation formed for battle, the intervals were 1m per man, half this period's typical Roman spacing, so that each Roman faced two Macedonians.

> So the Romans stand in three feet with their equipment. But in their battle, each man undertakes movement with his shield to protect his body, changing places continuously according to the occurrence of an attack and with his sword for the cut and thrust. It is clear that to fight it is necessary that the men have a space and an interval from the others at least three feet beside and behind (18.30.6–8).

Polybius' statement about the Romans needing 2m each reflected a loose style of heavy infantry in combat, while Vegetius' 1m referred to a tighter style of heavy infantry combat favoured by the late Romans, as shown by his advocating drawing troops up in a line and then 'the command should be given that immediately they double the line, so that in an actual attack (impetu) that the formation which they are accustomed to use may be kept' (1.26). Intervals of 1m suited pikemen and armies that stood still, but hand-to-hand combat with spear or sword and a shield needed more space, though certainty about how much more spaced was needed is impossible. The interval between ranks varied, but the dangers of injury from spears suggests that Vegetius' 2m was probably common, though pike phalanxes were more compact in this dimension too, at 1m per rank. Light infantry fought in loose and irregular formations rather than linear blocks, so that estimating how much space they took up is not possible.

For cavalry, Polybius expected a stade to hold 800 horsemen when deployed eight deep, i.e. 2m per man (Polybius 12.18.3–4). This is much looser than

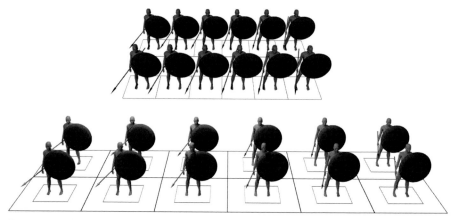

Figure 2.1: Spearmen spaced at 1m and 2m intervals.

Mauricius' suggestion of 3ft [1m] per man for battle (9.5) though he preferred a more open order for marching, defined as enough space to turn a horse easily (3.2–3.4). The differences resulted from Polybius referring to skirmishing cavalry and Mauricius to heavy cavalry. Between ranks, at least half a horse length, around 1.5m, was required, and a full length was common.

2.5 Deployment for Battle

Men and animals produced much dust during the approach march and deployment, especially in summer battles. Xenophon described the approach of Artaxerxes' army at Cunaxa in 401 BCE:

> And already it was the middle of the day and the enemy were not yet visible, but as the afternoon began some dust appeared, like a white cloud, and a long time later it was like something black over much of the plain. When they came nearer, very soon the bronze began to flash and spears and the formations started to be visible (*Anabasis* 1.8.8).

This battle began with the two armies separated by only 3–4 stades [600–800m]. At this distance the men could see each other, though they were still outside missile range. In good conditions, nineteenth-century manuals suggested that individuals had blurred into blocks at 1,000m and that infantry could only be distinguished from cavalry at about 1,300m (*1862 Army Officer's Pocket Companion*, 71–72). At Ruspina in Africa in 46 BCE, closely ordered cavalry appeared at first to the Caesarians to be infantry (*African War* 13). Rain or snow further restricted vision and Livy mentioned the difficulty of seeing what went on at Magnesia in 190 BCE because of the fog, while rain at the Crimisus in 341 BCE had a similar effect. So would looking into the sun in early morning or evening actions. Hills, woods, vegetation, and units of troops also blocked views, and though generals were usually mounted and could see over infantry, other cavalry would block their line of sight too. Generals might thus be expected to have difficulty in seeing what was happening at either end of a long battle line.

Classical and Hellenistic armies deployed in a single line of units known as a *phalanx* or acies, multiple ranks deep. From the third century BCE, Carthaginians and Romans usually fought in two or three lines, a practice sometimes also adopted by their enemies. We know little about the sorts of intervals between lines, although Mauricius in the sixth century CE suggested that first and second lines of a cavalry army should be about four bowshots (approx. 1,200m) apart (*Strategikon* 2.13).

Deploying for battle was a slow process. Troops on the march tended to move in long columns or hollow squares, but turning these into line of battle is not covered in any detail by ancient sources. Xenophon's *Lacedaemonian Constitution* seems to show a Spartan army marching in column and deploying by platoons (*enomotiai*) to the shielded (left) side, but leaves unclear precisely how this manoeuvre was to be accomplished (11.8). One of the diagrams in Mauricius (12.B.20) shows four parallel columns, a formation recommended for marching in open country. Here, the front of the units is marked on the left side of the two left hand columns, on the right side of the two right-hand columns, suggesting a wheel into line of battle. This would have been similar to sixteenth-century European practice, when columns marched towards the deployment line, then wheeled the column to march along this line until they reached a designated point at which the men would turn again to face the enemy. This is consistent with Polybius' description of Machanidas deploying his pike phalanx at Mantinea in 207 BCE, when he bent (*periekla*) his pike phalanx from column to the right, usually interpreted as wheeling it (11.12.4).

It seems likely to have taken an hour, if not longer, to get a marching army into a position where it could begin to fight, with well-trained men manoeuvring faster than the untrained, and larger armies being slower than smaller armies. There is little clarity about whether any ancient army practiced cadenced marching, in which men in a formation all moved off the same foot at the same moment. This practice developed in the mid-eighteenth century in Europe, allowing faster manoeuvring with ranks closer together. Herodotus referred to a unit of the Spartans moving *badēn* at Plataea, which could mean

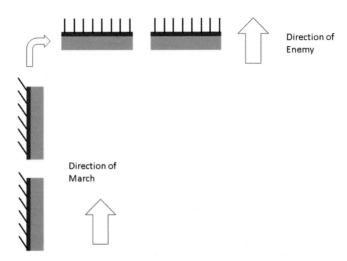

Figure 2.2: Moving from column to line.

'in step', or just 'at a walk' (9.57.1), while their use of flautists could have helped with marching in step. Vegetius also mentioned a 'military step' for Romans (1.9). As armies deployed, they tried to match the enemy to avoid being outflanked. At Marathon in 490 BCE, the Greeks stretched their formation to equal the frontage of the Persians, resulting in a thin centre that broke. At other battles, commanders were reluctant to spread out their army too much. At Cannae in 216 BCE, the Roman commander Varro deployed his troops in an unusually deep formation, suggesting a lack of confidence in their ability to stand against the Carthaginians at their regular depth.

The main line of a deployed army was normally continuous, but with small intervals (*diastēmata*) between any subdivisions. At Mantinea in 207 BCE, Philopoemen deployed his pike phalanx 'with intervals between the sub-units (*speirēdon*)' (Polybius 11.11.6). Roman armies in the Middle Republic deployed in a checkerboard formation with gaps between the front-line maniples equal to their frontage, the second lines standing behind the gaps. Intervals were standard in European armies in the seventeenth century, usually equalling their frontage, though this was a period in which there was more manoeuvring on the battlefield. For Hellenistic cavalry, Polybius suggested a space equal to the frontage of each unit 'so that they are able to perform wheels (*epistrophais*) and about-faces (*perispasmois*)' (Polybius 12.18.3). Mauricius recommended intervals between divisions (*merē*) of 100–200ft, and intervals of a bowshot (approx. 300m) between divisions (*Strategikon* 2.13, 12.B.17).

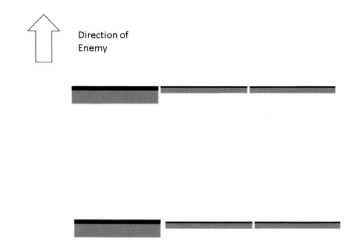

Figure 2.3: Spacing of units in two lines, with two units of infantry on the right with small intervals, two deeper units of cavalry on their left with intervals a unit wide, and a second line some distance behind.

From these sorts of details, we can make some estimates of how much space an army might take up. Polybius' rule of thumb imagined frontages of 10 and 20 stades [2 and 4km], while Vegetius mentioned a Roman mile [1.6km]. There were few flat and featureless plains in Europe several kilometres wide so that most battles would have involved some areas of difficult terrain: ditches, streams, hillocks, small woods, etc. During the Cynoscephalae campaign in 197 BCE, both Romans and Macedonians wanted to avoid the area around Pherae as it was 'under cultivation and full of walls and small gardens' (Polybius 18.20.1), and at First Cremona in 69 CE the battlefield included ditches, vineyards, and woods (Tacitus, *Histories* 2.42). Even in steppe and desert terrain, battlefields without some minor obstacles were rare. Our sources sometimes described certain types of terrain as being difficult for cavalry e.g. Herodotus described Attica as bad for cavalry and Boeotia good (9.13.3), Xenophon (*Agesilaus* 1.15) thought Caria was difficult for cavalry, and Diodorus described Cappadocia in the same way (18.40.6). What was good for cavalry was also good for heavy infantry who were also badly affected by minor obstacles. These comments are best seen in light of Late Roman manuals advising generals to fight on plains if they had good cavalry, but in more difficult terrain if their strength was in infantry, i.e. terrain increased the effectiveness of troops on it, but was not decisive (*Strategikon* 8.2.20–21).

These figures give a sense of the problems of controlling large armies since men on one flank of a large army could rarely see what was happening on the other flank. Typical practice was to have three commanders, one for the centre and one for each flank. Armies generally deployed in a linear fashion, with a centre of heavy infantry, supported by cavalry and light troops on the flanks, the heavier cavalry being deployed next to the infantry. This was the case even when the infantry centre was composed of multiple lines of units. Light troops might also form a screen in front of the heavy infantry. When present, elephants tended to be placed in front of the main lines, either on the flanks or in front of the main bodies. Finally, there was little concept of keeping a reserve of uncommitted troops in the Classical or Hellenistic period, though it was common for Roman imperial armies to do this.

The only significant divergences in large set-piece battles were for armies composed only of cavalry or where a flank was anchored on a river, as at Magnesia, Pharsalus, or Callinicum. Other variations in deployment were generally linear and did not involve manoeuvring. One possibility was to refuse (i.e. keep back) a part of the army, so that not all parts of the line began to engage at the same time, as the Carthaginians did at Cannae and the Alamanni did at Strasbourg. The Boeotians at Nemea in 394 BCE deployed far to the right deliberately with the intent of outflanking the Spartan alliance. This

Theban choice pulled the rest of the Boeotian army out of position, according to Xenophon, forced to move so that they would not have a gap in their line.

As a battle began, seeing what was happening would have become even more difficult as more dust was kicked up. Polybius' description of Mantinea in 207 BCE noted that

> for a long time the battle was evenly balanced so that the remaining troops, watching eagerly which of two ways the dust cloud turned, were unable to agree because they both held for a long time in the battle the place where they started (11.13.2).

Similarly, at Chettus in 559 CE, the Huns were unable to see because of the cloud of dust raised, so could not tell how few Roman troops there were (Agathias 5.19.9).

2.6 Manoeuvre During Battle

Heavy infantry units usually formed in lines varying in depth by army, troop types, and tactical situation. Mauricius in the late-sixth century CE adapted Aelian to say that 'more than sixteen is useless, less than four is weak' (12.B.17), which covers the majority of cases where we have details. For cavalry, Polybius suggested eight ranks was the maximum useful depth, while Mauricius noted that it was traditional for cavalry to deploy four ranks deep before recommending eight to ten ranks (2.6).

Although units were typically deployed as lines they could change formation in battle. The evolutions in the late Hellenistic manuals in the Polybian tradition, i.e. Asclepiodotus, Aelian, and Arrian, can be divided into turns, wheels, countermarches, and changes in spacing. This focus on changing formation was very different from Vegetius who suggested formations for particular battlefield instances, while Mauricius' suggestions focused on changes in spacing and turns. Instead of countermarching he recommended turning, suggesting a greater confidence that all men could fight, and omitted wheels.

Polybius, himself a cavalry commander, described the late-third century BCE Philopoemen teaching men how to carry out

> the wheel, the wheel-about 180 degrees, and the three quarter wheel by troop (*oulamon*). How to move out swiftly by files and double files from both flanks or from the centre; and then to reassemble when checked into troops, or squadrons, or regiments: and how to deploy on both flanks or through an interval or by a march alongside the rear ranks. A change in

direction did not need practice, he said, for it was close to their state on the march. After this it was necessary for them to become accustomed to advances against the enemy and retreats with all these manoeuvres so that they could carry them out at wonderful speed; as long as they continued to keep together by rank and file, and at the same time watched the intervals between the troops (10.23.3–7).

The technical terms used in military manuals were not always used correctly by ancient writers, while battle descriptions were often driven by stylistic considerations rather than accuracy.

- A turn changed the facing of individuals, either to the right (or spear) or to the left (shield). When a line 6 deep and 20 wide turned, it became a column 20 deep with a frontage of 6, with the previous front rank now standing on one side. If men turned 180 degrees then the rear-rank men became the front rank.
- A countermarch faced a unit to the rear with the front-rank men still in front. There were different types of countermarch depending on whether the new rear rank of the unit was to be ahead or behind the unit's original position. Carrying out a countermarch in battlefield conditions might also require opening the spacing of the unit.
- A wheel turned the whole unit forward on a pivot, so that unlike a turn or a countermarch it required more space than the frontage of the unit.

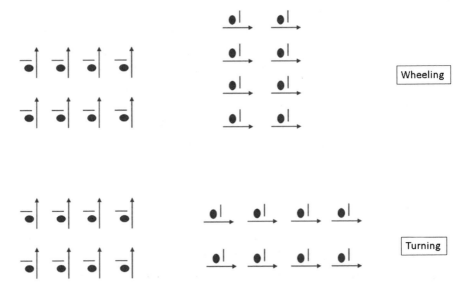

Figure 2.4: Wheeling the unit (top) and turning the men in a unit (bottom).

Wheeling becomes progressively harder as frontage and depth increase since the outside files have to move much further than the pivot man. In the nineteenth century, with much-better-trained troops, wheeling movements were typically conducted by company or squadron (around 100 men), not by battalion or regiment (around 500 men). A wheel about 180 degrees and a reverse wheel was possible, but required very well-trained troops and very flat terrain, and would have been slow
- Inclining involved marching at an angle.
- Changes in spacing could close up or expand a formation, altering either ranks or files.

The linear mode of engagement dominated, so that all troops on the battlefield usually did the same thing. Occasionally, however, generals were able to intervene in the events on the battlefield. At the River Sabis in 57 BCE, when the Nervii threatened to roll up the Roman line, Caesar not only noticed the problem, but was able to use some troops just arriving to restore the Roman line, and at Mons Graupius in 84 CE, Agricola ordered his cavalry to attack once the first infantry attack bogged down. More complex manoeuvring was very rare and almost always initiated by the general, not by a regimental commander. Once units had completed a manoeuvre they always had to pause to dress ranks, causing further delay and something risky to do close to the enemy. Polybius described Philopoemen ordering an Achaean League phalanx at Mantinea in 207 BCE to turn and then move, after which they must have again turned to face front (11.15.2). These troops had time to prepare for the enemy attack, but this was not always possible. Because of these dangers, at First Mantinea and Cunaxa officers refused to move their regiments across the battlefield, perhaps wisely. At Amphipolis in 422 BCE, Cleon 'since he thought he had plenty of time, turning to the right and offering his unshielded side to the enemy, he began to lead his army away' (Thucydides 5.10.4). However, he had misjudged the timing and when the Spartans sortied, his men panicked and ran. Manoeuvres on the battlefield, as at Ilipa in 206 BCE, were thus rare, needing good leadership and well-trained troops. It was only in exceptional circumstances that we find regimental commanders making such decisions.

2.7 Light Infantry and Missile Weapons

Light infantry with missile weapons covered flanks but could harass heavy infantry who did not have their own missile troops, light infantry, or cavalry support. Thucydides' description of light troops at Syracuse in 415 BCE suggests he thought they were of little value. 'First there was the skirmishing between the stone-throwers and the slingers, and the archers of both sides and they kept on putting each other to flight, as is usual with *psiloi* (6.69.2). In most periods it was only in unusual situations that heavy infantry were unsupported, but if so, they could suffer badly, as happened to several commanders in the Classical period. From the Hellenistic period, the use of light infantry to screen the front of the main line of battle became very common, mostly equipped with javelins with a range of about 30m. When both armies were properly screened the light troops had little effect on the battle itself, which makes them appear ineffective. Occasionally, however, armies well provided with light troops met those without, as with Roman armies of the Middle Republic when faced by armies of Celts or Gauls. At Telamon in Italy in 225 BCE, missile shot from Roman velites provoked the Celts into attacking the Roman heavy infantry (Polybius 2.30.4–6) and at Mount Olympus and Ankara in 189 BCE in Anatolia, Roman velites inflicted large numbers of casualties on Gauls who were unprotected by their own light troops (Livy 38.22, 26).

Even when light troops were armed with bows they were rarely important in battle, playing a major role only at Carrhae and Taginae. Many cultures made little use of military archery, e.g. classical Greece, Republican Rome, and European enemies of Rome, although the Persians and the steppe tribes made extensive use. Others, like Hellenistic and Roman imperial armies, had specialist contingents, with Cretans having a good reputation.

Ancient bows were either self bows, made from a single piece of wood, or composite bows, made from a wooden core with horn additions. Most military archers used composite bows, which were more efficient transmitters of human energy than self bows, so were less tiring to use and thus able to achieve higher rates of shot for longer periods with greater accuracy. Composite bows could be made smaller for use on horseback, but these took longer to make and cost more. There are occasional assertions in ancient authors about the supremacy of certain cultures' bows. Procopius when describing Callinicum in 531 CE noted:

> For their missiles were certainly more numerous, since the Persians are nearly all archers and they are taught to make their shots much faster than all other men, but they shoot from weak bows not drawn very much, so that whether they hit body armour or helmet or even a shield of a Roman, they snapped off and in no way bothered the man who was hit. But the archery of the Romans is always slower, seeing that they shoot from bows that are extremely stiff and very tightly drawn, and one might add that they are stronger men, much more than the Persians, and they

easily hurt those they hit, for no armour is an impediment to their assault (*Wars* 1.18.32–34).

We find the opposite in Plutarch's *Crassus* where he claimed that Parthian arrows were 'shattering armour and being borne through every kind of covering equally, both hard and soft' (24). More balanced was Livy on some Cretan archers in 200 BCE who

> if someone made an attack could shoot their arrows against horses and riders open to wounding, but against Roman shields they did not have enough force to penetrate, nor were there any unexposed parts which they might look for. And so, when they realized that this type of weapon was useless … (Livy 31.39.12–13).

For infantry archers shooting at individuals maximum effective archery range, i.e. the sort of range where most shooters could hit their targets frequently, was about 100m. Most military archery involved shooting by formations at units or areas, often at a high angle, sometimes over other troops or fortification walls. For formation targets, maximum effective range was around 300m, which is what ancient sources refer to as a bowshot. Shooting at longer distances was possible, but of little value militarily. For horse archers, these ranges were much shorter. Even when standing still horses were not stable shooting platforms, and when they were moving accurate shooting was difficult. The Mamluk Egyptian writer Taybugha wrote a manual of archery in the thirteenth century CE recommending infantry archers train with targets at 75m, horse archers with targets at 10m. Getting this close to any missile-armed heavy infantry would be very dangerous for horses and riders, suggesting that most horse archery was harassing shot at formations, not aimed shot at individuals. When Xenophon claims that the Cretan archers in the Ten Thousand shot shorter than the Persians, he was comparing the Cretans within the dense block of infantry shooting at dispersed and faster moving Persian skirmishers (*Anabasis* 3.3.7, 15).

In shooting at units, all archers had to estimate the angle required to achieve the desired range, and every shot was different, made in a new stance by men who grew tired over time, shooting handmade arrows with slightly different weights. The target's formation was important, with shallow formations taking up less space and so being less vulnerable than deep formations. All these variations were more pronounced if either the shooter or target was moving, and although many ancient archers were experienced huntsmen, game generally ran across or away from the shooter, not towards him, so they would be less practiced at shooting at advancing units. Wind also affected shooting, so that at the Frigidus in 394 CE, Eugenius' troops' missiles were blown back on themselves. Similarly, rain, snow, fog, or mist could make bowstrings damp, reducing the effectiveness of archery or even prohibiting it, and Livy invoked this as a factor at Magnesia in 190 BCE. Finally, the ever-present dust on the battlefield might also make it difficult to see well enough to shoot accurately.

Placing infantry archers in the line of battle was rare. Experiments in the American Civil War (1861–1865) suggested that it took infantry about two minutes to cover the final 200yd to the enemy (*1862 Army Officer's Pocket Companion*, 72). Extrapolating from this, with a maximum effective range of 300m there would be no more than three minutes' shooting time if the archers were attacked by infantry and probably less. This shooting would have been at formations until attackers were within 100m, after which shooters could start to aim at individuals. Around this point, however, the archers would have to choose between running or fighting; if they chose to fight, they would need to replace their bows with melee weapons and prepare to fight. If infantry archers were attacked by cavalry, a range of 300m allowed at most a minute for shooting. We can say little about ancient speed of shot, though the idea of passing through the danger zone rapidly was commonly expressed and Mauricius emphasized the need to shoot swiftly. His recommendation that light infantry and cavalry should carry thirty to forty arrows suggests that prolonged or speculative shooting was uncommon.

Harassing shot at area targets was intended to provoke an enemy into moving out of position. It was unlikely that most defenders would be seriously damaged by a short barrage of arrows, and as long as troops were well-disciplined, the best defence against this sort of archery was to raise shields and wait out the barrage, a formation known as the tortoise (testudo) to the Romans, but used by all armies. However, horses and poorly disciplined or unarmoured men would suffer more, eventually being forced to choose to advance or retreat. Psychologically, it was hard to resist the urge to charge out to disperse the harassers, even when there was the possibility of getting surrounded and shot up when doing so.

Some insights into the effectiveness of battlefield archery come from nineteenth-century peacetime trials in shooting muskets or rifles at canvas targets. These produced hit rates of 40–60 per cent at 200m, which was a common range for infantry to start shooting (although waiting until the enemy was closer was preferred). Reality was very different. In the Napoleonic Wars, approximately 0.5 per cent of shots fired by infantry muskets produced a casualty, while in the American Civil War, the increased lethality of rifles increased this figure to around 1 per cent. While it is possible that ancient archers shot more accurately than Early Modern soldiers, the enormous difference between the later tests and reality suggest that being close to an enemy reduced the effectiveness of shooting.

The effect of hitting the target varied greatly. Arrows had a curved trajectory at most ranges over about 50m, so much aimed shot and most indirect shot hit the target at an angle, increasing the chance of being deflected by armour and reducing the penetrative effects. Range also had a significant impact, with air resistance slowing the speed of the arrow. Finally, the type of material used to make the arrow (iron, bronze, wood, stone, and bone, though most ancient arrows were iron) made little difference. As might be expected, unarmoured or shieldless men and horses suffered most. At a siege near Dyrrachium in 48 BCE, Caesar claimed 30,000 arrows were shot and no more than 20 men were killed, though many were injured and one centurion had 120 arrow holes in his shield (*Civil War* 3.53).

These limitations to archery also applied to slings. These tended to be found in specialized units, with a similar effective range as archery against individuals and formations. Sling projectiles were either stones or lead bullets, both of which had a blunt-force effect on targets. As with archery, there are some optimistic reports on their effectiveness, with Xenophon apparently claiming that the Rhodian slingers among the Ten Thousand outranged the Persian archers (*Anabasis* 3.4.16 although the word 'archers' is not found in all manuscripts). Despite Xenophon, their infrequent use in all periods of antiquity suggests that their effectiveness was less than that of archery.

2.8 Morale and the Will to Engage

As bodies of men approached each other, their readiness to engage in hand-to-hand combat was critical. Ancient writers were rarely explicit as to what happened as men came close together, but there is a consistency in what they say about combat which fits well with more detailed accounts of battle in later periods. They also fit well with the work of the nineteenth-century military theorist Charles Ardant du Picq, a French officer who had extensive experience as a regimental commander in the Crimean War, as well as in smaller wars in Syria and Algeria. His work placed great emphasis on morale and discipline as critical factors in battle, emphasizing that soldiers entered battle for victory, not to fight, and that it was a rare human who was enthusiastic about facing a confident enemy. Keegan cited du Picq approvingly on this point, but it does beg the question of whether ancient battle was like battle in the era of firearms. This book argues that an emphasis on morale is consistent with the ancient sources and that it explains the critical importance of unit-level leaders and the paradox of a general reluctance to enter combat, whether attacking or defending, and the urge to get the battle over with which led to rushing into battle.

Many accounts describe only the outcome of combat and involve men who did not hesitate to come into contact, like this account of a skirmish in Spain in the Roman Civil War.

> When the forces of both sides had attacked this tall hill, the enemy, being kept off by our men, were thrown back to the plain. After this, the battle was successful for our men. Everywhere as the enemy retreated our men were engaged in no little slaughter (*Spanish War* 24).

Fortunately, many other accounts are more detailed, like Xenophon's description of the opening phases of Coronea in 394 BCE.

> As they met for a while there was complete silence from both sides, but at the time when they were about a stade [200m] from each other, the Thebans shouted and advanced at a run (*dromō*). There were still three *plethra* [100m] between them when [the Spartans] ran out from the line of Agesilaus … and coming to the spear they turned to flight those opposite them. However, the Argives did not wait for the attack of those with Agesilaus, but fled to Helicon (*Hellenica* 4.3.17).

Xenophon gives a good sense of the closeness of lines as first the Thebans and then the Spartans began to run, as well as describing both contact and breaking before contact. With both armies moving forward at Coronea, they met in about a minute after beginning to attack. The precision of these times, speeds, and distances is less important than the fact that when the battle began, contact could happen very quickly indeed.

2.9 Infantry Combat

The model of infantry combat presented here is similar to the views of Zhmodikov, Goldsworthy, Van Wees, and most succinctly of Sabin. Although these authors have usually focused on one period, the model is applicable to battle in all periods of antiquity, with 'model' meaning a simplified generalization of processes. Any model of ancient combat needs to take into account that battle was unpredictable, leadership was very important, it was difficult to get men to fight hand-to-hand, and disorder or gaps in the formation were very dangerous. These factors were usually more important than the more easily described and quantified factors like numbers, depth of formation, length of weapon, or types of armour, factors less often discussed by the primary sources and of little interest to experienced soldiers like Xenophon or Caesar. The model should also account for most battles lasting for several hours, though they might be over very quickly or take all day, and resulting in few casualties for the victor but many for the defeated.

Most battles were over relatively quickly with Vegetius suggesting two or three hours was typical (3.9). When Pydna in 168 BCE was over in less than an hour it was to the surprise of all concerned (Plutarch, *Aemilius Paullus* 22.1) and the Tearless Battle in 370 BCE was probably also quite short. Other battles took longer, like Himera in Sicily in 480 BCE which lasted from dawn to late evening (Herodotus 7.167) and Bibracte in 58 BCE from the seventh hour (i.e. just after noon) until evening (Caesar, *Gallic War* 1.26); Gabiene, Carrhae, and Adrianople also started in mid-day and were only finished by nightfall. In long battles men began to run out of missiles, and Caesar reported that after five hours of infantry fighting at Ilerda in Spain in 49 BCE, all the throwing weapons of his infantry had been used up (*Civil War* 1.46.1).

Attacks were usually described as <u>impetus</u> in Latin, *ephodos* in Greek, often translated into English as 'charge', though neither ancient word has a required sense of running. More common were vague phrases describing men engaging, driving forward, pushing back, advancing and retiring. More important than speed in the attack was confidence. Faced with a confident attack, defenders often wavered and then broke rather than standing to fight, like the Argives at Coronea. If the defenders ran, then the battle was over quickly, but if they faced the charge then the attackers might stop moving forward. It was only if the will to engage was similar on both sides that hand-to-hand fighting would take place. Fighting in these cases began as a series of clashes between small groups of men, the bold rushing forward to engage, the less bold hanging back. At the beginning of a battle, it was possible to engage in a line, but if neither side forced the other back in the first moments, then fighting became prolonged in a series of clashes rather than non-stop combat. Ammianus described infantry fighting at Adrianople as moving backwards and forwards like the sea (31.13.2), similar to Mauricius warning commanders that

> like water which flows forwards or backwards, not to react immoderately to any little push (*ōtheseōs*) by the enemy or themselves ... for it is not a complete victory to push the enemy back a little so that they withdraw nor is it a defeat to retreat a little and then turn again (*Strategikon* 3.11).

The most important single theme in ancient accounts of battles is of order, of keeping one's formation intact. Polybius noted that Philopoemen 'thought nothing was more dangerous or more useless than cavalry who have lost order in their troops (*oulamois*) choosing to fight' (10.23.8), while Vegetius stressed that men too close to each other got in their way, but men too far from each other allowed the enemy to breach the formation (1.26). Maintenance of order and control was critical, an exposed flank was vulnerable, and gaps between formations were a great danger. Trained men thus stayed in their ranks as much as possible and cavalry officers looked for such opportunities.

2.10 Cavalry Combat

Cavalry were generally deployed on the flanks where they could either skirmish with other cavalry if deployed loosely or, from the Hellenistic period onwards, fight hand-to-hand if deployed more compactly. They were especially dangerous to light infantry, to heavy infantry who had lost formation, or when attacking from the flank or rear. The only major variation was with cataphracts, i.e. armoured men on armoured horses, who might be used to intimidate heavy infantry from the front. Stirrups were not used until the later-sixth century CE, at which point they were seen only as aids to mounting the horse. Most cultures had saddles with deep seats or horns at the corners which helped keep the rider in place so that shooting bows, throwing javelins, and fighting with spears, lances, and swords are all well attested.

As with infantry, cavalry combat was dominated by the readiness of both horses and men to engage. When cavalry attacked cavalry, one side might break rather than fight. If both groups were ready to engage then they would slow down before contact and begin fighting hand to hand. The mid-nineteenth-century British cavalry officer Nolan, at a period when cavalry combat was still dominated by swords, wrote:

> Cavalry seldom meet each other in a charge executed at speed; the one party generally turns before joining issue with the enemy, and this often happens when their line is still unbroken (1853, 279).

With looser formations the two groups could pass through one another if their formations were shallow. Mauricius described cavalry 'pursuits and counter-pursuits' (3.15), like Procopius 'they each kept making quick-turning pursuits against each other, since they were all cavalry' (*Wars* 1.15.15). Feigned flights were often used in these situations. Good generals tried to be aware of this and not commit all troops to the pursuit, but it was up to the regimental commander to keep his men under control.

We don't know whether ancient cavalry typically charged at the canter or at the gallop, or how practices differed between cultures. In the sixth century CE Mauricius, recommended charging 'at a canter and not forcefully so that order might not be lost by the speed of riding before mingling in hand-to-hand combat' (3.5). Losing formation was inevitable as cavalry galloped, even over short distances, with stronger horses moving faster, small variations in terrain, and varying levels of training and riding skills.

Heavy infantry who kept close formation were able to resist cavalry attacks, so cavalry were only rarely deployed in the centre of armies. If cavalry did attack formed heavy infantry, the infantry might begin to waver, with gaps opening in their formation. In this case, the cavalry would complete the charge, penetrating the infantry formation who would then break and run. But if the infantry held firm then the cavalry turned away. Cavalry attacks against heavy infantry thus required lots of space. The looser formations of light infantry meant that they were generally unable to stand up to cavalry, unless they were also supported by cavalry or were able to evade in difficult terrain.

Cavalry attacks could take place very quickly, with horsemen able to cover 200m in about forty-five seconds at a canter (approx. 20kph = 5.5m/second), about twenty seconds at a gallop (approx. 40kph = 11 m/second). Commanders of cavalry regiments could exploit fleeting opportunities provided by disorder very rapidly indeed. Cavalry were at their most dangerous in these situations which were especially common as men were pushed back or even left battle.

2.11 Pursuit

When the battle had been lost, the slaughter began, with the victors hoping that this would avoid the need to fight again. Injured men were often not able to flee fast enough to avoid being cut down, though the winners were able to keep many of their casualties alive. Men often discarded their equipment, especially helmets and shields, to flee more swiftly. Like the fighting, pursuit was a fluid process. Men who showed fighting spirit were more likely to be left alone, whether small groups like those with Socrates at Delium in 424 BCE or the thousands of Roman troops able to fight their way off the battlefield after the Trebbia, Lake Trasimene and Cannae. Heavy infantry were not the best troops for pursuit, which was often left to light infantry and cavalry.

There were dangers associated with pursuing too aggressively and of meeting the enemy while disordered, as happened at Mons Graupius. Sometimes this could be generated by a deliberate action by the enemy, a manoeuvre known as the feigned flight, as at Carrhae and Casilinum. It was also often possible for a general to rally some of his defeated troops which might then prove dangerous to over-confident pursuers.

On some occasions, after commanders were successful on one flank they or their forces continued to pursue the enemy, rather than breaking contact and turning to roll up the line of the enemy main body. Controlling troops in this situation was difficult, and at Cunaxa in 401 BCE, the Greek mercenaries pursued the Persians on their flank for 6km before halting and at Magnesia Antiochus III ended up attacking the Roman camp rather than rolling up the Roman line, an error that cost him the battle. But moments when generals or regimental commanders could control their men and lead them into flanks, rear, or compressed troops, disaster followed for the defenders, as at Cannae and Adrianople.

2.12 Conclusion

The difficulties of manoeuvring on the battlefield meant that most ancient battles took place in a very linear fashion. There were occasions when outstanding generals or regimental commanders were able to manoeuvre on the battlefield, but these were exceptional. The role of regimental commanders varied greatly. For heavy-infantry leaders in the main line of battle keeping men motivated and under control was the most important task, and opportunities for manoeuvre were rare. For leaders of light troops and cavalry on the flanks, the opportunities were greater.

In thinking about ancient battle, we should not be looking for absolutes, but trying to define what was normal or typical, so that we can recognize what was unusual. For all interactions, we should consider the range of possibilities, rather than expecting a similar situation to produce the same result, thus reflecting the views of Greek and Roman writers who saw battle as unpredictable. In this respect, battle is like sporting events which often produce different results in successive contests between the same individuals or teams.

Chapter 3

The Classical Greek Period

The fifth and fourth centuries BCE was the period of the wars between the Achaemenid Persian Empire and the cities of mainland Greece, including the Battles of Marathon, Thermopylae, and Plataea, and a long series of wars between Greek cities before the rise of Macedon in the mid-fourth century BCE. Although much scholarship has suggested that the Classical Greek way of war was superior to the armies and fighting style of the Persian Empire, this chapter argues that there was little that was exceptional about how Greeks of the fifth and fourth century BCE fought. Here, I use 'heavy infantry' and 'line' where other scholars usually use 'hoplite' and 'phalanx'. Hoplite (*hoplitēs*) was consistently used throughout antiquity for heavy infantry, i.e. those fighting in the main line of battle. Outside the Classical period, Polybius used hoplite for Carthaginian infantry and Macedonian pikemen (3.53.1, 18.29.4), Arrian used it for Macedonian pikemen, and Cassius Dio used it for Roman legionaries (49.29.4). Phalanx was used loosely to mean any linear formation, with Arrian using the term to describe Porus' infantry in India (6.15.5), Josephus to describe Romans (*Jewish War* 3.95), and Caesar to describe the Helvetii in Gaul (*Gallic War* 1.24.4). It could even be used for cavalry (Xenophon, *Hellenica* 3.4.13; Arrian 1.14.4). 'Hoplites in phalanx formation' sounds technical, it means only 'heavy infantry in a line'.

3.1 Sources

For the Greco-Persian Wars, we are dependent on Herodotus (*c.*490–420 BCE) from Halicarnassus on the west coast of Anatolia. He had no military experience himself, but did talk to many of the Greek participants in the Ionian Revolt (499–493 BCE) and the Greco-Persian Wars (490 and 480–479 BCE). By the time he was writing, the story was already established and Herodotus was reporting what he was told, not analysing events. He wrote with style and took great joy in colourful anecdotes, but he was not a military historian, as his account of Marathon showed.

Our models of what happened on the Classical Greek battlefield thus come from Thucydides and Xenophon. Thucydides (*c.*460–*c.*400 BCE) was an

Athenian aristocrat who was elected as a general in 424 BCE to fight in Thrace. He was exiled for poor performance and then began a *History* covering the Peloponnesian War from its outbreak in 431 down to 411 BCE, at which point the work breaks off, unfinished, although Thucydides saw the end of the war. We can say very little about the sources used since his history was so highly polished. He had a strong but often difficult style and was very interested in the role of chance in war and politics. The Athenian point of view and the unfinished analysis are easy to forget when reading as the language and details sway the reader into thinking that Thucydides' account is the only possible version. He provided detailed accounts of Delium in 424 BCE and First Mantinea in 418 BCE, as well as many smaller actions.

Thucydides' *History* was continued by Xenophon (428–354 BCE), another wealthy Athenian. After fighting in an Athenian civil war, in 401 BCE he joined a force of Greek mercenaries hired by Cyrus, brother of the Persian king, and soon found himself involved in a Persian civil war. When Cyrus was killed at Cunaxa near Babylon in 401 BCE (below 3.6), the mercenaries, subsequently known as the Ten Thousand, carried out a long march back to friendly territory. Xenophon described this expedition in the *Anabasis* ('The march up country'). Then Xenophon became friends with the Spartan king Agesilaus and fought for him against the Persians in Asia between 396 and 394 BCE. When Agesilaus returned to Greece, Xenophon accompanied him and fought at Coronea against Athens in 394 BCE for which he was exiled. Xenophon's prose style was simple, but very clear. He wrote two major historical works, the *Anabasis* and the *Hellenica*, the latter a continuation of Thucydides' *History* covering Greek politics between 411 and 362 BCE, and two short works, *The Cavalry Commander* and *On Horsemanship*, the earliest surviving military manuals. Not only did Xenophon have extensive military experience, he was an eyewitness of much combat in the 390s BCE and described Nemea and Coronea in 394, Leuctra in 371 (below 3.7), and Second Mantinea in 362 BCE, as well as numerous smaller actions.

Finally, contemporary playwrights and poets often give some details of the experiences, emotions, and perceptions of individuals, but their words should not be pressed too strongly. Of later authors, the most often cited is Plutarch, writing in the second century CE, who wrote biographies of several important fifth- and fourth-century BCE figures, but as a non-soldier his understanding of battle was often weak.

3.2 Greek Equipment and Organization

The classical style of heavy infantry equipment was not peculiar to mainland Greece, but was found widely across the Mediterranean in this period, with art in Etruria in Italy and Lycia in Anatolia showing similar warriors. The primary offensive weapon was a spear wielded in one hand, around 2–2.5m long. The striking end was an iron point, around 0.25–0.3m long, and there was a bronze butt-spike about 0.25m long. Most men also carried a sword or large knife, with those shown in artwork usually being short (approx. 0.5–6m) and single-bladed, chopping weapons rather than swords used for thrusting.

Defensive equipment included shields, helmets, body armour, and leg defences. The typical shield was large and circular, around 1m in diameter with a thin bronze facing and wooden core of edge-jointed thin strips of wood,

Figure 3.1: Greek heavy infantryman wearing a Corinthian helmet, linen body armour and greaves. Not all of his colleagues would have been as well equipped. He has a sword on his left hip, barely visible behind his shield, which is decorated with a Sigma for the city of Sikyon. (© *Philip Sidnell*)

often poplar, weighing 5–7kg. These were similar in size and weight to shields in the Roman Empire. It was, from the user's perspective, concave, its curves encouraging blows to slide off. Unlike Roman or medieval shields held by a central horizontal handle, the Classical heavy infantry shield was held by a central arm strap (*porpax*) and a handle (*antilabē*) at the outer edge. This arrangement of handles appears limited to the Classical Greek period and since no later culture used this technique it could have offered few advantages.

The full-face Corinthian helmet was common in art, as was the *pilos*, a dome-shaped, open-faced helmet of bronze or felt. We can say little about which type was more common, though the *pilos* would have been easier and cheaper to make. The helmet was often supplemented by a bronze cuirass, rarely used by the fifth century BCE, or a corselet of layered linen or metal scales attached to a cloth backing, all types being described as a *thōrax*. Men often wore greaves, thin bronze leg defences. The total weight of a full panoply including body armour was around 20kg.

Figure 3.2: Greek light infantryman, wearing a tunic unpinned at one shoulder to free his throwing arm, and with bare feet. He is lightly equipped, without shield or armour, throwing a javelin and carrying a couple of spares. Despised by many writers, feared by many veterans. (© *Philip Sidnell*)

Figure 3.3: Peltast, hired out of Thrace, with a flamboyant cloak. He's unarmoured, apart from a small shield, but has several javelins for throwing and carries a nasty-looking scythe-like rhomphaia for close combat. (© *Philip Sidnell*)

The range of equipment is well understood, but how any given force was equipped is a more difficult problem, especially as individuals rather than the state tended to provide equipment. When Xenophon described the Ten Thousand on parade at Tyriaeum in 401 BCE, 'they all had bronze helmets and dark red tunics and greaves and uncovered shields' (*Anabasis* 1.2.16). He does not mention armour, but when a cavalry force was formed out of infantry later in the expedition, Xenophon stated specifically that they were given armour, suggesting it was not universal. When the Athenian state began to supply soldiers with equipment at the end of the fourth century BCE, it provided only spears and shields (*Athenaion Politeia* 42.2), i.e. the state only issued what was needed, leaving it to individuals to provide optional and more expensive items like helmet and armour.

Figure 3.4: Greek cavalryman, lightly equipped, with a cloak (some might also have a large floppy sun hat), boots, a javelin, and a sword. A few men might be more heavily equipped, as recommended by Xenophon, with breastplate, helmet, longer spear (and perhaps a javelin) and sword. (© *Philip Sidnell*)

Light infantry (*psiloi, kouphoi, euzōnoi*) were equipped with bows, slings, or javelins, usually without shields or other defensive equipment. Some javelin-armed light infantry had small shields (*peltai*), from which they were called 'peltasts'. These are only described from the late-fifth century BCE, but we have no idea when they first began to be used.

Classical Greek cavalry sometimes wore body armour and helmets, but did not carry shields. They were usually equipped with javelins for throwing and a sword. Saddles were rudimentary and stirrups were not used. There was little to no use of horse archers.

With the exception of Sparta, there were no standing armies in the Classical Greek world. Armies were thus created for expeditions, and though many individuals were experienced at fighting, regiments and officers were barely organized; at Athens, troops fought by tribes, the ten political divisions of the city. Occasionally we hear of groups of soldiers, e.g. the 'Five Regiments (*lochoi*)' of the Argives (Thucydides 5.67.2, 72.4), or groups of selected men, and a few cities had a small standing force like the Theban Sacred Band. At Sparta, however, there were permanent regiments, with Thucydides suggesting that a full-strength regiment (*lochos*) at Mantinea in 418 BCE had 512 men. His methodical listing of the sub-units and their commanders emphasized how different Sparta was from his experience in commanding Athenian soldiers.

Most Classical Greek armies were mixed forces of heavy infantry supported by small numbers of cavalry and larger numbers of light infantry. When Gelon of Syracuse offered to send help in the face of Xerxes' invasion, he listed 20,000 heavy infantry, 2,000 cavalry, 2,000 archers, 2,000 slingers, and 2,000 light troops to support the cavalry (Herodotus 7.158.4) and at Plataea in 479 BCE, Herodotus reported that the Greek alliance assembled 38,700 heavy and 69,500 light troops. At First Mantinea in 418 BCE, the Boeotian part of the Spartan army was composed of 5,000 heavy infantry, 5,000 light troops, 500 cavalry and 500 infantry trained to operate with the cavalry. This suggests that Herodotus' description of the army at Marathon (below 3.4), when he mentioned only heavy infantry, was atypical, if not wrong.

In mainland Greece it was possible to get away with small numbers of cavalry, with Theban and Thessalian cavalry having a good reputation (Xenophon, *Hellenica* 7.5.16; cf Herodotus 7.196). Elsewhere more cavalry were needed; after Agesilaus had arrived in Asia in 396 BCE and met the Persians, he realized he needed to raise a larger cavalry force (Xenophon, *Hellenica* 3.4.15).

3.3 Persian Equipment and Organization

Greek armies of the fifth and fourth centuries often fought against the Achaemenid Persians whose enormous empire stretched from Thrace and western Anatolia to India. The Persians had a small standing royal army supplemented by regional levies. Herodotus' description of Xerxes' army in 480 BCE emphasizes the different equipment of these ethnic contingents, while Xenophon's description of Artaxerxes' army at Cunaxa is similar, including Egyptian 'hoplites with wooden shields coming down to their feet' (*Anabasis* 1.8.9). Persian and Median troops made up the infantry core of the army, equipped with spears, shields, and body armour, many of them also having bows. Modern authors often follow Herodotus in ascribing Greek success to their equipment since at Plataea he noted 'the Persians were no less in courage and strength, but they were unarmoured' (9.62.3). However, this conflicts with other parts of his own account, e.g. a description of Persian infantry:

> on their heads they had soft hats called tiaras, and on their bodies they had sleeved tunics of various colours, with iron scales similar to fish, on their legs they had trousers; in front their shields were wicker, quivers hung beneath these; they had short spears, large bows, reed arrows, and daggers on the right thigh that hung from a belt (7.61.1).

Herodotus was telling his stories half a century after the events, at which point most Greeks had become convinced of their military superiority to the Persians. Such a perspective privileged the results of recent battles, but during the Ionian Revolt (499–493 BCE) the Persians defeated Ionians and Carians

Figure 3.5: Persian heavy infantryman with scale body armour mostly covered by his tunic and a large wicker shield. In addition to his short axe, he's also got a bow partly hidden behind his shoulder. (© *Philip Sidnell*)

Figure 3.6: Persian infantry archer, lightly equipped with no armour and only a knife in addition to his composite bow. This might be used for skirmishing, but this man is engaging in long-range unaimed shooting at an area target. (© *Philip Sidnell*)

Figure 3.7: Persian horse archer, inspired by the Tatarlı tomb paintings from Lydia, shooting behind him and reloading his bow from a quiver on his left hip. He's unarmoured, though his trousers might have distracted some enemies and if they failed he also has a long knife. (© *Philip Sidnell*)

who fought in the same way as men from mainland Greece. During this war, the Persians were successful in four land battles, at Ephesus in 498 BCE, two battles near the River Marsyas in 497 BCE, and Malene in 493 BCE. Herodotus provides few details, though he records that Malene was won by a Persian cavalry attack (6.29.1). Thus, Persian generals involved in the Marathon campaign had recently won a number of battles against Greek armies equipped and fighting in the same way as those they were about to face. There were no technological or financial reasons why many Persian infantry could not have worn armour or used long spears if they thought this was important, while Herodotus' attributing success in battle to equipment was very different to the emphases of experienced soldiers like Xenophon.

Persian light infantry was similar to Greek light infantry, i.e. equipped with bows, slings, or javelins and unarmoured. Some fought with shields like Greek peltasts; Herodotus described the Paphlagonians and Phrygians as being equipped in this fashion (7.72.1, 7.73.1). Contemporary Persian art shows bows with distinctly curved ears, i.e. composite bows.

Some Persian cavalry were equipped with javelins, like the light cavalry harassing the Greeks at the beginning of Plataea (Herodotus 9.49, 52) and illustrated on the paintings from the Tatarlı tomb in Phrygia while others used bows, especially Scythians. Other Persian cavalry were more heavily equipped; at Cunaxa, Cyrus' bodyguard wore armour and rode on armoured horses (Xenophon, *Anabasis* 1.8.6–7). Like contemporary Greek cavalry, they did not carry shields. Some of these troops were ethnic Persians, but there were also large numbers of troops from parts of the Empire.

We know little about Persian organization, with both Herodotus and Xenophon naming only ethnic contingents which had unit standards (Herodotus 9.59.2). Herodotus identified two groups of Persians, the Immortals 10,000 strong and an elite group of 1,000 armoured spearmen, the Apple-Bearers, and there was also an elite cavalry regiment, the Kinsmen (*suggeneis*).

3.4 The Battle of Marathon, 490 BCE

The Battle of Marathon, when the Athenians and Plataeans defeated the Persians, is a culturally significant battle that preserved the freedom of the Greek cities of the mainland and inspired the resistance of 480 BCE to a second Persian expedition. As the first detailed account from classical antiquity of a battle, it provides a good illustration of the problems with the primary sources. Herodotus is the only writer worth serious consideration, but there are other sources. Cornelius Nepos who wrote in the first century BCE was not a historian but a biographer focusing on the character of his subjects, in this case the Athenian commander Miltiades, rather than analysing their actions. Justin, writing a universal history in the second century CE, covered Marathon in a paragraph. Pausanias, also working in the second century CE, described a fifth-century BCE painting of the battle, i.e. a snapshot, not a description of a dynamic event. And finally, the *Suda*, a tenth-century CE encyclopaedia, contained the proverb 'the cavalry are separated' (*chōris hippeis*) which it related to Marathon, suggesting that when the Persian cavalry re-embarked on the ships, the Athenians attacked. None of these later works add anything to Herodotus' account.

After the Persians had landed at the bay of Marathon, the Athenians camped a few kilometres away. Herodotus did not say how many Persians there were or how they were equipped and although he had mentioned their cavalry earlier, they do not appear in his account of the battle. The numbers often cited for the Athenians, of around 10,000, come from both Nepos and Justin, but only by extrapolation from Herodotus' statement that there were ten Athenian tribes. Since we don't know how many Greeks or Persians there were, or where their camps were, drawing diagrams of the battle on maps of the area is of no value.

Neither side attacked for several days, with Herodotus suggesting that some of the Athenian commanders did not want to fight. On the day that the battle was fought both armies had deployed, the Greeks stretched to match the Persian frontage. Then battle began as the Greeks charged, running, Herodotus said, for 8 stades, around 1.6km. The majority of commentators have suggested that carrying military equipment and running for close to ten minutes in the heat of August or September leads to severe exhaustion and breaks up the formation. A swift advance to catch the Persians off guard, with a run at the end seems possible, and it may have been intended to strike before the Persian cavalry had deployed on that day. This problem is typical of those posed by Herodotus' account, i.e. the narrative is plausible, but we have to provide a lot of interpretation.

His description of the fighting was very compressed.

The fighting at Marathon lasted a long time. In the centre of the army, the barbarians won, where the Persians themselves and the Sacae were deployed. Against the centre the barbarians won, and having broken it they began to pursue inland. But on each flank the Athenians and the Plataeans won and having won, they allowed the enemy who had turned to flee, but with those who had broken through in their centre, bringing both flanks together, they kept on fighting and the Athenians won. They followed the fleeing Persians, cutting them down (6.113).

The Athenians and Plataeans won the battle, although their centre was broken and the right-flank commander Callimachus was killed. Herodotus does not say how the Greeks reformed after their centre was broken. We might suggest that Greek light armed troops or cavalry were present, since otherwise the Persians would have harassed the Greek camp continuously, as they did before Plataea and during the march of the Ten Thousand, but they are not mentioned.

What of the regimental commanders, whom we might assume to be the generals in charge of each of the ten Athenian voting tribes? They might have decided how deep to deploy their men, and then fought in the front rank once the battle started, with one of them, Stesilaus being killed. A few would probably have played some part in the reorganizing of the flanks to attack the Persian centre. With so few details of Persian activity we can say nothing about what their leaders would have been doing, other than managing troops as they fought and then withdrew from the battlefield. Casualties are recorded as 192 Greek and 6,400 Persian. A great disparity between winner and loser was typical of ancient battles, though the figure for Persian losses may be so much larger than typical because of the difficulties of loading men onto ships as they left the battlefield.

3.5 The Battle of Delium, 424 BCE

The first major land battle of the Peloponnesian War (431–404 BCE) was at Delium in 424 BCE, giving Thucydides a good opportunity to describe a battle in detail (4.90–96, 101). His is the only detailed account; Diodorus Siculus has a short account on similar lines (12.69–70), based on the lost, and also short, version of the fourth-century BCE universal historian Ephorus.

The battle took place in Boeotian territory between the Athenians led by Hippocrates and an army of the Boeotian League, an alliance of cities, led by Pagondas. It started late in the day, when the Athenians were attacked as they were marching away from Delium. Hippocrates had 7,000 Athenian heavy infantry and some cavalry at hand; most of his light troops had already been sent away to Athens, suggesting a failure of intelligence or scouting. At the start of the battle, the Athenian infantry were deployed 8 deep, thus taking 1,800 x 20m if at 2m per file, half that if at 1m spacing. The cavalry and the few light troops remaining were deployed on the flanks.

Pagondas led 7,000 Boeotian heavy infantry, more than 10,000 light infantry, 1,000 cavalry, and 500 peltasts. The Boeotians were deployed on a hill, with their heavy infantry arranged by cities. The Thebans on the right flank stood 25 deep, but the other contingents were in varying depths so the Athenian line would have been a little longer than the Boeotian army. The cavalry and light troops were placed on the flanks. Thucydides noted that the flanks did not engage because of streams (ruakes); these are unlikely to have stopped the Boeotian light troops from outflanking the Athenians, so he may have meant that they constrained the heavy infantry.

The main clash started as the Boeotians came over the hill and sang a type of pre-battle song known as a 'paean', and then the two lines ran towards each other, the Boeotians having the advantage of coming downhill. 'With fierce fighting and a pushing (ōthismos) of shields they joined with each other' (4.96.2). This is a nicely balanced phrase in Greek, but it is the only use of the noun ōthismos in Thucydides. The Athenians were successful on their right, despite fighting uphill, while the Thebans were successful on the Boeotian right. Thucydides did not explain why either side was successful in the combat or whether the Theban deeper formation was important, but he did say that in the confused fighting on the Boeotian left, a number of Athenians were killed by their own men, suggestive of fluid lines of battle.

The battle then came to a sudden end when two units of Boeotian cavalry appeared at the end of the ridge on the Athenian right, with Thucydides saying that they were sent by Pagondas when he saw his left flank being pushed back. When the Athenians saw the cavalry they panicked, fell back all along their line, and then broke. The Athenian philosopher Socrates was on the field, and Plato described his courage in the retreat. Nonetheless, the Athenians were harassed by the Boeotian cavalry who heavily outnumbered the Athenian cavalry, though more serious losses were avoided because of nightfall.

The Athenians lost their commander Hippocrates, almost 1,000 heavy infantry, and a large number of light troops, but we are not told when Hippocrates fell or where the many light troops fell when none are listed in the order of battle. The Boeotians lost nearly 500 men. Thucydides ignored the actions of the Boeotian light troops making up half of their army, but it is hard to avoid thinking that they were able to outflank the Athenians. Regimental commanders would have been involved in leading their own units, but apart from Pagondas' orders to his cavalry, we see only two lines of heavy infantry coming into contact with each other. The failure of Athenian morale when they saw the flanking Theban cavalry was the decisive event in the battle. This was not inevitable, but the outnumbering and outflanking of the Athenians made this panic more likely.

3.6 The Battle of Cunaxa, 401 BCE

The Battle of Cunaxa was fought near Babylon in Mesopotamia in 401 BCE during a civil war begun by Cyrus, the younger brother of the Persian king Artaxerxes II (404–358 BCE). Our main account comes from the participant Xenophon. Since his main interest was in the Greek mercenary contingent often known as the 'Ten Thousand' it is easy to forget that the battle was between two Persian armies, one of which had some Greek mercenaries attached. The Greek doctor Ctesias was present with Artaxerxes, and though his account is lost, it was used by Xenophon. Diodorus Siculus' account (14.19–24), despite a few differences, was derived from Xenophon, and finally, Plutarch's *Artaxerxes* leaned heavily on Xenophon but also used Ctesias.

Xenophon claimed that Cyrus' army was composed of 100,000 Persians, while Diodorus estimated 70,000. This force included the Greek mercenaries, 10,400 heavy infantry and 2,500 peltasts, who were deployed on the right end of Cyrus' infantry line, with Paphlagonian cavalry beyond them by the banks of the Euphrates. Cyrus also had 20 scythed chariots. Artaxerxes' army was larger, though Diodorus' figure of 400,000 and Xenophon's figure of 900,000 should both be rejected as too large to be supported by ancient logistics. Xenophon's observation that Artaxerxes, in the centre of the line of battle, stood beyond Cyrus' left flank suggests that Artaxerxes' army was at least twice as big as that of Cyrus if both sides had deployed at about the same depth. Some 150 scythed chariots screened the front of Artaxerxes' army which also had cavalry on the flanks.

Cyrus' army had been surprised on the march, so was forced to deploy rapidly from marching column into line. As it did so, Cyrus ordered Clearchus, the leader of the Greek mercenaries, to move from the army's right flank into the centre. Clearchus refused, not wishing to expose his right flank as he crossed the battlefield. This made good sense from his perspective, but shows poor preparation for battle by Cyrus and insubordination by Clearchus.

At this point, Xenophon focused on the Ten Thousand, noting that when the two lines of battle were 3–4 stades (600–800m) apart, the Greeks sang the paean and then began to advance. 'As they advanced, some of the line (*phalangos*) began to bow and the part left behind began to run at speed' (*Anabasis* 1.8.18). Xenophon suggests the run was spontaneous, although Diodorus has it planned by Clearchus to reduce the exposure to Persian arrows. The Persians opposite the Greeks broke before contact, no different from many Greeks when charged by the enemy.

Xenophon then described Artaxerxes' right flank encircling Cyrus' left flank, as expected given the deployments. At this point, Cyrus led his cavalry against Artaxerxes, hoping to kill his brother, but was killed himself. With the news of Cyrus' death, his left flank withdrew from battle and Artaxerxes occupied Cyrus' camp. Xenophon then returned his focus to the Greeks, noting that by now they were 30 stades, approximately 6km, from their camp, and admitted that Artaxerxes' left-flank commander Tissaphernes had not only got past both the Greek peltasts and the Paphlagonian cavalry, but had also reached Cyrus' camp. Although Xenophon claimed that the Greeks were able to scare off more Persians, his narrative is unconvincing and is better interpreted as the Persians screening the Greeks with cavalry.

Xenophon writes beautifully, but this is a challenging account of the battle. As a skilled participant, one would hope for better, but the description of the battle as a whole is subordinated to the story of the Ten Thousand, and Cyrus' death is emphasized more than the defeat of his army. Terrain played little role in the battle itself, though the Greek commander Clearchus was very wary of moving too far from the Euphrates, probably fearful of being surrounded by Persian cavalry. The Ten Thousand were divided into a number of mercenary groups, but we can see little of their activity in the battle, nor of the Persians, so can say little of the actions of any regimental commanders.

3.7 The Battle of Leuctra, 371 BCE

The Battle of Leuctra was fought in Boeotia in mainland Greece in summer 371 BCE, with the Spartans being defeated by the Boeotian League led by the Theban Epaminondas. Previous, Spartan military excellence did not make them invincible, just more likely to be successful, and though they had defeated the Boeotians at Nemea and Coronea in 394 BCE, they had lost smaller actions at Haliartus in 395 BCE and at Tegyra in 375 BCE, while the Athenians had outfought Spartan forces at Sphacteria in 425 BCE, in 409 BCE at the Horns, and again at Lechaeum in 391 BCE. The Boeotian victory at Leuctra had great strategic significance, leading to the loss of Spartan control over the enslaved Messenians and thus their economic ability to train regularly.

The main account of Leuctra comes from the contemporary Xenophon's *Hellenica* (6.4), though we also have accounts in Diodorus (15.52–56) and Plutarch's *Pelopidas* 20–23. These accounts are very different from each other, leading to scholarly disagreement with modern commentators looking for the causes of Boeotian success in the genius of Epaminondas, the Theban deployment fifty ranks deep, or the Theban deployment with their greatest weight on the left flank.

Although Xenophon's description does not give numbers for either side, he said that the Spartans, led by king Cleombrotus, deployed twelve deep, and there were some Spartan cavalry and allied troops. The Theban contingent stood opposite the Spartans, deployed fifty deep. There were also other troops of the Boeotian League including some cavalry. Unusually, both armies deployed their cavalry in front of the infantry in the centre, with Xenophon noting that the Theban cavalry were experienced and the Spartan cavalry were in poor condition. He did not mention light troops or Epaminondas.

Xenophon then described the disruption as the Spartan cavalry were pushed back by the Theban horse.

Fleeing, they collided with their own heavy infantry (*hoplitais*), and already the regiments (*lochoi*) of the Thebans were attacking. Nevertheless, the men around Cleombrotus at first were winning the battle, as is shown by this clear evidence: they would not have been able to pick him up, still living, to carry away if those fighting in front of him were not winning at that time. When, however, there died Dinon the polemarch and Sphodrias a royal tent companion and Cleonymus his son, then the cavalry and the staff officers of the polemarch and all the rest, being pushed by the crowd, began to retreat, but those on the left flank of the Lacedaemonians when they saw their right pushed back, gave way (Xenophon, *Hellenica* 6.4.13–14).

For Xenophon, the main causes of the Spartan defeat were the disorder caused by the cavalry in the early phases of the battle, followed by the king being injured and a series of deaths among the Spartan leaders. Casualties among the Spartans were heavy, including 400 of the 700 elite Spartiates, the result of Spartan resilience which led them to fight on when others might have retreated or routed. And even after all this, the Spartans were still able to retire in good order. Xenophon also commented on the importance of chance since 'for the Lacedaemonians everything happened against them, but for the others everything was successful, especially matters of Fortune' (*Hellenica* 6.4.8). Xenophon's account explains the events of the battle and as an informed contemporary we should take his words seriously.

Problems arise only when we come to the later sources written within a tradition of attributing Theban success to their leaders. Diodorus wrote in the first century BCE, based on the fourth-century Ephorus, listing 6,000 Thebans among the Boeotians, as well as 1,500 Thessalian infantry and 500 cavalry, all led by Epaminondas. He also had Cleombrotus' army reinforced by a second Spartan contingent under Archidamus, though in Xenophon's account this force was sent only after the battle. Diodorus attributed Epaminondas' success to his putting his best men on one flank and his weaker men on the other flank which withdrew as the battle began, and then added the Spartans attacked in a crescent formation. His account compressed a longer version, as during the battle he referred to a force of picked men (*epilektōn*, 15.56.1–2) that is probably Plutarch's Sacred Band. Diodorus gave casualty totals as more than 4,000 Spartans and about 300 Boeotians. The only thing in common with the account of Xenophon is the judgment that the death of Cleombrotus was significant.

Plutarch's account in his biography of Pelopidas was different again, based on another fourth-century BCE historian, Callisthenes, with Cleombrotus leading 10,000 Spartan infantry and 1,000 cavalry into Boeotia. In this account, as Epaminondas deployed, extending his formation to the left, Cleombrotus reacted and prepared to envelop the Thebans, perhaps a consequence of the deep formation mentioned by Xenophon. Epaminondas, however, was saved by the charge of Pelopidas, leader of the Sacred Band, an elite force of 300 men, who ran out at the double and contacted the Spartans while they were still changing formation. After fierce fighting, the Spartans were defeated. Plutarch's account focusses on Pelopidas rather than on Cleombrotus or Epaminondas.

If, as is often done, we create a composite account of the battle, we lose the emphasis that each author placed on events. More productive is thinking about the details that we have, like Xenophon's focus on luck and leadership or Plutarch's focus on the aggression of Pelopidas. It is unfortunate that his account has few details, as this is an example of a regimental commander taking the initiative in battle. Diodorus' focus on Epaminondas' stratagem of advancing his best troops and refusing the weaker ones reduced success in battle to planning. He was dependent on Ephorus whose description of this battle was criticized by Polybius as 'laughable' (12.25f).

We could speculate that Cleombrotus had deployed the Spartan cavalry to screen moving troops across the battlefield, repeating the successful Spartan strategy from the Nemea in 394 BCE. The lack of gaps between infantry regiments for the defeated Spartan cavalry to fall back through suggests this was an experimental deployment. Xenophon did not record any Spartan changes in response to their defeat and they continued to fight in the same way as they did at Leuctra. Only three years later in 368 BCE, Sparta defeated an Argive and Arcadian force at the Tearless Battle without losing a man (Xenophon, *Hellenica* 7.1.31–32). Then in 362 BCE Sparta fought an allied Athenian and Boeotian force at Second Mantinea where the Thebans, led by Epaminondas, were on the allied left flank, deployed in depth. If the Boeotian victory at Leuctra had been the result of the reversed flank or the deep formation, one might have expected their success to be repeated, but in this battle, it was Epaminondas who died, and both sides claimed victory. Epaminondas had become famous because of his defeat of the Spartans at Leuctra, but mostly because Cleombrotus died and he did not. As was so often said by the ancients, battle was risky and unpredictable.

3.8 Battle in the Classical Period

With these case studies in mind, what can we say about the mechanics of battle in the fifth and fourth centuries? Thucydides and Xenophon emphasized luck, leadership, confusion, and courage, not weapons, numbers, and tactics.

3.8.1 Who was a regimental commander?

Among the Greek cities, the most common regimental commander was the leader of part of a city's heavy infantry contingent. He could read and write and might have fought before, but would have little, if any, training. Fighting on foot, his ability to see the battlefield or manoeuvre untrained men was limited, especially as his men had no subordinate officers. By the end of the Peloponnesian War experienced mercenary commanders began to appear, like Xenophon, Chabrias, or Iphicrates, who had long associations with their troops. A third group was Spartan regimental commanders who had subordinate officers and trained men who could manoeuvre in formation.

Among the Persians, regimental commanders were similar to those of the Greek city states, fully literate with perhaps a few professionals among Persian royal troops, especially the Immortals.

3.8.2 Training and discipline

Apart from the Spartans, Classical Greek armies had no training as formations and little as individuals, so that they are best characterized as amateur militias. As Konijnendijk wrote recently, 'Simply put, the Greeks refused to train for war' (2017, 3). The Athenian youth training programme (*ephēbeia*), which lasted for two years and included weapons handling, was not established until 335 BCE; its establishment three years after the defeat at Chaeronea suggests it addressed a shortcoming. Xenophon's manual *The Cavalry Commander* focused on individual training in riding, long distance marches, and javelin throwing, although his wish for Athens to pass a law banning vicious horses from service suggests that there was little discipline (*Cavalry Commander* 1.13–15). When fourth-century BCE generals trained their men, like Iphicrates or Jason of Pherae, it was commented on, but was still mostly individual training.

Sparta was different, troops being marked out by red cloaks and long hair, as well as formal regiments with officers which were trained to manoeuvre. But Spartans were also driven by individual honour, sometimes manifested in insubordinate behaviour. In the preliminary phases of Plataea in 479 BCE, an order to retreat was disobeyed by the regimental commander Amompharetus, and orders for two regiments to redeploy at First Mantinea were also disobeyed by their commanders, similar to Clearchus' refusal to obey Cyrus at Cunaxa.

Otherwise, without permanent units, men focussed their loyalty on their city. Within these larger identities, most shield blazons were individual, though city emblems became more common in the fourth century BCE. Prizes for being the most courageous in battle were often given. Citizen troops were not always paid and usually had to provide their own food, while mercenaries were not always paid on time. When the Spartan Mnasippus was attacked at Corcyra, many of his mercenaries had not been paid for two months (Xenophon, *Hellenica* 6.2.19). There was no formal medical care. Nor was punishment common for poor behaviour, and after Clearchus had flogged a man in another unit of the Ten Thousand, an axe and stones were thrown at him (*Anabasis* 1.5.11–14).

Amongst Persian armies, the standards of training were similarly low, with most of the troops being contingents levied from the local population or mercenaries. Persian royal troops, i.e. the king's cavalry bodyguard, the Apple-Bearers, and the Immortals, were standing bodies, so perhaps trained as individuals and units.

3.8.3 Infantry and cavalry spacing

No Classical writer discussed spacing between heavy infantry in combat, so that everything we say about the intervals between ranks and the intervals between files is an argument. As discussed above (2.4), a loose 2m spacing for a spearman is preferred here, though 1m is possible. Many modern authors quote Thucydides' description of how the Spartan and Argive armies closed at First Mantinea in 418 BCE:

> All armies do this: they push out somewhat to their right flank when moving, and both surround the enemy's left with their right, through fear each man as much as possible wanting to protect their shieldless side by the shield of the man ranked to their right, thinking that he will be best protected by the closeness of the formation (5.71.1).

No other ancient author remarked on this unplanned drift to the right during the advance to combat, although Thucydides' logic suggests it would have been true of all shielded formations. It is thus not a generalization for antiquity but a description of how the untrained troops that he knew advanced.

Advocates of close spacing often argue from Asclepiodotus in the first century BCE who mentioned three spacings for infantry: the most open at 4 cubits [2m] apart, a spacing he qualified as 'natural' (*kata phusin*), the intermediate or 'compact' (*puknōsis*) at 2 cubits [1m], and the most compact, with 'shields together' (*synaspismos*) at 1 cubit [0.5m]. Although Asclepiodotus referred to these as 'hoplite' formations, he described men with weapons that were 10 or more cubits long, i.e. pikes used in two hands, with five ranks of weapons projecting past the front rank (*Tactica* 5). He also thought that these three spacings applied to both depth and width equally. Asclepiodotus is thus of little use in understanding what fifth-century BCE spearmen did.

Intervals between ranks were determined by the weapons used. The balance point of the typical 2.5m-long infantry spear was a little behind the centre, so about 1.5m of the spear projected in front and about 1m behind the soldier. This gives a minimum interval so that men were not at risk of being injured by the weapons of the men in front. The distance that the spear could extend to the front suggests that only the front rank was directly engaged in combat at any one moment, since the spears of the second rank would barely reach the shoulders of the men in the first rank and getting any closer risked getting injured by their butt-spikes, only rarely recorded. As the fighting developed, openings in the front rank or between files would give the second rank opportunities to engage.

Greek heavy infantry formed up in lines varying between four and sixteen ranks deep. At First Mantinea Spartan regiments 'were not all drawn up in the same depth, but as each commander (*lochagos*) wished' (Thucydides 5.68.3). Greater depth did not guarantee victory, and at Syracuse in 415 BCE, eight-deep Argives and Athenians defeated sixteen-deep Syracusans (Thucydides 6.67–70). The costs and benefits were understood, as Xenophon noted:

> If we advance deployed in depth, the enemy will outnumber us and will use their extra men for whatever they wish. But if we are deployed in a few ranks, it would not be a shock if our line (*phalanx*) were cut through by a crowd of missiles and many men falling on us; and if this happens at some point, it will be bad for the whole line (*phalanx*) (*Anabasis* 4.8.11).

The Thebans sometimes used deeper formations, twenty-five deep at Delium and fifty deep at Leuctra, but the lack of imitators suggests it brought no consistently significant advantages. These blocks were easier to move than long lines, but as Xenophon observed, they increased the risk of being outflanked.

We have no evidence for Persian heavy infantry but might cautiously conclude from their also being spear-and-shield armed that their spacing was similar. Light infantry spacing was looser, in clouds rather than blocks.

The minimal attention paid in our sources to Greek cavalry means we can say little about their formations. Xenophon in the *Cavalry Commander* envisaged Greek cavalry being deployed in lines of multiple ranks, consistent with his descriptions of Agesilaus' cavalry in Asia deploying in a line four deep and Spartan cavalry at Second Mantinea deployed six deep (Xenophon, *Hellenica* 3.4.14, 7.5.23). Cavalry usually fought by skirmishing in loose formations. Persian cavalry deployed in the same way, though the more heavily equipped men like Cyrus' bodyguard may have fought in linear formations.

3.8.4 Deployment for battle

Typical Greek deployment was a single line of heavy infantry units ordered by city, with cavalry and light troops on the flanks. The best troops were usually on the right, occasionally on the left as with the Spartans at Olpae in 426 BCE (Thucydides 3.107–108) and the Boeotians at Leuctra. With most armies consisting of untrained troops, it would take a long time to get into position, especially for armies containing contingents from different cities. Before Plataea, Herodotus described debates about who should stand where on the battlefield and at Coronea Xenophon described a delay as the allies debated about how deep each contingent should deploy.

Cavalry were normally on the flanks, but unusually deployed in front of the main body by both Spartans and Thebans at Leuctra (Xenophon, *Hellenica* 6.4.10–13). This feels more like advanced guards engaging, as at the Lyncus in Thrace (Thucydides 4.124.3), rather than deliberate deployment in the centre. Light troops could screen the front of armies, but it is often hard to tell whether they were deployed in front of the main body or on the flanks. If units were defending on hills, the light troops could be deployed behind them, further up the slope so they could see and shoot overhead (Xenophon, *Hellenica* 2.4.12).

Reserves, i.e. a group of men deliberately kept back to change the flow of the battle, were rare though the concept was understood. With most generals distracted by their own involvement in fighting and the likelihood of armies collapsing rapidly, i.e. before a reserve could stabilize the situation, it was not the best allocation of resources. However, during the first battle at Syracuse, half of the Athenian force was held back to support the front line (Thucydides 6.67.1) and some forces arriving later in battle with good results may have been reserves, like Pagondas' cavalry at Delium and some Corinthians at Solygeia (Thucydides 4.43.1–4).

Most generals preferred to fight on flat and open ground which would have had the least impact on their formations. Even at Delium, where the Boeotians had the advantage of higher ground, they chose to attack the Athenians rather than waiting, although in an action before First Mantineia an Argive force stood uphill and the Spartans chose not to engage. At Cunaxa, Artaxerxes deployed with a flank anchored on the Euphrates. Once deployed, Greek armies usually advanced to contact rapidly, eager to get the fighting over with. This gave little time to adjust the deployment if the enemy had drawn up for battle in an unexpected fashion. At First Mantinea, the Spartan king Agis thought that his left flank was vulnerable to being encircled, while his right flank had more men than it needed. Both armies had already begun to advance when he ordered two regiments on the left to extend their order and two regiments from the right to move behind the battleline to fill the gap. The right flank regimental commanders refused to obey the order, leaving a gap in the Spartan line, and though Agis then ordered his left flank troops to close the gap, they were not in time to stop the line being penetrated (Thucydides 5.71–72). Most recorded adjustments after deployment were by Spartans, though one was ordered by Cyrus at Cunaxa.

Army commanders could engage with their best troops first in the hope of winning the battle quickly, a tactic favoured by the Thebans and perhaps accounting for their preference for deeper formations. At Nemea, as the Boeotians tried to outflank the enemy, they risked opening a gap in their own line, and although this was covered by the Athenians, the whole army slewed to the right. Spartan generals often tried to defeat the enemy on one flank and then turn to roll up the enemy's battle line which they did at First Mantinea, Nemea, and Coronea. They could do this because of their trained regiments, but also because Spartans were less prone to retire after seeing other parts of their armies defeated. Thus, at Nemea they successfully engaged the allied right as it returned from pursuit.

3.8.5 Manoeuvre during battle

Heavy infantry fought in linear formations. With no officers or formed units, and with most regimental commanders fighting in the front ranks, it was difficult for anyone except the Spartans to manoeuvre. For the Spartans, the most common manoeuvre came after defeating the enemy on one flank and, after dressing ranks, they wheeled in order to roll up the enemy line, probably after a signal from their general. They were able to do this successfully at First Mantinea and Coronea, even though their allies were defeated. Manoeuvre in front of the enemy was risky. At Corcyra in 373 BCE a Spartan unit

> being deployed eight deep and thinking that the end of the line (*phalangos*) was weak, tried to retire, but as they began to move backwards, the enemy attacked them, as if fleeing, so they no longer turned and those next to them rushed to flight (Xenophon, *Hellenica* 6.2.21).

The word translated here as 'retire', *anastrephein*, can also mean to wheel backwards, though this complicated manoeuvre was less likely to be what Xenophon meant. When Cleon at Amphipolis ordered his right wing to wheel (*epistrepsas*) they fell into disorder, prompting an attack by Brasidas that routed them, 'at the same time fearful from their disorder and amazed at his daring' (Thucydides 5.10.7).

There were occasional exceptions in difficult terrain, e.g. the experienced mercenaries of the Ten Thousand forming what Xenophon describes as columns (*orthious*) on a hill. These behaved as if they were small lines, with individual column commanders responsible for their own flanks (*Anabasis* 4.8.10–15). When moving under attack from skirmishers armies often formed a hollow square, but these moved slowly.

There is no Classical evidence for use of triangular wedges or diamonds for cavalry, despite the claims in the later Asclepiodotus and the derivative manuals. The word *embolon* is usually translated as wedge, but its only use in the Classical period for land battle was in Xenophon's account of the Theban attack at Second Mantinea where he used the image of a ship breaking the line, i.e. using *embolon* in another accepted meaning, that of 'ram' (Xenophon, *Hellenica* 7.5.23–24).

Contemporary Greek attitudes towards light troops were often dismissive, so that Thucydides omitted them from his account of Delium and Xenophon recorded Spartan contempt for the Mantineans, 'saying that their allies feared peltasts the way children fear monsters' (*Hellenica*, 4.4.17). These elite attitudes were badly misplaced and numerous actions showed the vulnerabilities of heavy infantry who were not supported by light troops and cavalry. One of the first land battles in the Peloponnesian War took place at Aegitium in Aetolia in 426 BCE, about 150km from Athens. The Athenian commander Demosthenes was severely defeated.

> The Aetolians who had come to help were already at Aegitium and attacked the Athenians and their allies, running down upon them from the hills from here and there and began to throw javelins. And when the army of the Athenians attacked, they fell back; and when the Athenians retired, they attacked. The battle was like this for a long time, pursuits and retreats in both of which the Athenians were inferior. But as long as the Athenian archers had arrows and were able to use them they endured, for the Aetolian light troops held back when shot at. But when the leader of the archers was killed they scattered and they were tired from the work of keeping formation for a long time, but the Aetolians were pressuring them and throwing javelins, so that the Athenians turned and fled, falling into ravines with no exits and places they did not know, and were destroyed (Thucydides 3.97.3–98.1).

In this case of poor generalship by Demosthenes and good leadership on the part of the anonymous Aetolian commander, 120 of 300 Athenians were killed and 'many' of their allies. This small battle was unusual in its detailed description, not in the skilled Aetolian use of light troops. Demosthenes learnt from his experience and in the following year used Athenian light troops effectively against Spartan heavy infantry at Pylos (Thucydides 4.29–38).

Even in flat terrain, heavy infantry when faced with harassing light troops could only stand in formation and take casualties or, providing no enemy cavalry was present, charge out to drive off the light troops temporarily. Since the range of javelins was around 30m, a space which could be crossed in ten to fifteen seconds, the margins were very fine, and pursuers sometimes caught some of the light infantry. More often, well-led light troops wore down heavy infantry, famously at Lechaeum near Corinth in 391 BCE when an Athenian force of heavy infantry and peltasts defeated a regiment of 600 Spartans with no light troops. The Spartans suffered heavy casualties and Xenophon observed that the Spartan horse stayed too close to their own foot as they drove off the Athenian harassers, poor practice by their commander (Xenophon, *Hellenica* 4.5.12–17).

3.8.6 Morale and the will to engage

Most battles began as the heavy infantry advanced towards the enemy. This advance often turned into a run, as at Marathon, Cunaxa, and Coronea, even though it spread men out, with stronger men running faster than their colleagues, especially the older ones, and risked the ranks becoming entangled and men getting hit by a butt spike. Controlling this behaviour without training and officers was very difficult. The Spartans were unusual in that they advanced 'slowly and with many flute-players … so that they came forward evenly walking in time and their formation (*taxis*) was not torn apart, as large armies usually do in their advances' (Thucydides 5.70.1). Battles rarely took place on featureless plains; many fields had drainage channels, softer and harder areas, slopes and areas of lower ground, bushes, occasional trees etc., bringing further disruption to any movement of troops, the more so the faster or further a unit moved. Aristotle noted that crossing even the smallest water course 'tore apart a phalanx' (*Politics* 1303b), using the same verb as Thucydides. Apart from the Spartans then, Greek armies often met with ragged formations.

If it was dangerous to meet the enemy in disorder, why did Greek armies often run into battle? Running was often the response of less-confident armies unable to stand the stress of waiting and wanting to 'get it over with', but at Sardis in 395 BCE, in Xenophon's account, the Spartan king Agesilaus ordered his men to run (*Hellenica* 3.4.23). Closing with the enemy was stressful and in the preliminaries to First Mantinea, a Spartan force did not attack some Argives on a hilltop, though they came within a stone's throw. Thucydides' explanation, of an older Spartan suggesting at this point that the attack was a mistake, is a nice literary flourish but reluctance to engage is a more compelling explanation for cancelling the assault (5.65.2).

At the Battle of Mycale, and perhaps at Marathon, the Persians waited to receive the Greek attack. In both attack and defence their heavy infantry archers shot from the main line of battle, protected by their wicker shields (Herodotus 9.99). Well-disciplined Greek troops, like Chabrias' mercenaries at Thebes in 378 BCE, might also wait in a good defensive position (Diodorus 15.32.4–6).

The same nervousness often resulted in troops not standing when attacked. Thucydides has the Spartan general Brasidas at Amphipolis in 422 BCE say of the Athenians 'these men will not stand up to us. That is clear from the moving of spears and heads, for when this happens they are not accustomed to stand up to their attackers' (5.10.5). At First Mantinea, when the Spartans turned their right flank against the Mantineans who had been victorious on their flank, the Mantineans did not stand to face them. It was the same at Coronea, the Spartans' Peloponnesian allies broke their Argive opponents in the centre: 'the Argives, however, did not wait for the attack of those with Agesilaus, but fled to Mount Helicon' (Xenophon, *Hellenica* 4.3.17). Finally at the Tearless Battle in 368 BCE, 'when Archidamus led the attack, the few of the enemy who received them with spears were killed, but the others who fled died, many from the cavalry, many from the Celts' (Xenophon, *Hellenica* 7.1.31). The flight of the Persians facing the Ten Thousand at Cunaxa was neither unusual nor a reflection of Greek superiority in battle.

3.8.7 *Infantry combat*
Armies might not stand, but on many occasions, violent clashes took place. As the heavy infantry closed, the runners slowed down and then the two groups began fighting with spears. This contact was noisy and terrifying. Then one side usually pushed back the other, sometimes quickly, sometimes after long and bitter fighting like that described around the body of Cleombrotus at Leuctra, and sometimes after a series of smaller advances and retreats. Many descriptions of infantry combat are very literary. Xenophon wrote about the main clash at Coronea: 'bringing together their shields, they pushed, fought, killed, died' (*Hellenica* 4.3.19), words he liked so much that he repeated them verbatim in his *Agesilaus*. Like the seventh-century BCE poet Tyrtaeus 'placing foot against foot, pressing shield to shield, crest against crest, helmet against helmet, chest against chest' (fr. 11.31–34) and the third-century BCE Roman writer Ennius 'foot is pressed by foot, weapons are beaten by weapons' (quoted in *Spanish War* 31), Xenophon was emulating Homer's 'making a fence spear to spear, and shield (*sakos*) overlapping with shield; shield (*aspis*) pressed on shield, helmet on helmet, man on man' (*Iliad* 13.130–131).

With no really detailed accounts, the nature of the fighting is controversial, with some scholars advocating a physical pushing match. I prefer to see most fighting as duels between individual spearmen or small groups, with the battle lines swaying backwards and forwards depending on the outcome of these fights. A small action at Solygeia in 425 BCE illustrates this sort of battle well.

> The right flank of the Athenians and the Carystians, for they were deployed at the end, received the Corinthians, and drove them back with difficulty. But the Corinthians, retiring to a stone wall, for the whole place was steep, threw stones from above and sang the paean and advanced again. When the Athenians received them, the battle again was hand-to-

hand. But a regiment (*lochos*) of the Corinthians coming to help their left flank, turned the right flank of the Athenians to flight and pursued them to the sea, but again the Athenians and Carystians drove them back from the ships (Thucydides 4.43.3–4).

There might also be a steady movement in one direction, but on other occasions a sudden collapse of confidence led to a rout or equally matched men wore each other down. The lack of training and officers in all armies except the Spartans meant that armies were very brittle, so that battles were over very quickly.

3.8.8 Cavalry combat

Xenophon described battle between two lines, using the word 'phalanx', of cavalry as involving turning, pursuing, and retreating (*Cavalry Commander* 8.23–24). Greek cavalry often fought in conjunction with light troops, who were sometimes organized with them and known as *hamippoi*, used at Second Mantinea. Cavalry could also fight on foot, so that at Corinth in 390 BCE, some Spartan cavalry dismounted and took shields from some allied infantry (Xenophon, *Hellenica* 4.4.10).

When heavy infantry kept together in close formation, cavalry could do little to them. Before Plataea, Persian cavalry in successive waves harassed Greek infantry with bows and javelins (Herodotus 9.20–23, 49), similar to Xenophon's description of fifty Sicilian cavalry fighting in the Peloponnese against the Thebans.

> But the horsemen from Dionysius, as many as they were, scattering here and there riding along, began to throw javelins and attacking, and when the enemy rushed at them, they retreated and after turning round began to throw their javelins again.... But if anyone pursued them far from the army then as those men retired [the Sicilians] pressing them and throwing javelins did terrible things to them, and by themselves compelled the whole army both to advance and to retire (Xenophon, *Hellenica* 7.1.21).

Such harassment had little impact on the heavy infantry as long as the defenders had enough light troops and were well led. Against unsupported light infantry, however, cavalry were very effective. At Thebes in 378 BCE some Spartans were ambushed.

> The cavalry of the Thebans, not being seen for a while, suddenly advancing through the gates in the palisade, attacked. And since the

peltasts were going away to dinner or preparing for it, and the horsemen were either still dismounted or mounting, they attacked them; and they cut down many of the peltasts, and from the cavalry the Spartiates Cleas and Epicydidas, and Eudicus one of the Perioeci, and some Theban exiles who had not yet mounted their horses (Xenophon, *Hellenica* 5.4.39).

Similar situations occurred if heavy infantry became disordered. At Plataea,

When the Megarians and Phliasians were near the enemy, the Theban cavalry, whose commander was Asopodorus son of Timander, seeing them rushing forwards in no order, attacked. Bursting in, they trampled 600 of them, and broke the rest, pursuing them to Cithaeron (Herodotus 9.69.2).

3.8.9 Pursuit

When one side was pushed back, low levels of resilience meant that they often broke and ran, and this rout frequently persuaded others in their army to retire too. It was at this point that the majority of casualties were inflicted, mostly by the light infantry and cavalry among the pursuing forces. Sometimes fleeing men were saved by a fortified camp or the coming of night, but on many occasions, they were cut down in their hundreds.

Not all defeated men ran in disorder; Socrates was famous for his courage in the retreat at Delium. Cavalry could also help to cover a retreat, like the Boeotians protecting their infantry after Plataea (Herodotus. 9.68–69) or a Syracusan cavalry force intervening as the victorious Athenians were pursuing the Syracusan infantry (Thucydides 6.101.4–5).

Keeping the pursuers under control was difficult, and the Ten Thousand at Cunaxa chased the fleeing Persians far off the battlefield. The Spartan ability to stay in formation after defeating the enemy in front of them was unusual, and though it avoided the risks of pursuit, failed to reap the benefits. According to one of Xenophon's characters, 'When cities defeat their enemies in battle, it is not easy to say how much pleasure they have in routing the enemy, how much in the pursuit, and how much in the killing an enemy' (*Hiero* 2.15).

3.9 Conclusion

There was little about the Greek way of battle in the fifth and fourth centuries that differed from the way that contemporary Persian, Etruscan, or Carthaginian armies fought. In mainland Greece, most troops were untrained, with the exception of the Spartans, and our sources often neglected light troops. Warfare was conducted by citizen-farmers who lived close to one another, so armies were small and brittle, soldiers provided their own equipment, and campaigns were short. In the plains and hills of the Peloponnese, Attica, and Boeotia, armies could sometimes get away with fewer light troops or cavalry. But not elsewhere.

Battles were linear, with planning and manoeuvring mostly confined to deployment. A second stage of possible manoeuvring occurred after breaking the enemy in front, though not all troops were capable of this and pursuit in this situation was common. Any breaks in formation gave an opportunity to win or lose a battle, though neither was unique to the Classical period and the failure to preserve order or to be outflanked continued to be critical features at all periods of ancient warfare.

What could the regimental commander typically expect to do? Since few troops had any training, and without permanent structures of units and sub-officers, regimental commanders could do little to affect the flow of the battle except to lead from the front and try to stop troops from pursuing in dangerous situations. Commanders of light troops and cavalry had more opportunities than leaders of heavy infantry to make tactical decisions, but these tended to affect only the flanks of armies.

Chapter 4

The Hellenistic Period

The story of Alexander the Great (336–323 BCE) was a popular subject in antiquity, as were the wars between his Successors. This was a period of great kings fighting each other with large armies built around a core of well-trained pikemen supported by a multiplicity of light troops, cavalry and, often, war elephants. Then, in the second century BCE, the Successor kingdoms met Rome (covered in Chapter 6).

4.1 Sources

The best ancient historian for Alexander is Arrian of Nicomedia, writing in Greek in the second century CE. Arrian conducted extensive research, using as his main sources Ptolemy and Aristobulus, both of whom had fought alongside Alexander. Arrian wasn't a stylist but did record details of military operations and the names of regimental commanders. He had some military experience of his own from when he was governor of Cappadocia under the Roman Emperor Hadrian (117–138 CE), defending the province against an attack by some Alani (see below 8.6). Arrian also wrote a now-lost *History of the Successors of Alexander*, based on the lost work of the contemporary Hieronymus of Cardia, which was also used by Plutarch for his *Lives* of Eumenes, Demetrius, and Pyrrhus. Hieronymus served several Hellenistic rulers, including Eumenes, Antigonus Monophthalmus, and Demetrius Poliorcetes and wrote a *History* which covered 323 to 272 BCE. He was seen by the ancients as a poor stylist because he recorded numbers, quoted documents extensively, and used technical terms.

The other significant Alexander historian is Diodorus Siculus who wrote a world history in the first century BCE, covering events from the Trojan War to his own day. He often provides a useful complement to Arrian, making heavy use of the late-fourth-century BCE historian Cleitarchus, a popular author, but not one with any knowledge of warfare. Although Diodorus used to be thought of as a copyist, modern assessments of his work are more generous, but he knew little about how battle worked in antiquity and his accounts of Alexander's battles should not be favoured over Arrian's. However, for the period after Alexander's death, Diodorus used Hieronymus, so that we are very well informed about military activity between 323 and 301 BCE, though our texts become fragmentary just before Ipsus.

The best source for later Hellenistic warfare is Polybius (c.200–118 BCE). He came from Megalopolis in the Greek Peloponnese; the Battle of Sellasia, in which his father's friend Philopoemen played an important role, took place only a few kilometres away (see below 4.6). Before the defeat of the Macedonian king Perseus at Pydna in 168 BCE (see below 6.5), Polybius was the cavalry general for the Achaean League, and then he was taken to Rome as a hostage where he met Aemilius Paullus and became tutor to his sons Fabius and Scipio Aemilianus. He remained close to Aemilianus, saw Carthage sacked in 146 BCE, and was at the siege of Numantia in Spain in 133 BCE. Although we do not know if Polybius had taken part in battle himself, he lived among soldiers for most of his life.

Polybius wrote extensively, though many works, including a *Tactica*, are lost. His most important work was the *Histories*, written to explain the Roman conquest of the Mediterranean for a Greek audience. This originally covered 220–167 BCE, though was later extended down to 146 BCE, and had descriptions of earlier events including the First Romano-Punic War (263–241 BCE) as background. We have most of his account of the Second Romano-Punic War (218–202 BCE), and full versions of Raphia and Cynoscephalae, but only fragments dealing with Panium, Magnesia, and Pydna. Polybius was a remarkably modern historian, very interested in causation. He used numerous sources, including Fabius Pictor, an early Roman historian who fought in the Second Romano-Punic War, and Sosylus of Sparta and Silenus of Caleacte, both of whom accompanied Hannibal in his Italian campaigns. He also interviewed participants, such as Gaius Laelius, one of Scipio Africanus' cavalry commanders at Zama. Stylistically Polybius can be disappointing, writing a clear Greek with few literary flourishes, but he was a very critical writer, so his *Histories* are studded with comments on other authors, in particular tirades against Ephorus, Timaeus, and Callisthenes. He believed that 'it is not possible to write well about what happens in war for someone having no experience of warlike matters' (12.25g.1). Polybius was also very reflective, with numerous digressions on military matters and comments on best practice, often to explain Roman institutions for his Greek audience. As a contemporary historian, well-informed, and with a good technical understanding of warfare, what Polybius says about ancient battle should be taken very seriously.

4.2 Equipment and Organization

Armies of the Classical period were built around a line of heavy infantry equipped with spears, but in the Hellenistic period armies were built around the pike phalanx. This was such a fearsome weapon system that Polybius claimed 'it is not possible to resist the charge of the phalanx which maintains its formation and capability' (18.30.11). As we have seen, the Greek word 'phalanx' was originally employed to mean a formation of men in the main line of battle, but from the later-fourth century BCE it was often used in a more technical sense to mean the infantry core of an army equipped with pikes, i.e. 'in the Macedonian style'. The Macedonian pike phalanx is usually thought to have been introduced during the reign of Alexander the Great's father, Philip II (r.359–336 BCE). The pike (*sarissa*) was a long spear held in two hands, with a wooden shaft 5–6m in length and a small penetrating head, weighing approximately 4–5kg. Since both hands were used to hold the pike, only a small shield could be used, strapped to the left arm. Most pikemen were also equipped with a helmet and sword or dagger. Body armour was the *linothōrax*, which made this a cheap panoply, important at the beginning of Philip's reign, though less important later when kings had access to greater financial resources.

The infantry core of Alexander's army was six regiments (*taxeis*, singular = *taxis*) of 1,500 men, identified by the names of their commanders. This was a theoretical strength, and campaign losses would rapidly have shrunk these units. Three of these *taxeis* were *asthetairoi*, and a good argument has been made that they were equipped as spearmen rather than as pikemen. Alexander's elite infantry *hypaspists* were normally organized as three regiments of 1,000 men, the first of which was also known as the *agēma* under Alexander and later as the *argyraspides* (Silvershields). The *hypaspists* fought in large battles next to the infantry *taxeis*, but we cannot be certain whether they were normally equipped with pikes or spears. Alexander's army also included large numbers of mercenary heavy infantry, equipped as in the Classical period. The heavy infantry was supplemented by light infantry who included javelinmen and archers, in Alexander's case the Agrianians and Cretans, and peltasts.

The armies of the Successors were initially similar to those of Alexander. The core of Macedonian infantry was soon replaced by a mixture of Greek colonists and local recruits, all still pike-armed. Less wealthy and smaller states were not able to afford the training needed to field an effective phalanx, so tended to continue to field spear-armed heavy infantry as in the Classical period. Sometimes these were described as *thureophoroi* (after their large rectangular shields) or *thōrakitai* (after their body armour). These troops became more

Figure 4.1: Macedonian pikeman, heavily armoured with linen body armour, helmet, and greaves. He also carries a shield with an eight-pointed Macedonian star and a short sword. Veterans found it easier to manage all this equipment, but new recruits might have been more tempted to dispense with some of it as they grappled with a pike measuring more than twice their height. (© *Philip Sidnell*)

common following a series of defeats by Rome, after which the pike phalanx was often replaced by heavy infantry equipped in the Roman fashion, i.e. heavy infantry wearing mail and fighting with javelins and swords.

Hellenistic armies contained large numbers of cavalry, with Alexander fielding a ratio of about 1:6 cavalry to infantry. Following his reign, the proportions of cavalry drifted back to where they had been in the Classical period, around 1:10 cavalry to infantry. As in the Classical period, most horsemen were light cavalry, equipped with javelins for skirmishing, although there were specialized regiments of horse archers. However, a consistent feature of Hellenistic royal armies were regiments of Companions, initially Macedonian heavy cavalry, though later including men recruited from elsewhere, with the highest status regiment known as the royal squadron or *agēma*. They were armed with spears and wore body armour and helmets, but had no shields. At the beginning of his campaigns, Alexander's Companions were organized into 8 squadrons (*ilai*, singular = *ilē*), of about 250 men, later expanded to form *hipparchiai* 500 strong, each of two *ilai*.

There were two significant developments in cavalry equipment during this period. One was the introduction of shields for cavalry, initially by a type of light cavalry known as Tarantines, armed with javelins and shields. Tarentum (modern Taranto) lay in southern Italy where cavalry had carried shields in the fourth century BCE, but they spread more widely into the Hellenistic world in the third century BCE, so that Polybius assumed that all cavalry had shields. The second development was the appearance of cataphracts, armoured men on armoured horses, equipped with lances but no shields, in the later Hellenistic

Figure 4.2: Macedonian Companion cavalry, wearing linen body armour and a metal 'Boeotian' helmet. He's got a *sarissa* in one hand that he would use as a lance since it was too long to throw, and a sword in case the *sarissa* broke. (© *Philip Sidnell*)

period. They seem first to have been introduced by the Seleucids after Raphia in 217 BCE, being first heard of at Panium in 200 BCE.

The Persian armies that Alexander faced were generally similar to those of the fifth and fourth centuries (see above 3.3). There was a contingent of Cardakes at Issus, described by Arrian as heavy infantry (*hoplitai*) (2.8.6).

The result of these changes was armies that were far more effective as combined arms formations than in the Classical period, with trained pikemen supported by Companion cavalry who focused on charges rather than skirmishing. The orator Demosthenes contrasted the Athenian army with the Macedonian king who was 'not leading a line of heavy infantry (*phalangg' hoplitōn*), but an army composed of light infantry, cavalry, archers, and mercenaries' (9.49).

Figure 4.3: Tarantine light cavalryman, equipped with a large shield, unlike earlier Greek light cavalry, with several javelins for throwing. He might be a little better than the Greek cavalryman at skirmishing, but still preferred to fight at a distance. (© *Philip Sidnell*)

4.3 The Battle of Issus, 333 BCE

During the fourth century BCE, the kingdom of Macedonia became increasingly important in Greek affairs. A combination of great natural resources, some lucky mineral finds, and several talented monarchs allowed the creation of a powerful army under Philip II (359–336 BCE) and his son Alexander the Great (*r.*336–323 BCE) which won five major battles: Chaeronea (338 BCE) against a Greek alliance, Granicus (334 BCE), Issus (333 BCE), Gaugamela (331 BCE) against the Achaemenid Persians, and the Hydaspes (326 BCE) against the Indian king Porus. Alexander was a great warrior and an inspiring leader, at the head of a well-trained and increasingly experienced army with excellent low-level leaders. The pike phalanx was successful because of its training, not its equipment, while the Companion cavalry were important because of their willingness to charge home, not because of their lances or formation.

Our knowledge of Chaeronea is minimal, and with only the sparsest of details in Plutarch and Diodorus it is best to admit our inability to discuss what happened on this battlefield. The evidence is better for the first meeting of the Persians and Alexander at the Granicus River in Anatolia when the Persians deployed on the banks of the river, forcing Alexander to choose between an assault up a riverbank or a crossing elsewhere. According to Arrian, Alexander chose the assault, but Diodorus had Alexander cross the river first, then fight the battle. After his victory at the Granicus, Alexander occupied the rest of Anatolia and by November 333 BCE, he was in Cilicia. The Persian king Darius III (r 336–330 BCE) was able to place his army between Alexander and Macedonia, so that Alexander was forced to fight with little hope of retreat if he were defeated. The battlefield was a narrow coastal plain, about 14 stades (approximately 2.8km) between the Mediterranean and the foothills, but its exact location is uncertain, and with significant coastline change since antiquity, the location of the River Pinarus is disputed.

The battle is described by Arrian and Diodorus, though their accounts, as at Granicus, are irreconcilable; Arrian's account (2.8–2.11), with details of terrain, deployment, and sequence of events, is followed here. Diodorus is dramatic but does not mention the strategic situation or the terrain, and has the battle fought entirely by cavalry, so that 'the phalanx of the Macedonians and the infantry force of the Persians were engaged only for a short time' (17.33–34).

The Persians had a similar plan as at the Granicus, attempting to disrupt the Macedonian army by fighting behind the Pinarus, which had steep banks in some places and stakes added in others. Arrian described the Persians as sending 30,000 cavalry and 20,000 light troops across the Pinarus on their right, with Darius and 30,000 Greek mercenaries in the centre with 30,000 Cardaces on each side, and a further 20,000 foot in the hills on the left. These numbers add up to 160,000, but Arrian said there were 600,000, though using a phrasing suggestive of doubt.

Alexander's army approached in column along the coast, around 30,000 infantry and 5,000 cavalry. The left flank, commanded by Parmenio, lay on the Mediterranean, its right extended into the foothills. As the army advanced, Alexander brought units forward to make a line. The infantry centre was composed of the *hypaspists* on the right, then the six *taxeis* of the heavy infantry (here called 'hoplites' by Arrian). Polybius was very critical of Callisthenes' lost account of this battle, which had the phalanx first at thirty-two deep, then at sixteen and finally at eight ranks deep (12.17–22). When more space became available, the infantry formations were made shallower and cavalry were fed into the line, the Companions and the Thessalian cavalry on the right, the majority of the allied Greek cavalry on the left.

As the Macedonians advanced, the Persian screening forces fell back and the cavalry were sent out to their flanks, mostly on the Persian right by the sea. Alexander adjusted his deployment to match, moving the Thessalian cavalry behind his infantry from the right to the left flank. Skirmishers were now placed in front of the centre and the mercenary infantry formed a second line behind. On the Macedonian right, an angled force of infantry and cavalry faced the Persians in the hills, protecting the flank of the main line of battle. This force was at first supplemented by further troops, but following some attacks by the Macedonians, Alexander thought there was no danger of being outflanked and moved men back to the main body.

With all these preliminaries, the battle did not start until the afternoon. Then the Macedonians advanced slowly, to avoid breaking up their formation, until they were in missile range (around 300m), and then began to move into contact, with Arrian noting that this was at a run (*dromō*) to reduce the time they were under Persian missile shot. Alexander, leading the Companion cavalry, was successful on his right. However, in the centre, when the infantry *taxeis* 'finding the riverbanks precipitous in many places were not able to keep their front in formation, the Greeks [i.e. the Persians' Greek mercenaries] attacked where they saw that the phalanx had been particularly torn apart' (Arrian 2.10.5). While fierce fighting took place in the centre, the Macedonian right continued to advance, and then were able to turn (*epikampsantes*, meaning to move at an angle rather than wheeling) onto the flank of the Greek mercenaries, overlapping them and then rolling them up, leading to the collapse of the centre. On the Macedonian left, there was heavy cavalry fighting with the Persians crossing the river. Then the Persian centre collapsed and the rout became general. Arrian gave a figure of 100,000 Persian casualties, but did not offer a total for the Macedonians.

The terrain was an important feature in this battle in two ways. First, it neutralized the numerical advantage of the Persians, who might otherwise have outflanked Alexander's army on one or both flanks as they later planned to do at Gaugamela. However, it also gave the Persians the advantage of having a linear feature, the River Pinarus, which they could defend, and with Alexander cut off from Europe, he was forced to attack. Sending a force of heavy infantry to attack a defended riverbank was a difficult task. The crucial moment in the battle came once the right of the Macedonian centre had crossed the river. 'Here Ptolemaeus, son of Seleucus, fell [leading a *taxis*], a brave man, and another 120 well-regarded Macedonians' (Arrian 2.10.7). Because Alexander had taken care not to begin the battle before neutralizing the Persians on the right, he had no concern about being outflanked himself, but he was also able to control his forces sufficiently to turn some of the phalanx against the Persian centre.

In their third battle with Alexander, at Gaugamela in 331 BCE, the Persians fought on an open plain to maximize their numbers, planning to encircle the Macedonians on both flanks. Alexander deployed with a refused left, as at Chaeronea, but also with a second line of troops, as at Issus. The Persians were pinned by the phalanx while Alexander advanced on the right and having defeated the Persian cavalry he could now strike at their main line. While he was doing this, gaps appeared on the left end of the Macedonian line, but Alexander got lucky as the penetrating Persian cavalry looted his camp, rather than rolling up his line.

Following his conquest of the Persian Empire, Alexander moved into India where at the Hydaspes in 326 BCE he faced the Indian king Porus leading an army that included fifty or more elephants and chariots. The Greeks had known about elephants since Herodotus, though few had seen one. The elephants were deployed in front of the Indian infantry, whose line Arrian called a phalanx (Arrian 5.15.5). Alexander refused his centre and began the battle with cavalry action on the flanks, ordering his infantry not to engage until the Indian infantry had been thrown into disorder by the Macedonian cavalry. The Macedonian phalanx attacked the elephants with javelins (Arrian 5.17.3). As the battle developed, the elephants disordered the Macedonian phalanx, but after losing many of their drivers lost their effectiveness and the Indians were gradually driven back before breaking.

4.4 Elephants

The Battle at the Hydaspes was the first time a Mediterranean army fought elephants. They were quickly incorporated into the armies of Alexander's Successors, with Eumenes fielding 114 elephants and Antigonus Monophthalmus 65 at Paraitacene in 317 BCE, and spread rapidly westwards, first appearing in the central Mediterranean during Pyrrhus of Epirus' invasion of Italy in 280 BCE. Soon afterwards, the Carthaginians fielded around 50 elephants at Agrigentum in Sicily in 262 BCE, close to 100 at Bagradas in 255 BCE, and 140 in Sicily in 254 BCE. The Romans began to use African elephants in the second century BCE, with 20 at Cynoscephalae in 197 BCE, 16 at Magnesia in 190 BCE, and 22 at Pydna in 168 BCE, though their last significant Roman use was at Thapsus in 46 BCE, where Scipio had about 60 elephants. The rapid spread suggests elephants were seen as useful, though few modern scholars agree.

The Ptolemies and Carthaginians fielded African forest elephants which in antiquity were found along the Mediterranean coast, but now restricted to Central and West Africa. They are smaller and more docile than African bush elephants and also smaller than the elephants used by Indian rulers, the Seleucids, and later the Sasanian Persians. At Raphia, Ptolemy IV had 73 African elephants and the Seleucid king Antiochus III had 102 Indian elephants.

> Most of Ptolemy's elephants were fearful of battle, as is the habit of African elephants. For they cannot stand the smell and the noise, and are also panicked by their size and strength, so that it seems to me that they immediately flee from the vicinity of Indian elephants (Polybius 5.84.5–6).

Elephants were driven by mahouts, generically known as Indians. Turrets or towers were regularly used on Indian elephants to carry a small crew, less often on the smaller African elephants.

The typical deployment of elephants was as a screen across the front of an army, usually supported by light infantry in the intervals, to disrupt the enemy heavy infantry. This formation was used by Porus at the Hydaspes, by both Antigonus and Eumenes at Paraitacene and Gabiene, and by Carthaginian armies at Bagradas, the Metaurus, and at Zama. It was most useful when facing infantry with limited missile capacities. Placing elephants in the main line of battle itself was rare, but at Magnesia they were placed between units of the Seleucid pike phalanx (see below 6.2). Elephants were also used to support cavalry and light troops on the flanks, as at the Trebbia and at Ilipa, by both the Ptolemies and Seleucids at Raphia, and by Scipio at Thapsus. Elephants could also screen a flank and at Ipsus were used by Seleucus to keep Demetrius' cavalry away from the main battle.

Defensive tactics were difficult to carry out and required well-trained and confident troops. The most common was to use light infantry to harass the elephants and their drivers with missile shot. Since elephant skin is about 2.5cm thick, giving them some resistance to many weapons, light troops would need to get close. At Paraitacene Antigonus' horse archers were able to damage Eumenes' elephants, at Beneventum in 280 BCE javelin shot forced back Pyrrhus' elephants, and at Thapsus in 46 BCE Scipio's elephants were forced to retreat by the volume of sling and arrow shot. Other defensive measures included Scipio at Zama deploying his maniples directly behind each other, rather than in a checkerboard formation, creating lanes between the Roman maniples that allowed the elephants to move through, while at the Trebbia, some Romans were able to get close enough to hamstring the elephants.

Elephants were also vulnerable to caltrops, used successfully by Ptolemy at Gaza in 312 BCE (Diodorus 19.84.4).

Sometimes elephants panicked and then their movements were unpredictable. At Panormus in 250 BCE Carthaginian elephants were driven into their own men as a result of missile shot, and at Ilipa the panicked elephants rampaged through both Roman and Carthaginian ranks. The author of the *African War* noted that in battle they were 'a danger to everyone' (28) and the Roman writer Livy was unable to mention elephants without emphasizing their inability to be controlled, but he was more convinced of this than his main source, Polybius. But elephants did not always panic, and were effective at Paraitacene, Gabiene, Bagradas, Cynoscephalae, and Pydna.

Because elephants were of most use against tightly packed infantry formations like pike phalanxes, they were less used after the Roman defeats of the Hellenistic kingdoms. When infantry were more easily able to spread out, like most of Rome's later enemies, elephants were of less value on the battlefield. At all periods, they were part of a combined-arms formation, not weapons expected to win the battle alone, and always had a great psychological impact. As Ammianus wrote in the fourth century CE, 'the elephants looking like walking hills, and by the movement of their enormous bodies they threatened destruction to those nearby, being dreaded from previous experiences' (24.6.8).

4.5 The Battle of Gabiene, 316 BCE

With the fragmentation of Alexander's empire after his death in 323 BCE, his Successors fought for power in a period characterized by battles between armies built around pike phalanxes. In central Persia (modern Iran), Antigonus coming from Mesopotamia was contending with Eumenes in control of the eastern satrapies near India. At Paraitacene near Persepolis in 317 BCE, Eumenes was successful in the infantry clash in the centre and on his right, but this advance opened a gap on his left flank, where Antigonus threw in his cavalry and broke Eumenes' cavalry. The action ceased as night fell, allowing the armies to separate.

Antigonus and Eumenes regrouped over the winter and then in 316 BCE met again at Gabiene on the uncultivated salty plain of Gavkhuni, now a seasonal wetland. Diodorus' account (19.40–43) can be supplemented with some details from Plutarch's *Eumenes*, both based on the eyewitness Hieronymus of Cardia. Before the armies deployed, the camps were separated by 40 stades (around 8km), so that the battle started late in the day. Antigonus had 22,000 heavy infantry, an unknown number of light infantry, 9,000 cavalry, and 65 elephants. He led the centre himself, with his left under Pithon, and the right with the best cavalry under his son Demetrius. The front of the army was screened by the elephants with light troops in the intervals. Eumenes had 36,700 infantry (both light and heavy), 6,000 cavalry, and 114 elephants. He placed his best troops on his left flank opposite Demetrius, with a screen of 60 elephants and light troops. The centre was of pike-armed regiments, his hypaspists, the *argyraspides* (Alexander's former hypaspists), and the phalanx, also screened by elephants. On his right there were more cavalry and a further elephant screen under Philip, ordered to stay back and not engage. Diodorus focused on the heavy infantry, cavalry, and elephants, and said little about light infantry.

Antigonus was successful on his right flank after a fiercely fought cavalry battle, but once it was over, Eumenes was able to extricate some troops and cross the battlefield to his own right flank. In the centre meanwhile, Antigonus' infantry had been defeated by the assault of the *argyraspides*.

> As for the infantry, the tightly packed *argyraspides*, attacking very forcefully those deployed against them, killed some in hand-to-hand fighting and forced others to flee. They were not to be checked in their rushes and fought against the whole phalanx of the enemy, exceeding them so much in skill and strength that they lost none of their own, but killed more than 5,000 of the enemy and turned to flight all the infantry who were much greater in number (Diodorus 19.43.1).

Antigonus, however, had sent a force of cavalry around Eumenes' flank, hoping that this would not be detected in the dust of the battle, and they captured Eumenes' camp. As night fell, the battle was over, but any further military action was superseded by the *argyraspides* handing over Eumenes to Antigonus in exchange for their families captured in the camp.

Diodorus' account focused on numbers, deployments, and aims, rather than on a detailed account of the fighting itself. In both battles, reported troop numbers have the total of Eumenes' foot exceeding the heavy infantry of Antigonus, but with no details we are unclear as to how the two groups of pikemen clashed with one another. Eumenes was probably successful because of the experience of the *argyraspides*. Unlike Alexander who led his cavalry in person, the generals kept a distance from the fighting and at both battles Eumenes was able to detach cavalry from one flank and transfer them to the other. Eumenes' army was 1:6 cavalry to infantry, while Antigonus may have had an even higher proportion of cavalry.

The rivalries between Alexander's generals continued until the defeat of Antigonus at Ipsus in 301 BCE, after which the Antigonid kingdom based in

Macedonia contended for supremacy with the Seleucids based in Syria and the Ptolemies in Egypt, as well as struggling to keep control of mainland Greece.

4.6 The Battle of Sellasia, 222 BCE

In the Greek Peloponnese in 222 BCE, the Macedonian king, Antigonus III Doson (r.229–221 BCE), and allies from the Achaean League attacked Sparta, their army totalling 27,600 infantry and 1,200 cavalry. The Spartans, led by King Cleomenes III (r.235–222), fielded 20,000 infantry and 650 cavalry. After their defeat at Leuctra (see above 3.7), Sparta had lost its dependent territories and thus the ability to maintain large numbers of professional soldiers. Following recent reforms by Cleomenes, they were now equipped in the Macedonian fashion, i.e. as pikemen. The main source is Polybius who had talked to participants and probably visited the battlefield (2.65–69). Plutarch used Polybius and one of his contemporaries, Phylarchus, in his biographies of Cleomenes and of Philopoemen. Plutarch tells a good story, but his assertion that 'skill in deploying an army is the acme of military matters' (*Philopoemen* 14.5) cannot be accepted.

The two armies met in a pass about 10km north of Sparta where Cleomenes had fortified two hills on either side of the road and river with a trench and palisade. The Spartan centre was held with cavalry and mercenary infantry, an unusual deployment, but this battle would be won or lost on the flanking hills, rather than in the centre. Cleomenes led the troops on the right hill, his brother Eucleidas those on the left. By standing uphill, Cleomenes sacrificed the initiative and waited to be attacked, while Antigonus chose to fight instead of withdrawing to take a different route.

After several days preparing Antigonus launched his attack. The right flank of his army composed of the Illyrians and *chalkaspides* (Bronzeshields), arranged alternately by regiments, with a unit of Achaean infantry kept back for use as a reserve (*ephedreia*). The cavalry were deployed in the centre with supporting infantry. On the left, which Antigonus led himself, mercenary light infantry preceded the remainder of the phalanx who were deployed at double the normal depth, i.e. thirty-two ranks rather than sixteen, because of the narrowness of the terrain. The cavalry were placed in the centre because the fighting here was not expected to be significant.

The battle began with the Macedonian phalanxes climbing both hills. As they advanced, an attack by Spartan light troops from the centre threatened the Illyrians at the rear of the Macedonian right flank, but was defeated by an attack led by some cavalry led by Philopoemen of Megalopolis, later the subject of biographies by Polybius and Plutarch. With their rear secure, the victory of the Macedonian right was quick, When Cleomenes on the other hill saw the defeat of Eucleidas

> he was compelled to tear down the fortifications and to lead out his whole force for battle from one side of the camp. After calling the light-armed troops of both sides from the space between them by trumpet, shouting war cries and lowering *sarissai*, the phalanxes began to engage each other. Then a fierce struggle arose: at one time the Macedonians made a retreat backwards being pressed hard by the courage of the Laconians, at another time the Lacedaemonians were pushed back by the weight of the Macedonian formation. At length those around Antigonus closing up their pikes and using the formation of the doubled phalanx with a strong attack pushed the Lacedaemonians out of the fortifications. Most of them fled headlong and were slaughtered (Polybius 2.69.6–10).

Both armies were notable for the very small numbers of cavalry, though this was not important because of the constrained nature of the battlefield. Polybius faulted Eucleidas for sacrificing the initiative and standing to receive the Macedonian assault rather than attacking downhill, but says nothing about the failure of Cleomenes to do this and the ability of Antigonus' phalanx to fight its way uphill. In both clashes of pike phalanxes, Polybius described movement backwards and forwards. Finally, Philopoemen's decision to intervene in the centre was praised by Antigonus, a good example of initiative by a regimental commander.

4.7 Battle in the Hellenistic Period

Warfare in the Hellenistic period differed from the Classical period by involving larger, better-trained and thus more-resilient armies, often with more experienced generals, and larger numbers of cavalry and light troops.

4.7.1 Who was a regimental commander?

There were several types of regimental commander. One was the veteran Macedonian aristocrat who fought for first Philip, then Alexander, and then divided his Empire between them. This first generation was characterized by their ambition and competition for the king's favour and later Macedonian commanders may not always have been so driven. There were also numerous professional soldiers, often commanding mercenaries, either of their own or another ethnicity. Literacy in Greek would have been normal for these men, and over the course of Alexander's campaigns they would have acquired much experience. Later Hellenistic commanders often had fewer opportunities to gain experience, though many of Philip V's officers would have had long careers and the armies of Sparta and the Achaean League had much experience in the late third century BCE.

4.7.2 Training and discipline

Philip II's acquisition of silver mines at Mount Pangaeum near the Chalcidice allowed the development of a paid force that trained regularly. This professional standing army was inherited by Alexander and became the standard model for the Hellenistic kingdoms, though it was only slowly adopted in mainland Greece. Polyaenus reported that 'Philip accustomed the Macedonians to constant exercise before they went to war so that he would frequently make them march 300 stades, carrying with them their helmets, shields, greaves, and spears; and, besides those arms, their provisions likewise, and utensils for common use (*Stratagems* 4.2.10). This training allowed Alexander even in his first year as king to manoeuvre the phalanx on the battlefield, dividing it into parts, turning, and advancing in echelon (Arrian 1.6.1–3). We also hear of training for later pike phalanxes, e.g. the Ptolemaic army before Raphia and Philip V's army before the Cynoscephalae campaign (Polybius 5.64.1.4; Livy 33.3.4–5). Other troops began to be trained too; for example, the Athenians adopted youth training after their defeat at Chaeronea and Polybius commented favourably on Philopoemen's training of the Achaean League cavalry in the late third century BCE (10.22.6). Food for troops was provided by the state, though there was no medical care. Standing armies allowed permanent units to begin to appear, with standards and an increase in effectiveness and tradition. Sometimes, however, this *esprit de corps* meant that units looked after themselves rather than their general, as the desertion of Eumenes by the *argyraspides* after Gabiene or of Antigonus' mercenaries to Ptolemy in Egypt in 306 BCE showed.

4.7.3 Infantry and cavalry spacing

Polybius described normal spacing for heavy infantry in a pike phalanx:

> A man with his equipment stands in 3ft [approx. 1m] in close order (*puknōsis*) for action … Each man of the first rank has five *sarissai* projecting beyond him, differing in length from each other by two cubits [approx. 1m] (18.29.2–7).

Alexander's phalanx regiments were about 1,500 strong, perhaps six *syntagmata* of 256, with a frontage of 96 men, making them 96m wide when 16 deep. For other infantry the spacing was the same as earlier, i.e. 2m for spear-armed heavy infantry, with looser spacings for lighter troops. For cavalry, Polybius expected a stade (approx. 200m) to hold 800 horsemen when deployed 8 deep, i.e. a spacing of 2m per man (12.18.3–4). Cataphracts were probably arranged more compactly.

4.7.4 Deployment for battle

Better logistics often meant there was less immediate need to engage, so generals sometimes waited for several days before fighting. A centre of infantry, built around the pike phalanx, was flanked with cavalry and light troops. Sometimes there was a screen of light infantry ahead of the main body, a practice that became increasingly normal after Alexander. The right of the line continued to be the post of honour, so that Alexander always deployed his *hypaspists* on the right of his infantry line. Second lines of troops are found occasionally, under Alexander at Issus and at Gaugamela. Centres could be refused, as by Alexander at the Hydaspes, so could flanks, as by Philip at Chaeronea, Antigonus at Paraitacene, and Eumenes at Gabiene. Most battles opened with a period of skirmishing followed by the advance of the main bodies of infantry in the centre and the cavalry on the flanks.

Larger armies were less able to find broad open plains to accommodate their forces. Both commanders during the Cynoscephalae campaign were 'displeased with the country near Pherae, because it was thickly wooded and full of walls and gardens' (Polybius 18.20.1). However, fighting in difficult terrain was often necessary and the Persians defended riverbanks at Granicus and Issus, as did Porus at the Hydaspes, and at Sellasia the Spartans deployed on fortified hilltops. Nonetheless, confident leaders could successfully attack such positions with pike phalanxes, as at Issus and Sellasia, though an enthusiastic Spartan phalanx at Mantinea in 207 BCE had begun to cross a shallow dry ditch when it was broken by a well-timed attack of the Achaeans under the capable Philopoemen (Polybius 11.15–16).

4.7.5 Manoeuvre during battle

With better trained troops and more experienced generals than in the Classical period, there was an increasing amount of manoeuvring by generals on the battlefield, though usually on the flanks. The pike phalanx had two different modes on the battlefield, pikes held upright for movement and lowered for combat. When pikes were lowered, the shafts reached past the front rank locking the first six ranks together, so only forward movement was possible. For a unit to do any manoeuvring there would have to be a pause so that they could return their pikes to an upright position before changing formation.

Philip II withdrew part of his 'phalanx' at Chaeronea (Polyaenus, *Stratagems* 2.2), but we cannot say whether this consisted of pikemen or other parts of his line, and in India, Alexander turned (*epitrepsas*) his phalanx when already within arrow shot of the attackers, then led it into the attack at a run (*dromō*) (Arrian 4.26.3). Earlier practices of trying to outflank the enemy continued. At Gabiene Antigonus exploited the poor visibility caused by the dust of the dry plain to launch a flanking operation to capture Eumenes' baggage and Antiochus III sent out cavalry and infantry round both ends of his line against Molon near Apollonia in 220 BCE (Polybius 5.53.4). Like the Ten Thousand earlier, Ptolemy formed columns for an attack up a hill in India (Arrian 4.25.2) and Alexander used columns (*orthiai*) in a skirmish against horse archers in Asia who were shooting from circles (Arrian 4.4.7), and moved cavalry across the battlefield from one wing to another at Issus, similar to Eumenes at Paraitacene and Gabiene.

Generals sometimes attempted to take advantage of gaps in the enemy line, with the Persian cavalry at Granicus and Alexander's pike phalanx in the Balkans forming attack columns (Arrian 1.15.7, 1.6.3). These columns were described in Greek as an *embolon*, often translated as 'wedge', but better thought of as 'ram'. Livy even used the equivalent word in Latin (<u>cuneus</u>) as he described Roman attempts to penetrate the 'Macedonian <u>cuneus</u> (ram), which they call a phalanx' (Livy 32.17.11). These wide columns were very different from the theoretical triangular wedges of the tactical manuals. In the second century CE, Arrian noted that:

> We hear that the Scythians in particular used wedge formations and the Thracians, having learned from the Scythians. Philip of Macedon also trained the Macedonians to use this formation (Arrian, *Tactica* 16.6).

The lack of triangular wedges in Classical or Hellenistic battle accounts suggests that they appeared in the works of Asclepiodotus, Arrian, and Aelian for their mathematical interest and were not actually used.

As the use of light troops to screen the central bodies of infantry become widespread, they tended to cancel each other out in major battles, as at Sellasia. Their presence also protected armies from elephants and scythed chariots, which otherwise could have had a significant disruptive effect on closely formed lines of heavy infantry. Artillery was occasionally used on the battlefield, notably at Mantinea in 207 BCE when Machanidas used catapults to shoot at an Achaean phalanx deployed behind a ditch (Polybius 11.11.6, 12.4–5), but it was more often used in sieges or for defending passes or river crossings.

4.7.6 Morale and the will to engage

The close formation and interlocked weapons of a pike phalanx resulted in a steady walk to contact, rather than an undisciplined run. Although the difficulties in individual action made the pike phalanx an inflexible formation, this also made them much easier to lead forward in battle without hesitation. This closely-formed hedge of pikes was terrifying to those facing it. Although Polybius' account of Pydna is lost, it was used by Plutarch's *Aemilius Paullus*. This claimed that when Paullus saw

> the strength of the close formation (*synaspismou*) and the speed of the advance, terror and fear grasped him. No sight that he had ever seen was more fearful. Often later he used to reminisce about his emotions and what he had seen (19.1–2).

Polybius was tutor to Paullus' sons, so this is Polybius' own memories of Paullus describing the battle.

Leadership was critical for all troops in battle; it was especially important for a pike phalanx if it became disordered. Several unit commanders were killed during Alexander's campaigns, including Ptolemy, son of Seleucus, who led a *taxis* of the phalanx at Issus, while Coenus, Menidas, and Perdiccas were hit by arrows and Hephaestion by a spear at Gaugamela (Arrian, 3.15.2; Quintus Curtius Rufus 4.16.32).

4.7.7 Infantry combat

As two pike phalanxes approached, there were moments of decision as to whether to go forwards. At Apelaurus in the Greek Peloponnese in late 219 BCE, a force of Eleans were prepared to fight as long as they thought they were facing other Greeks, but 'as soon as the Macedonians advancing on them drew close, they realized the truth and all took to flight throwing away their shields' (Polybius 4.69.6), while at Menelaium near Sparta in 218 BCE, a Spartan pike phalanx fled from another Macedonian attack (Polybius 5.23.4). In descriptions of Hellenistic battle, as in the Classical period, writers often used verbs like push (*ōtheō*) or drive (*elaunō*) to refer to success, so that at Thebes in 335 BCE, the Macedonian phalanx 'pushed back' the Thebans (Arrian 1.8.5). When pike phalanxes did get close to each other, there would be a period of prodding at one another with pikes, the battle lines moving forward and backwards as at Sellasia. Not all members of the phalanx would fight and Polybius noted:

as far as the fifth rank they raise their *sarissai* and are not able to join in the fighting. Therefore, they do not attack individually, but hold them slanting over the shoulders of those in front, so that they protect the formation from above, keeping off by the close formation (*puknōsis*) of the *sarissai* the flight of missiles which, carried over the front ranks, are able to fall on the rear ranks. In an advance the rear ranks by the weight of their bodies pushing those in front make a very strong charge, but it is impossible for the front ranks to change place with those behind (18.30.1–4).

Since Polybius had just said that there was 1m ('two cubits') between each rank, this reference to the 'weight of bodies' must be figurative rather than literal. In this fighting, experience and steadiness were important, and this is where Alexander's veterans had an advantage. At the heart of Eumenes' army in 317–316 BCE were the *argyraspides*, many of whom had fought under Philip II.

At this time the youngest of the Silver Shields were around sixty years old, and many of the others were around seventy, and some even older, but all of them were irresistible because of their experience and strength, so great was their skill and daring through continuous fighting (Diodorus 19.41.2).

Casualties in these clashes were low and they were rarely the decisive factor.

When a pike phalanx faced men equipped with shorter weapons, a different sort of battle ensued. Spearmen or swordsmen were initially faced with multiple rows of pikes which were hard to get past, but missile weapons or terrain often created gaps which could be exploited, as at Issus and later at Pydna (below 6.3).

4.7.8 Cavalry combat

Much cavalry activity consisted of skirmishing with other cavalry as in the Classical period, but we can see the beginning of shock cavalry with Alexander and his Successors often leading their Companions directly at the enemy. This was a high-risk tactic, requiring precise timing to exploit momentary gaps or wavering in the enemy formation. Only well-led cavalry were capable of doing this, and there was a risk of the king losing his life in the combat that followed. At the Granicus, for example, Alexander was injured, but these tactics brought success at Issus and Gaugamela, and charges by Antigonus restored the situation at Paraitacene and Eumenes hoped to do this at Gabiene. These elite cavalry units were usually better armoured and often equipped only with lances and swords for hand-to-hand to combat.

As in the Classical period, since cavalry could not defeat formed and confident heavy infantry, they remained deployed on the flanks, either used as skirmishers or waiting for an opportunity. Although dangerous opportunists, there are no clearly described cases of cavalry breaking heavy infantry from the front, but when the infantry were in a loose formation, disordered, or could be attacked from the flank or rear they were more vulnerable. At Caphyae in 220 BCE, an Aetolian force of light troops and cavalry defeated a similar Achaean force and then the disordered heavy infantry (*thōrakitai*) who arrived to support them (Polybius 4.11–13).

4.7.9 Pursuit

The larger and more professional standing armies of the period were much more resilient than in the Classical period, so that aggressive pursuits were needed to stop them reforming to fight again. More effective pursuits resulted from larger numbers of cavalry provided that they were kept until control. At Issus, Alexander did this so well that he could intervene in the central battle against the Persian infantry, but Antiochus III was not able to restrain his pursuing troops at Raphia after being victorious on the right. This was similar to Machanidas at Mantinea in 207 BCE; while his victorious right flank pursued the Achaean cavalry, the central Achaean phalanx led by Aratus remained on the battlefield to fight. But pursuing too eagerly could be dangerous and in an earlier battle with Sparta in 227 BCE

> Lydiadas the Megalopolitan rushed out with his cavalry, and pursuing into a place full of vines and ditches and walls, was shaken and disordered badly by these, and began to fall into difficulties. Seeing this, Cleomenes sent the Tarentines and Cretans against him, at whose hands Lydiadas fell, defending himself bravely (Plutarch, *Cleomenes* 6.3).

4.8 Conclusion

Hellenistic battles often involved prolonged fighting and lasted longer than most Classical battles which were often over soon after the initial clash. The armies involved were much larger than earlier, with more cavalry and more trained troops, and with generals who were regularly able to make decisions on the battlefield. These armies were also more difficult to handle, with numerous different troop types requiring specialist commanders.

The battles of Issus, Gabiene, and Sellasia between pike-based armies show that experienced troops, like the *argyraspides*, were more effective than inexperienced troops and that close coordination between the pike phalanx and the faster-moving troops on the flanks was critical. If the flanks lost coordination with the centre, then gaps appeared as at Issus, and if not covered, as by Philopoemen at Sellasia, disaster could strike. At Issus, Alexander was saved by winning so rapidly in his sector that he could roll up the Persian line before it defeated his centre. At Paraitacene, Eumenes' troops, despite winning in the centre and on one flank, were still upset by the arrival of Antigonus' flanking cavalry. And as Sellasia showed, pike phalanxes could fight successfully on hills if their flanks were adequately covered.

What could the regimental commander typically expect to do? Although armies were larger, the opportunities for heavy infantry leaders remained limited. Training and formal units were needed for a pike phalanx to function, but they had little opportunity for manoeuvre. As in the Classical period, it was the commanders of light troops and cavalry who had the most opportunities to make tactical decisions, but these still tended to affect only the flanks.

Chapter 5

The Second Romano-Punic War

In a remarkably short period of time, from the middle of the third to the middle of the second century BCE, Rome grew from a central-Mediterranean power to become the largest power in the Mediterranean region, having defeated Carthage, Macedonia, and the Seleucid Empire. In the subsequent two centuries, the Romans gained control over the whole of the Mediterranean and much of Europe. This growth prompted the second-century BCE Greek historian Polybius to ask 'who is so indifferent or so idle that they would not wish to know how and under what form of government almost all the inhabited world came under the single rule of the Romans in less than fifty-three years?' This expansion began during the First Romano-Punic War (264–241 BCE) during which Rome took control of Sicily from Carthage. Carthage then began acquiring territory in Spain, but when she threatened Saguntum, the Romans offered the city protection. Hannibal occupied Saguntum, and then in spring 218 BCE left Spain, crossed the Rhone and the Alps, and entered Italy, starting the Second Romano-Punic War (218–202 BCE). This chapter examines three battles in this war: Cannae in 216, Ilipa in 206, and Zama in 202 BCE.

5.1 Source Material

The two major historians of this war are Polybius and Livy. Polybius and his universal history were discussed earlier (see 4.1). Writing in the 160s BCE there was a substantial interval between the war and memories of it, so he was mostly dependent on literary sources (all lost to us), some from a Carthaginian perspective like Sosylus of Sparta and Silenus of Caleacte, some Roman sources like Fabius Pictor, though he did talk to a few aged survivors.

Titus Livius (59 BCE–17 CE), better known as Livy, was very different. An aristocrat from Padua in the Po valley in northern Italy, no details are preserved of his career or any military experience. At the beginning of Book 31, he remarked 'I too am pleased, as if I myself had taken part in the work and the danger, to have reached the end of the Punic War', something that could only be said by a writer with no military experience. Livy's massive *History* covered the period from the foundation of the city of Rome in 753 BCE as far as 9 BCE in 142 books. Although much is lost, we have Books 21–45, covering the Second Romano-Punic War and the Romano-Macedonian Wars. Livy based his narrative on Polybius, supplemented by some of Polybius' sources like Silenus of Caleacte, Fabius Pictor, and other (now-lost) Latin sources. Stylistically, Livy's Latin is a delight, but for our purposes the major question is how he used his source material. Since we have both Livy and Polybius' accounts of the Trebbia, Lake Trasimene, Cannae, Ilipa, Zama, and Cynoscephalae, we can be confident that Livy normally stuck to Polybius' narrative but added sentences here and there which changed the tone to fit his grand narrative. Thus, he added material about the Numidians at Cannae pretending to desert to the Romans and about Macedonian pikemen at Zama (below, 5.6). Polybius often included a weighing up of a battle and Livy did the same, but often adapted Polybius' analytical points. Livy liked to add dramatic tension and, whereas Polybius focussed on what commanders did, he frequently made commanders appear to be less effective through lack of preparation or misjudgement. When Livy changed the tone of Polybius, he was using his literary judgement, but we might be reassured that his battle descriptions have much in common with those of Caesar, at least until we remember that Livy had read Caesar too.

The high quality of Polybius and Livy means that most later historians chose to rely on them, so the accounts of Diodorus Siculus, Dionysius of Halicarnassus, Appian and Cassius Dio add little. There are some biographies by Cornelius Nepos and Plutarch, though as biographers they were more interested in the character of their subjects than in military matters. Thus, Nepos' *Life of Hannibal* says nothing about the fighting at Cannae, but there are occasional useful anecdotes in Plutarch's biography of Marcellus.

5.2 Roman Equipment and Organization

Both Polybius (6.19–26) and Livy (8.8) described legionary organization and equipment. From the mid-third century BCE Roman armies were raised annually for a particular campaign. Each of the two annual magistrates called consuls was assigned command of two legions. These were usually supported by two regiments (alae) raised from their Italian allies, organized and equipped similarly. Although in many cases the men were released at the end of the year, in some campaigns armies continued to exist over the winter so that by late in the Second Romano-Punic War there were at least twenty legions.

The internal organization of a legion was complex and there are inconsistencies between the descriptions of Polybius and Livy that cannot be reconciled. I have followed Polybius who wrote that each legion was nominally

4,200 strong, but sometimes stronger, and that it normally deployed in three lines. The first line was composed of 10 maniples of 120 hastati, heavy infantry fighting with pilum and sword, and the second line was 10 maniples of 120 principes, equipped in the same way. A third line was formed by 600 triarii, also in 10 maniples, with the same defensive equipment as the other maniples but armed with spears. Men were assigned to maniples by age, youngest in the hastati, oldest in the triarii. Maniples were led by two centurions. The front of a legion was normally screened by 1,200 velites, light infantry attached to maniples in some fashion. A unit of 300 cavalry was also part of the legion. Each legion had 6 tribunes who were supposed to have at least 5 years' military experience. The lack of a formal commander for both legions and cohorts suggests that the dominant mode of battle was thought of as being linear.

The few Roman cavalry squadrons were of aristocrats equipped with helmets, body armour, shields, and spears. There were also some allied infantry cohorts and cavalry alae, probably 500–1,000 strong, usually with ethnic names. Even with the allies, proportions of cavalry to infantry were 1:10 or even fewer.

Soldiers provided their own equipment. Offensive weapons for the first two lines of heavy infantry were a combination of javelin and sword, very different from the spear- or pike-based systems used in Classical and Hellenistic warfare. Polybius noted that Roman heavy infantry carried two javelins, one heavy and one light (6.23.9–11). The heavy javelins are traditionally known to scholars as 'pila', although the various words preserved in our sources (Latin: pilum, telum, iaculum; Greek: *hyssos, grosphos, akontion*) cannot be mapped closely to troop types, usage, or finds. Though intended to be thrown, pila could also be used as spears. Roman infantry swords were primarily stabbing weapons with short blades around 60–75cm, though they could also be used to cut. The spears used by triarii were similar to those used in other cultures, i.e. about 2.5m long with an iron blade and a butt-spike.

The defensive equipment consisted of metal chest-plates or for wealthier men mail shirts, helmets, and in some cases greaves. This was in addition to a large rectangular shield, which Polybius described as being made of two layers of wood glued together, 4 Roman feet (1.18m) high and 2.5 Roman feet wide (0.74m). These dimensions are similar to a shield from Egypt (excavated in 1900, now lost), which was 1.28m tall and 0.635m wide, made of laminated birch covered in felt and weighing about 10kg. These dimensions are similar to the shields depicted on the mid-second century BCE monument of Aemilius Paullus from Delphi and the late-second century BCE altar of Domitius Ahenobarbus from Rome, both of which show shields reaching from the shoulder to the ankle with horizontal handles.

Figure 5.1: Roman heavy infantry, equipped with a shield that was larger and heavier than those of contemporary Greek and Carthaginian infantry, and thus quite cumbersome. He also has a helmet and a pectoral, though others would have had a full mail shirt. This man is a *princeps* or *hastatus*, armed with a heavy javelin for throwing, after which he would fight with his short sword. (© *Philip Sidnell*)

Figure 5.2: Roman *veles*, equipped with a small shield, short sword, and some javelins. This man wears a wolfskin as a headdress, in the hope that he will be recognized by his officer and then be rewarded for his bravery. (© *Philip Sidnell*)

Figure 5.3: Roman cavalryman, wearing mail shirt and helmet and carrying a round shield. His offensive weapons are a spear to fight with (or perhaps throw) and a short sword as backup. (© *Philip Sidnell*)

Light infantry were equipped with a sword and javelins, with Livy suggesting as many as seven javelins (26.4.4). They had helmets and a circular shield 1m in diameter, but no body armour. Roman and Italian allies did not usually use long-range missile weapons like slings or bows. The Romans often used non-Italian allies, some recruited from Spanish tribes, but also peltasts and Cretan archers from the Sicilian kingdom of Hiero, and Numidian cavalry provided by King Masannasa (aka Masinissa).

5.3 Carthaginian Equipment and Organization

Our knowledge of Carthaginian practice is not as good since almost all our source material is Roman, presenting similar problems to understanding the Persians in the Classical period or the enemies of the late Roman Empire. Another difficulty is that the Carthaginian state recruited troops from many different cultures rather than having a centralized military system like the Romans.

Figure 5.4: Carthaginian heavy infantry, a spearman from early in the war before they started using scavenged Roman equipment. This man has a *pilos* helmet, linen body armour, and greaves, as well as a large round shield with an elaborate blazon. (© *Philip Sidnell*)

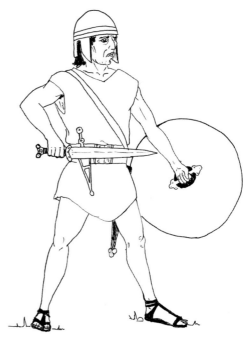

Figure 5.5: Spanish *caetratus*, unarmoured but with a helmet possibly made of felt or linen instead of metal. Some of these men might also have javelins. They were similar in terms of equipment and role to Roman *velites*, despite the visual differences. (© *Philip Sidnell*)

Figure 5.6: Carthaginian citizen cavalry like the men led by Hasdrubal at Cannae. This rider is equipped with a spear that could be thrown in some circumstances, after which he could still fight with his sword. His defensive equipment is linen body armour, helmet, and a small shield. (© *Philip Sidnell*)

At the core of most Carthaginian armies were African heavy infantry (sometimes described as Libyans or Carthaginians), cavalry, and African forest elephants. We can say nothing about typical unit sizes or command structures. These African troops were supported by mercenary infantry and by Spanish and Gallic allies, the latter from both Transalpine and Cisalpine Gaul, Numidians, and a few Italians. Livy emphasized the mixed contingents more than Polybius did. Some of these allies were heavy infantry, but there were also light infantry (with slingers from the Balearic Islands being notable) and cavalry. The proportions of cavalry were much higher than in Roman armies; Hannibal arrived in Italy with 20,000 foot and 6,000 horse (Polybius 3.56.4).

Since Polybius normally described the Africans as heavy infantry using spears (*longchophoroi*) their defensive equipment was probably mail shirts and large shields. Spanish troops were equipped with javelins and short swords. Once Hannibal was in Italy, he used captured Roman equipment to outfit some of his men, so that over time the men in his army would have looked a lot like a Roman army. Light troops were equipped with javelins and slings, but made no use of archery. We can say little about Carthaginian cavalry, but the Numidians, unarmoured and without shields, saddles, or bridles, usually fought by skirmishing with javelins.

5.4 The Battle of Cannae, 216 BCE

After entering Italy, Hannibal defeated Roman armies at the Trebbia in 218 BCE and at Lake Trasimene in 217 BCE. At the Trebbia, Hannibal was successful on both wings, outnumbering the Romans greatly in cavalry, while at Lake Trasimene he was able to ambush the Roman column. Roman strategy briefly changed to attritional warfare, but soon reverted to a strategy of confrontation, leading to Cannae in 216 BCE where the outnumbered Hannibal destroyed a Roman army commanded by Paullus and Varro. The battle is traditionally described in terms of the genius of Hannibal engaging with a deliberately weak centre first, which as it fell back sucked the Romans into a pocket while his superior cavalry won on both flanks and were able to encircle most of the Romans in a double envelopment. Then, according to Polybius, 'those on the edges were continuously being killed, and little by little being confined, until at length all of them … fell there' (3.116.11). This is a clear narrative, but we need to know much more for an analysis of what happened on the battlefield. The only sources we should consider are Polybius and Livy, with Frontinus, Appian, and Plutarch being derived from them.

The Carthaginian army was the surviving part of Hannibal's expeditionary force that had entered Italy at the end of 218 BCE, supplemented by some Gauls and a few Italian cities who had defected from the Roman alliance. His cavalry was particularly strong, but all of the elephants that had crossed the Alps had been lost. Culturally and linguistically, the army was diverse, but several years of campaigning in Spain and Italy had sorted out most of the issues of command. Confidence in their leader and their own abilities was also high following their victories at the Trebbia and Trasimene. Hannibal had about 40,000 infantry and 10,000 cavalry. His African infantry were now equipped with Roman arms, presumably mail shirts.

The Roman army was commanded by the two consuls for 216 BCE, C. Terentius Varro and L. Aemilius Paullus. The nature of Roman political careers meant that both had extensive military experience and Paullus had recently fought successfully in Illyria. They led about 80,000 men, organized into eight Roman legions and an equivalent force of Italian allied legions, as well as some 6,000 cavalry. Most of these men were new recruits, although Polybius reported that the Romans thought before the campaign started that 'newly recruited and completely untrained' troops were one of the major causes of their earlier defeats (3.106.5). This army was four times as large as a typical expedition of two Roman legions and allies led by a single consul, and the resulting command structure was unwieldy, with the consuls commanding on alternating days. In the battle, Paullus led the right flank and Varro the left. According to Livy, the centre was under the surviving consul for 217 BCE, Gn. Servilius Geminus, though Polybius has two generals for the centre, Geminus and M. Atilius Regulus. Following Polybius would give each of the four generals command of a group of two Roman legions and their allies, i.e. a typical consular army.

After several days of skirmishing, the battle took place when Varro was in command. Since the suggested generals of flanks and centre were the same regardless of who was overall commander, we should not put too much emphasis on the differences between Varro and Paullus. As usual, the Roman velites were deployed in front of their heavy infantry, with the Roman cavalry on their right flank against the River Aufidus, the allied cavalry on the left flank. Polybius noted that Varro was 'placing the maniples closer together than before and making the depth in the maniples many times that of the front' (3.113.3), probably because so many of his men were raw recruits; Livy said nothing about this deep deployment. The battle took place on an open plain, so Varro's decision to deploy in depth was not forced on him because of the terrain. If the Romans had followed a normal deployment they would have outflanked the Carthaginians, but exposed their raw infantry to the Carthaginian cavalry. Varro may also have been concerned about the ability of his infantry to hold back the Carthaginian infantry if they were deployed more shallowly.

The Carthaginians deployed with a centre of Spanish and Gallic infantry, flanked on both sides by African infantry, screened by light infantry in front, with the Spanish and Celtic cavalry on the left flank and the Numidian cavalry on the right. Hannibal commanded the centre, while the left-flank cavalry was under Hasdrubal and Hanno led the right. After deploying, Hannibal then advanced the Spanish and Gallic infantry in the centre, forming a crescent.

The battle opened with clashes of light infantry in the centre and cavalry on the flanks. The Roman cavalry was significantly outnumbered and were soon defeated on their right; the lack of space by the river limited opportunity for manoeuvre and led to some dismounted combat. Livy explained the defeat here by treachery from the Numidians who pretended to desert before turning on the Romans. At the same time as the flanking cavalry battles, the skirmishers withdrew and the Roman infantry began first pushing back and then breaking the Spanish and Gallic centre of the Carthaginian army. The significance of deploying these troops in a crescent (according to Polybius: Livy turned this projection into a <u>cuneus</u>) was to keep the Romans engaged so that they could not break off from fighting once their cavalry were defeated. This plan did depend on the Carthaginian infantry holding until their cavalry had been successful, but also of the rest of Hannibal's army not breaking when his centre began to crumble. As the Romans pushed forward against the retreating Spanish and Gauls, the Africans began to engage them from the flanks.

While the infantry combat continued in the centre, Hasdrubal kept his men under control rather than pressing the pursuit and brought them across the battlefield behind the Carthaginian army to assist the Numidian cavalry. Once the outnumbered allied cavalry were defeated here, he left the Numidians to pursue and turned his attention to the infantry battle in the centre. The Carthaginian cavalry fell on the already engaged Roman infantry from the flanks and rear. Although the <u>triarii</u> should have been able to protect the rear of the army, the Carthaginian cavalry probably hit the withdrawn Roman <u>velites</u> first. With no Roman reserve, a slaughter of the closely packed Romans followed. At both the Trebbia and Lake Trasimene many Romans kept their formation and fought their way out of Carthaginian encirclement, but few did so at Cannae, perhaps because many of the troops and their leaders were less experienced. The Roman failure to surrender and the Carthaginian decision not to take prisoners are both worth remarking on.

Roman casualties were huge. Livy claimed 45,500 infantry and 2,700 cavalry, though less than Polybius' 70,000 infantry and 5,630 cavalry. Livy also mentioned the loss of twenty-nine Roman tribunes. Paullus died bravely in both accounts, with Livy adding a dramatic final speech for him, but Varro survived. Livy gave many reasons for the Roman defeat at Cannae: the dust that blew into their faces, Varro's aggression, and claiming that Hannibal thought 'that the generals differed from and dickered with each other, and that almost two-thirds of the army was recruits' (22.41.5). Polybius had a much simpler explanation:

> the greatest benefit was provided to the Carthaginians in victory, both
> then and earlier, by the number of their cavalry. It was clear to later men
> that is better in times of war to have half the infantry and complete

cavalry superiority rather than fighting with complete equality to the enemy (3.117.4–5).

Beyond the analysis provided by our sources, we can see changes in Roman strategy with a return to avoiding direct confrontation with Hannibal but no changes in Roman armies themselves; and later in the war Roman generals were successful with the same types of armies. This suggests that Roman defeat was not simply the result of being outnumbered in cavalry, but that Hannibal's leadership and Hasdrubal's control of his men were critical. Success on a flank did not always translate into victory, as shown by the Ten Thousand at Cunaxa, the Persians at Issus, and Antiochus at Magnesia. There was also a failure by the Romans to make good use of the river, very different from Caesar's deployment at Pharsalus, when he too was outnumbered by the enemy's cavalry, so anchored his infantry on the river and concentrated all his cavalry on the other flank (below 7.6).

5.5 The Battle of Ilipa, 206 BCE

Following Cannae, Hannibal continued to campaign in southern Italy, hoping to detach more Italian allies from their allegiance to Rome. The Romans avoided confrontation as much as possible, though they defeated a reinforcing army led by Hasdrubal at the Metaurus in northern Italy in 207 BCE. Instead, the Romans concentrated on Spain where, despite some minor defeats, they slowly gained the upper hand. These efforts were led by the P. Cornelius Scipio who had fought at Cannae as a military tribune. After Scipio's victory at Baecula in 208 BCE, he met a Carthaginian army commanded by Mago, another of Hannibal's brothers, and Hasdrubal, son of Gisco, at Ilipa, 15km north of Seville in spring 206 BCE.

As with Cannae we can compare the accounts of Polybius (11.20–24) and Livy (28.12–16). The Carthaginians had 70,000 infantry, 4,000 cavalry, and 32 elephants according to Polybius. Livy claimed 50,000 infantry, 4,500 cavalry, and 32 elephants from Roman annalistic sources, but otherwise followed Polybius very closely. Scipio's army of 45,000 infantry and 3,000 cavalry combined Romans and Spanish allies. Scipio was not particularly confident in the fighting value of the Spanish but needed them because he was significantly outnumbered, suggesting that Polybius' figures for the Carthaginians should be preferred. The proportions of cavalry to infantry in both armies were below the more common 1:10.

For several days the armies left camp and deployed to fight. The Carthaginians placed their Libyan infantry in the centre, and on the flanks cavalry and light troops with the elephants in front. The Romans, deploying after the Carthaginians, placed their Spanish allies on the flanks and the Romans in the centre in the <u>triplex acies</u> formation with the <u>velites</u> in front. On the day that he decided to fight, Scipio varied the Roman routine, leading his army out earlier than on other days and forcing the Carthaginians into a hurried deployment with men who had not eaten before fighting started. Scipio also inverted his deployment, placing the Spanish troops in the centre and the Romans on the flanks. A prolonged period of skirmishing followed which allowed the Carthaginians to see the Roman deployment, suggesting that Scipio was most interested in exacerbating the effect on the Carthaginians of not eating.

When Scipio withdrew his skirmishers though the intervals between the maniples, he sent them to the flanks, deploying them and then the cavalry behind the main infantry line, rather than next to them as was usual practice. He then ordered the Spanish infantry centre to advance. With his cavalry and light troops screened by the main body he began a manoeuvre to outflank the enemy. Polybius was very clear about what Scipio intended, but his description of how it was done is hard to understand and was thus simplified by Livy. On both flanks Scipio first wheeled his troops to their flanks, then advanced, extending the line from the centre, then wheeled back into line before advancing against the Carthaginians. The degree of the wheel is unspecified by Polybius, but seems likely to have been only a few degrees, not the 90 degrees that is often suggested.

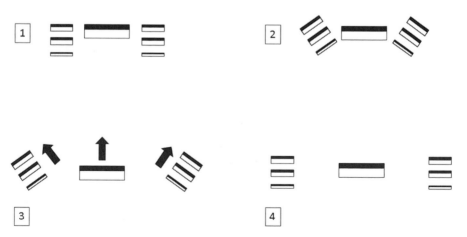

Figure 5.7: Scipio's manoeuvring to his flanks at Ilipa. 1: Initial position; 2: Romans wheel to their flanks; 3: Romans advance to their flanks; 4: Romans wheel back into line and advance to contact.

The result was that the Romans reached the Carthaginian battle line on the flanks first with the Spanish troops in the centre slower to engage. As the Roman flanks came into contact, the Carthaginian centre was reluctant to advance. The Romans were eventually victorious on the flanks where the Carthaginian elephants panicked under the Roman assault and fled uncontrollably in all directions, disordering friend and foe alike. Then, after long fighting, the Carthaginians fell back, first step by step, then routing to their camp. As the Carthaginian flanks were retreating to their camp, a sudden rainstorm erupted, making it difficult for the Romans to pursue effectively.

Scipio's plan was to attack rapidly on the flanks, in the hope of defeating the enemy there before his weaker centre was engaged, a similar plan to that of Hannibal at Cannae. While the Romans were manoeuvring, the Carthaginians were very passive, not attacking the Spanish in the centre or trying to disrupt the flanking Romans as they changed formation. Polybius also noted that the lack of food before combat was significant. These factors alone are enough to explain the Roman victory, and the early end to the battle made it less damaging than Cannae. The most unusual feature was Polybius' very detailed description of Scipio's manoeuvres, possible for units of a trained army used to operating together, but not typical.

5.6 The Battle of Zama, 202 BCE

The victory at Ilipa gave the Romans control of Spain and Scipio returned to Italy. He crossed to Africa in 204 BCE where he defeated the Carthaginians at the Great Plains in 203 BCE, forcing Hannibal to withdraw from Italy. The final battle of the war took place near Zama, about 125km southwest of Carthage, in late 202 BCE. We have the accounts of Polybius (15.9–19) and Livy (30.32–36) for this battle, as well as the versions of Frontinus (2.3.16) and Appian (*Punic Wars* 7.43–45). Polybius' main source was detailed, but differed from those used for Cannae and Ilipa, now using technical terms like <u>hastati</u> and <u>principes</u> transliterated into Greek. Frontinus only knew what he read in Livy, while Appian's version added a duel between Hannibal and Scipio.

Hannibal led a Carthaginian army that included more than 80 elephants, 12,000 mercenary infantry, and 2,000 Numidian cavalry.

> Hannibal placed the elephants in front of his whole force, there being more than eighty, and behind them the mercenaries, about twelve thousand in number. They were Ligurians, Celts, Balearic Islanders, and Moors. Behind these he placed the native Libyans and Carthaginians, and last of all those coming from Italy with him, standing more than

a stade [approx. 200m] from the front ranks. He secured his flanks by cavalry, placing on the left the Numidian allies and on the right the Carthaginian cavalry (Polybius 15.11.1–3).

Livy's version provides a good example of how he added material (shown here in **bold**) to Polybius.

> Hannibal **for terror** deployed his elephants in the front line. There were eighty of them, **more than he had ever before used in a battle line.** Then he placed his auxiliaries, Ligurians and Gauls, mixed in with Balearic Islanders and Moors. In the second line were the Carthaginians and Africans **and a legion (legionem) of Macedonians.** A short distance behind he placed a supporting line of Italian soldiers, **mainly from Bruttium, of whom more from necessity than of their own will followed his withdrawal from Italy.** He also put his cavalry on the flanks, the Carthaginians held the right, the Numidians the left (Livy 30.33.4–7).

The Macedonians played no role in Livy's account of the fighting and were not mentioned by Polybius; most modern scholars attribute their involvement to subsequent Roman justification of the war against Philip of Macedon that started in 200 BCE. Livy has also turned the Italian veterans of Hannibal into conscripted Italian soldiers and added subjective material about the elephants. Other than these additions, Livy's passage is a very close translation of Polybius, providing only the same information about numbers.

Scipio led an army of two Roman legions and two of allies, perhaps 20,000 infantry, some Italian cavalry, and 6,000 Numidian infantry and 4,000 (or 6,000) Numidian cavalry, to make an army of around 30,000 men, outnumbered by the Carthaginians. The high proportion of cavalry was the result of the presence of the allied Numidians. When he deployed, Scipio

> placed in front the hastati with intervals between the maniples and behind them the principes, placing their maniples not opposite the intervals of the front maniples, as is the custom of the Romans, but directly behind at a distance because of the great number of enemy elephants. Finally, he placed the triarii. On the left flank he deployed Gaius Laelius with the Italian cavalry, and on the right flank Masannasa with all the Numidians that he commanded. The intervals between the front maniples he filled up with the units of velites (Polybius 15.9.7–9).

This was the standard Roman <u>triplex acies</u> deployment, modified to make it easier to withdraw the <u>velites</u> in the face of the elephants.

The battle began with skirmishing on the flanks between the Numidian cavalry of both armies before Hannibal sent his elephants against the Roman line. Polybius was explicit that Hannibal had planned for them 'to confuse and tear apart the formations of their opponents' (15.16.2). Some of them panicked. This resulted in the Carthaginian left flank becoming exposed to the Roman Numidians, while in the centre the elephants 'both inflicted and suffered much loss', before some went through the gaps between the Roman maniples, and others went right, harassed by the Roman <u>velites</u> and cavalry. The Romans were quickly successful on their right flank, while Laelius was able to push the Carthaginian cavalry back on the Roman left. Meanwhile the first line of the main bodies of the two armies, both called 'phalanxes' by Polybius, came into contact. Initially, the Carthaginian first line was successful, but it was soon pushed back by the Romans in Polybius' version, though Livy has the Romans immediately breaking the enemy. Rather than passing through the second line, the defeated Carthaginians were squeezed out to the flanks, suggesting that there were no gaps in the Carthaginian formation. Then the Carthaginian second line of African infantry engaged the Roman <u>hastati</u> and fought well for a while before breaking. Scipio was reluctant to pursue too aggressively, so reformed his line, moving groups of <u>principes</u> and <u>triarii</u> out to either flank which would have required a break in the fighting. With his troops reformed, he launched an attack on the Carthaginian third line, which according to Polybius contained Hannibal's best troops. This was hard fought until the Roman cavalry returned from pursuit on both flanks. Then the Carthaginian infantry were attacked from flanks and rear and collapsed, a pattern similar to Cannae. Casualties according to Polybius were more than 1,500 Romans, but 20,000 Carthaginians were killed and 20,000 more taken prisoner in an effective pursuit.

The Romans were successful, but it was a hard-fought battle. If the Carthaginian elephants had been more successful or if the Roman cavalry had not returned to engage the Carthaginian infantry after pursing the enemy, things might have turned out differently. When Polybius wrote his conclusion about the battle, he felt that Hannibal was unfortunate.

> If [Hannibal] after doing everything possible for victory failed, though he was undefeated until that time, we must forgive him. This is a moment when even Fortune acted against the plans of good men (15.16.5–6).

Polybius also praised Scipio and gave the impression that a lesser Roman general might have been defeated.

5.7 Battle in the Second Romano-Punic War

We have good descriptions by Polybius as well as Livy's versions for most of the battles during the Second Romano-Punic War as well as numerous smaller actions. These battles were characterized by combat between multiple lines of heavy infantry, with the actions of the cavalry on the flanks often being decisive.

5.7.1 Who was a regimental commander?

Roman tribunes were all supposed to have at least five years' campaign experience, though as they suffered heavy casualties in the early fighting in the war many of those at Cannae had less. Later in the war, at Ilipa and Zama, however, many tribunes had much experience of campaigning and of fighting major battles. Allied tribunes were similar to Romans, and all were literate. Most Carthaginian officers were quite experienced, with Hannibal's army in 218 BCE already practiced at working together before it entered Italy, though in the final phases of campaigning in Africa, some units would have been commanded by less-experienced leaders. As literate aristocrats, commanders were similar to the Romans.

5.7.2 Training and discipline

Roman soldiers of this period were an annually levied militia, though once enlisted could serve for many years, acquiring extensive experience. After armies were raised and the men formed into units there was some training, sometimes supplemented by training in the field, e.g. in Italy in 215 BCE by T. Sempronius Gracchus or in Spain by Scipio after the capture of Carthago Nova in 209 BCE (Livy 23.35.6–9; Polybius 10.20.1–4). New recruits were usually mixed with veterans, but losses at the Trebbia and Trasimene led to the army that fought at Cannae having a large number of inexperienced soldiers.

Roman armies were able to stay in the field for long periods of time because the soldiers were paid and supplied by the state. These long campaigns allowed the development of unit cohesion, focused on maniples, each of which had its own standard and two centurions. Bravery was encouraged, with Polybius describing velites as wearing conspicuous headgear so that their actions could be recognized (6.22.3). Discipline was fierce, sometimes with execution by comrades, a practice referred to as decimation.

Carthaginian armies were less-well structured but still effective. Hannibal's army had learned to work well together, accommodating the different contingents and so was well practiced even if not formally trained. How divergent it really was after years of living together is unclear, though Livy emphasized these mixed contingents more than Polybius.

5.7.3 Infantry and cavalry spacing

Polybius described typical Roman infantry spacing in the Middle Republic:

> Now the Romans with their equipment stand in a space of 3ft [approx. 1m]. In their battle each man must move separately, protecting his body with his shield, always turning to meet the expected strike, and as he uses his sword to fight by both cutting and thrusting it is clear that the men need to have a gap and an interval, so are at least 3ft in depth and breadth from each other, if they are to be of proper use (18.30.6–8).

Neither Polybius nor Livy suggested that the Carthaginians fought in a tighter spacing, so we can accept a 2m spacing for their heavy infantry too. The light infantry that screened the front of heavy infantry formations fought in a looser formation. We have no details of cavalry spacing, but no reason to think that it was different from Hellenistic practices.

5.7.4 Deployment for battle

Both Roman and Carthaginian armies normally deployed with a heavy infantry centre flanked by cavalry, screened in front by light infantry. Roman armies usually deployed in three lines (triplex acies) of heavy infantry, while the Carthaginians fought in multiple lines at Zama, but in a single line at the Trebbia and at Cannae. The use of multiple lines was a change from Hellenistic practice in which a single line was typical, providing much greater resilience. Carthaginian elephants could be deployed in front of the flanks or in front of the heavy infantry.

Typical Roman armies were made up of two legions of Roman citizens and two regiments (alae) of allies, both equipped and fighting in the same way so

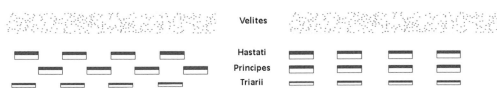

Figure 5.8: Middle Republican Roman Legion showing the maniples deployed in multiple lines, with intervals of a maniple frontage.

it is rare that we can distinguish them in battle descriptions. In each legion or ala, the maniples of the hastati and principes were usually deployed six ranks deep and twenty files wide, those of the triarii three deep and twenty wide. The interval between the three heavy infantry lines or between the velites and the hastati is unknown. Polybius described the maniples of the second line as normally placed in the intervals between the maniples of the first line, with intervals the same frontage as a maniple. This arrangement allowed the second line to support the first, but also allowed both the velites and the first line to retire through the second line. However, at Zama, the maniples lined up directly behind one another, a pattern in which each group of three maniples was known as a cohort (Polybius 11.23.1, 15,9.7; cf. Livy 8.8.9–12).

The Romans were very aggressive, attacking regardless of the circumstances, whereas the Carthaginians were generally cautious, preferring to wait for the Romans to come to them. This allowed Hannibal to make good use of terrain. At the Trebbia in 218 BCE he finessed the Romans into crossing the river in a cold and snowy December to fight and then ambushed them using a small force hidden in a sunken stream bed. The following year at Lake Trasimene, he ambushed an entire Roman army. In other battles, terrain was of less importance and at Cannae, Ilipa, Great Plains, and Zama, flat ground was suitable for Carthaginian cavalry, but also provided the space needed for large numbers of Roman infantry. Both Roman and Carthaginian generals carried out successful outflanking manoeuvres before battle, Hannibal at Herdonea in 210 BCE (Livy 27.1.9–12) and Scipio at the Ebro in 206 BCE (Polybius 11.32–33). The lack of a commander for each legion suggests manoeuvring could only be initiated by the army commander.

5.7.5 Manoeuvre during battle

As the armies advanced, the velites fought other light infantry or harassed the main body of the enemy. When the two main bodies came into contact, the velites retired through intervals in the line. Now maniples of hastati engaged, advancing to throw their pila and then attacking with swords, led by their centurions and the boldest men. One of the fragments of Cato's lost military handbook from this period reads: 'or if perhaps there is a need for a cuneus or a globus or the pincers (forceps) or the towers (turres) or the saw (serra) in order to attack' (fragment 11). This suggests a series of choices open to a commander, in addition to deploying in a line or a testudo, but does not help us to know who might have issued these commands. Carthaginian heavy infantry fought in similar linear formations, also screened by light troops, though Livy did mention the use of a cuneus by Carthaginians, seemingly a blunt column (Livy 25.34.11).

As with Alexander at Issus and Eumenes at Gabiene, cavalry could be moved across the battlefield from one flank to the other, as by Hasdrubal at Cannae, Claudius Nero at the Metaurus in 207 BCE (Livy 27.48; Polybius 11.1) and Scipio at Zama. This required stopping successful cavalry from pursuing the defeated enemy, not an easy task.

Light infantry usually screened the main bodies of heavy infantry in the centre, but were also sometimes mixed with cavalry on the flanks. In smaller actions, as at Ticinum in 218 BCE, cavalry and infantry might fight alongside each other or the cavalry dismount.

5.7.6 Morale and the will to engage

The deployment of skirmishers in the centre meant that battles opened at the same time across the whole field, rather than starting on the flanks. Once the skirmishing ended, the main bodies came into contact. The extensive use of missile weapons among the Romans resulted in a slower but more continual engagement, quite different from the heavy infantry clashes of Classical Greek and Hellenistic armies, but similar to the way in which Achaemenid Persians fought. For Roman armies, the presence of two centurions in the 120-strong maniples of hastati and principes meant that there were numerous junior leaders. Their presence drove Roman armies forwards, and in later periods we hear of competition between centurions for valour. Occasionally we hear of the rapid collapse of an army, as at Ibera in Spain in 216 BCE, when the centre of a Carthaginian army routed rather than fight (Livy 23.29.9), and a Roman army collapsed at Herdonea in Italy in 212 BCE (Livy 25.21.8).

Generals were often engaged in combat, with Scipio, consul for 218 BCE and father of Africanus, being wounded in a skirmish before the Trebbia and being killed in Spain in 212 BCE, Flaminius dying at Trasimene, and Paullus at Cannae. Among the Carthaginians, Hannibal was wounded at Cannae and Hasdrubal was killed at the Metaurus.

5.7.7 Infantry combat

The Romans generally attacked, but Carthaginian infantry were more defensive in posture, e.g. after the first two lines had fought at Zama, Hannibal waited for the Roman infantry to assault. Roman heavy infantry fought in small blocks, with a legion having 10 maniples in its front line. Each maniple of hastati or principes was 120 men, deployed 6 ranks deep, so had a frontage of about 40m. Provided the enemy stood firm, both lines would end up standing perhaps 50m apart, beyond the range of javelins. Where the enemy lines looked ragged, where men were wavering or had suffered from the missiles of the velites, maniples of Romans would move forward encouraged by their centurions, and missiles would be exchanged. Depending on the effectiveness of both sides' missiles, either one group would fall back and the other advance, or sometimes both groups would engage in hand-to-hand combat for a while before one group fell back. The waves of probing would then start again, so that missile weapons were used through the battle, though in diminishing quantities as they were expended over several hours. As the battle went on, the lines might wash back and forwards in waves if evenly matched, or turn into a steady flow if one side became increasingly confident.

5.7.8 Cavalry combat

Cavalry were almost always deployed on the flanks of armies, with no records of cavalry attacking steady heavy infantry from the front. Polybius regarded lots of turning and wheeling as typical: 'the Numidians retreated readily and in a scattered manner, then attacked again in a bold and daring fashion after changing direction' (3.72.9). This pattern is also suggested by Livy's description of a battle in 200 BCE between Romans and Macedonians which also shows the involvement of light troops.

> The king's troops thought the style of fighting would be what they were accustomed to, ie that the cavalry in turn would pursue and retire, now using missiles, now pulling back, the speed of the Illyrians would be used in sudden rushes and attacks; the Cretans would shoot arrows at the enemy who was rushing forward to attack (31.35.3).

Some of these retirements might be deliberate feigned flights intended to draw the enemy out of position and formation, as by some Numidians in skirmishing near Casilinum in 217 BCE (Livy 22.15.5–10).

The ideal situation for cavalry was to be able to fall on the flanks or rear of the enemy infantry, as happened spectacularly at Cannae, but also at Zama. Although in theory the rear line of a multi-line formation could turn to face the enemy, this was difficult to achieve in practice, suggestive of the limits to vision posed by the large amounts of dust on battlefields as well as the limited command structures of these armies.

5.7.9 Pursuit

The proportion of cavalry in Carthaginian armies was much higher than that of Classical Greek armies which meant that their pursuits could be more effective. There were also several battles of encirclement, like Cannae and Zama, battles in which the victor kept firm control of their cavalry which were able to focus on the infantry rather than haring off in pursuit. This resulted in very high casualties for the defeated army, perhaps increased by the great resilience of the infantry on both sides who fought for a long time before breaking.

Conclusion

During the Second Romano-Punic War, the Romans won and lost many battles. They had transformed a fourth-century BCE army which was similar to Classical Greek armies with spear-armed infantry and round shields fighting in a single line, into a system where javelin and sword-armed infantry with rectangular shields fought in multiple lines. Equally important for Roman success were regular pay, supply of food by the state, and medical care for the wounded, practices that were to continue for all Roman armies, and very different from the practices of the amateur armies of Classical Greece or the non-state enemies of Rome.

In the war between Rome and Carthage, the two states were evenly matched in terms of resources and fighting power, so that generalship and luck played an even greater part in this war than in many others. Thanks to Polybius' descriptions of most major actions, we can see that all of these battles were linear and opportunities for manoeuvring were very limited; Ilipa was exceptional. Within this linear format, Hannibal made excellent use of his large numbers of cavalry. The numbers of cavalry varied greatly, with Carthaginian armies often reaching proportions of 1:4 cavalry to infantry, whereas Roman armies were typically 1:10 cavalry to infantry.

The options available for individual regimental commanders to influence battle were limited. Commanders of skirmishers might be successful locally, but had little chance to influence the flow of events. Heavy infantry officers provided low-level leadership, with the actions of Roman tribunes and centurions giving their armies much resilience, but centurions shared command of a maniple and within a legion tribunes had no fixed commands. Cavalry officers had the greatest opportunities to influence the course of a battle, with the ability to control their men in pursuits being of great importance, exploited to devastating effect by Hannibal at Cannae.

Chapter 6

The Romano-Macedonian Wars

The Romano-Macedonian Wars involved the Hellenistic kingdoms and Roman Middle Republic. The Roman armies in these wars were the same as those which fought Carthage (Chapter 5), though now supported by local Greek allies, while the Hellenistic armies were similar to those of Antigonus at Sellasia (Chapter 4.6). There were three great battles in the first half of the second century BCE, at Cynoscephalae in 197, Magnesia in 190, and Pydna in 168 BCE. Although the Romans won all of these battles, their victories were not easy. These confrontations are often described as 'legion vs phalanx', which suggests that equipment and organization were important in Roman success. Such an approach follows in the footsteps of Polybius, who described the Macedonian pike phalanx in detail following his account of the Roman victory at Cynoscephalae in a digression structured around the Macedonian system being successful in Greece and Asia, and the Roman system successful in Africa and Europe.

6.1 Sources

The most important source for these wars is Polybius, very interested in how Rome was able to defeat the Macedonian and Seleucid kingdoms. Although his *History* described Cynoscephalae, Magnesia, and Pydna, only his account of Cynoscephalae survives. Livy's accounts of these battles were all based on Polybius; comparing the versions of Cynoscephalae helps us to read Livy's versions of Magnesia and Pydna. Most later writing has little independent value, with the exception of Appian's account of Magnesia, which is based on Polybius.

6.2 The Battle of Cynoscephalae, 197 BCE

In spring 197 BCE, during the war between Rome and the kingdom of Macedon under Philip V (*r.*221–179 BCE), a Roman force with some Greek allies came out of winter quarters in Boeotia and marched north into Thessaly. Polybius' account (18.18–27) was based on a Macedonian source which named several

Macedonian regimental commanders; he could also have talked to many of the participants on both sides. Livy's account (33.7–10) was derived almost entirely from Polybius, whom he preferred to the Roman annalistic sources that gave much larger Macedonian casualty figures. In the early second century CE, Plutarch's *Flamininus* came mostly from Polybius but added some details from another source.

Figure 6.1: Hellenistic thōrakitēs. This man is heavily equipped with a mail shirt and helmet as well as a large shield often called a *thureos*, though others might not have worn as much armour. He has javelins for throwing and a spear for fighting; such men could be described as equipped in 'Roman style'. (© *Philip Sidnell*)

The Roman army was commanded by Titus Quinctius Flamininus who led two Roman and two allied legions, around 16,000 infantry, about 2,000 cavalry, and 10 African elephants provided by Numidian allies (Livy 32.27.2). Polybius' use of a Macedonian source meant that he described the Roman infantry generically, whereas at Zama his Roman source had divided them into hastati, principes, and triarii. Flamininus and many of his officers and men had fought in the war with Carthage. The Romans were accompanied by an allied force of 6,000 Aetolian infantry, 400 Aetolian cavalry and another 2,000 Greek infantry, bringing their total force to about 26,000 men. The Macedonian army was similar in size at 25,500 strong. It had as its core a pike phalanx of 16,000 men, supported by 2,000 peltasts, 2,000 Thracians, 2,000 Illyrians, and 1,500 mercenary infantry, and 2,000 cavalry. Both armies had equally low proportions of cavalry to infantry, about 1:10.

In late spring, both armies converged on Scotussa, marching on different sides of a long ridge and unaware of the enemy's precise location until their scouts located them. Neither Philip to the north of the ridge nor Flamininus to its south had planned a battle, but fighting began between the light troops and, as it intensified, first the Macedonians and then the Romans had the upper hand. Here Polybius named the Aetolian officers, a detail omitted by Livy. The Romans deployed for battle on the plain below the ridge, at which point Philip chose to cross the ridge to engage. Polybius claimed that

Figure 6.2: Seleucid cataphract, inspired by a relief from Pergamum. He's wearing a muscle cuirass with *pteruges* (but colleagues might have preferred linen body armour), helmet with bearded mask, and banded arm defences, as well as carrying a *sarissa* as an offensive weapon. His horse has lamellar armour on its forequarters and a transverse-crested chamfron. (© *Philip Sidnell*)

Philip was not happy with the ground, but was hoping to take advantage of early successes in the battle of the light troops.

Polybius said of Flamininus' deployment only that the elephants were placed on the Roman right flank in front of the troops and that the left advanced to support his light troops, very different from his detailed description of Zama. At the same time, Philip led his peltasts and part of his phalanx up to the crest of the ridge and, looking down on his light troops first advancing, then being pushed back by the Romans, deployed the troops he had with him into line and ordered Nicanor to bring the rest of the army to support him by deploying to his left. Livy here added emotive language about Philip hesitating about what to do. Although the terrain was not ideal for Philip's pike phalanx, he decided that the advantages of attacking downhill and the psychological boost of pushing back the Roman light troops were more important than the problems posed by the terrain and the fact that his pike phalanx was not fully present. Polybius describe the next stage:

Receiving those who were engaging, he began to assemble them all on the right flank, both the infantry and cavalry, and ordered the peltasts and phalangites to double their depth and close up to the right. Having done this and being close to the enemy, the order was given to the phalangites to lower their pikes (*sarisas*), to the light infantry [to go to] the flank. At the same time also Titus [Flamininus], having received his advanced troops into the intervals between his maniples, attacked the enemy (Polybius 18.24.8–10).

Livy's version, in which he added words (shown here in **bold**), is not as clear.

The cavalry and the light infantry who had been in the battle he placed on the right flank. He ordered the peltasts and the phalanx of the Macedonians, having put down their spears [hastis] **whose length was an impediment, to fight with swords.** At the same time, **so that the line of battle would not be broken easily,** he decreased its front by half and doubled it **by extending the ranks behind, so that the line of battle was more deep than wide.** At the same time he ordered the ranks to close up **so that man was joined to man, arms to arms.** Quinctius [Flamininus], when he had received those who had been in the battle into his standards and ranks, **gave the signal with the trumpet** (Livy 33.8.12–9.1).

In Polybius, the order to the pike phalanx to double its depth to the right is succinct, whereas Livy's version is hard to understand on its own. Livy misunderstood the lowering of pikes as meaning they were put down on the ground so was forced to add material to explain it. He also picked the wrong translation for *sēmaion*, which can mean both 'maniple' and 'standard', and added an allusion to Ennius or Homer. Since we have Polybius, we can see both his clarity and the limits of Livy's understanding of technical military phrasing.

Once the light troops were out of the way, to the flank for the Macedonians, through gaps in the main line for the Romans, the heavy infantry met and the Macedonians began pushing the Romans back. Flamininus then moved to his right flank where the Macedonians had not advanced as far. Polybius noted that the pike phalanx here

having no one to command them nor being able to organize and take the formation proper to the phalanx, because of the difficulties of the terrain and having difficulties coming near those fighting and were also not in the state of deployment (18.25.6).

Livy's version, 'in column rather than line' (33.9.5) is clearer than that of Polybius. Flamininus led his right-flank infantry uphill, and the screening elephants disordered the Macedonian left which began to fall back even before the Roman infantry had attacked.

As the Romans began to pursue on the right, 'one of the military tribunes with them, taking no more than 20 maniples and understanding what should be done at the critical moment' crossed the battlefield and came down on the rear of Philip's pike phalanx (Polybius 18.26.2). Once this was hit in the rear, the Romans in front rallied and were able to drive the Macedonians off. In a few moments, Philip went from believing he had won a victory to realizing that he had been defeated. The Romans lost 700 men, the Macedonians 8,000 killed and 5,000 captured.

The Romans won the battle for three reasons. First, they did not collapse when Philip was victorious on his right flank. Second, they won on the Macedonian left, which was not well led, was lagging behind the unengaged centre, and was disrupted by the Roman elephants. And third, a tribune on the Roman right saw an opportunity and then exploited it to attack the Macedonian right flank from the rear. It was rare for any army to survive being attacked in the rear and Roman success was a victory of resilience and leadership rather than of any strength or weakness of legion or phalanx. Polybius followed his account with a digression on the pike phalanx, which Livy omitted, in which he argued that it required clear and level ground, but did not connect this observation with Philip's success on the Macedonian right.

6.3 The Battle of Magnesia, 190 BCE

Although the Romans withdrew from Greece and Macedonia after Cynoscephalae, they had become entangled in the politics of the eastern Mediterranean. When the Seleucid King Antiochus III (r.222–187) attacked Pergamum, a Roman ally, in 196 BCE, this eventually led to a Roman army landing in western Anatolia. Magnesia-ad-Sipylum was fought in December 190 BCE by a Roman force under Lucius Cornelius Scipio, advised by his brother Publius, victor at Zama (see above, 5.6). The Romans were supported by their Pergamene allies under King Eumenes II.

Polybius' lost account was the basis of Livy's version (37.39–44). As at Ilipa and Zama, Polybius' close association with the family of the Scipiones may have led to some generous treatment of Scipio's decisions. Appian followed Polybius closely in his account (*Syrian Wars* 30–35) though the differences between his version and Livy's allow us to see some of their editorial choices. Both agree that Publius Scipio was ill and played no role in the battle, but in Appian, the

Roman plan was made by Domitius, in Livy by Lucius Scipio. Appian had the Roman centre led by Lucius Scipio, the left under Domitius, the right under Eumenes; Livy's decision not to mention the Roman commanders of centre and left suggests he preferred a simpler story rather than the complexities described by Polybius.

Heavily outnumbered, the Romans camped at the confluence of the Hermus and Phrygius Rivers where they faced Antiochus for several days. The king hoped the Romans would withdraw at the end of the campaigning season so he played for time and did not attack. When the Romans finally advanced into the plain, leaving their camp and no longer anchoring their right flank on the Hermus, Antiochus feared that not fighting would hurt the morale of his troops and so chose to engage.

Livy provided a detailed description of both armies' deployments. The Romans had 28,000 infantry, 5,000 cavalry, and 16 African elephants. Their left flank of 4 regiments of cavalry stood against the Phrygius. The centre was composed of 2 <u>alae</u> of allies, 1 on either side of two Roman legions, drawn up in 3 lines of <u>hastati</u>, <u>principes</u>, and <u>triarii</u> and screened by their <u>velites</u>. On the right were 3,000 Pergamene and Achaean peltasts, 3,000 cavalry, 500 Cretan archers, and 500 Trallian light troops. The elephants were deployed behind the infantry centre and played no part in the battle while the camp was guarded by a further 2,000 men.

The Seleucid army was much larger, totalling 57,000 infantry, 12,000 cavalry, and 54 Indian elephants. In the centre the pike phalanx was deployed in 10 separate units of 1,600 men deployed 32 deep. Each unit was separated from its neighbour by 2 elephants, carrying towers with a crew of 4 soldiers and a driver, to total 22 elephants, including those on the edges of the phalanx. On the right of the phalanx were the elite infantry *argyraspides* (Silver Shields), wrongly described by Appian as cavalry. The right flank, led by Antiochus himself, had the best cavalry including the 1,000 strong *agēma*, 3,000 cataphracts, and 1,200 Dahae horse archers, as well as 1,500 Galatian infantry, 16 elephants, and 11,500 light infantry, archers, and slingers. On the left were another 5,200 allied infantry, 3,000 more cataphracts, and 1,000 Companion cavalry. Beyond these were more cavalry, the Tarantines and 2,500 Galatians, as well as 16 elephants, and more light infantry: 2,500 archers, 4,000 peltasts, and 4,000 archers and slingers. The scythed chariots and some camelry (camel-mounted troops) were deployed in front of the left flank. The broad strokes are clear, but the exact arrangement of both flanks is less certain; Appian recorded the light infantry screening the Seleucid centre, a detail omitted by Livy.

It was a wet day, which had a negative effect on Antiochus' archers and Livy noted that the flanks of Antiochus' army were not visible from the centre. The

Romans deployed about halfway between the opposing camps which were 2.5 Roman miles (approx. 4.5km) apart, so that as the battle began the armies would have been separated by at most 2km.

The sequence of events as presented in Livy began on Antiochus' left, where the scythed chariots were shot up by Eumenes' light troops. As the chariots fell back, they disordered their own cavalry, who were then broken by Eumenes' follow-on attack. When Livy described this, he probably added his own emotive language (here shown in **bold**) to Polybius' description: 'The chariots were pushed from the field, and **with the silly show over,** then the signal was given and both sides closed in a **legitimate** battle' (37.41.12). A panic spreading from here reached the Seleucid centre, where the Romans advanced, threw their <u>pila</u> and almost defeated the pike phalanx. At this point, Livy's Romans learned that Antiochus had led the right-flank cavalry attack in person. He defeated the Roman cavalry on this flank, then turned on the allied regiment next to them and broke that too. Antiochus, however, then attacked the Roman camp, rather than continuing to roll up the main line of battle. Unable to capture the camp, and aware of the defeat in the centre where there were large piles of bodies, he withdrew and the battle was over. The reported losses were 53,000 Seleucids and 349 Romans and allies.

Appian's account was similar, but placed less stress on the scythed chariots. He described skirmishers in front of the Seleucid pike phalanx, which was soon encircled by the cavalry on the Roman right flank. In the centre, the Roman <u>velites</u> won the light infantry skirmishing and then used missile weapons against the pike phalanx, but did not engage in hand-to-hand combat, 'fearful of the experience of disciplined men and their compactness (*puknotēta*) and desperation' (Appian, *Syrian Wars* 35). The phalanx finally broke when some of the elephants panicked. Since both Livy and Appian derived their accounts from Polybius, Appian's detailed description of the fate of the phalanx should be preferred to Livy's version which avoided mentioning that the Romans did not engage the phalanx in hand-to-hand combat.

As at Issus and Cynoscephalae, each army was successful on one flank but in this battle the Romans were able to keep their right-flank forces focused on the battlefield, swinging round to put pressure on the Seleucid heavy-infantry centre, while on the Seleucid right after defeating an allied regiment Antiochus became embroiled in an attack on the Roman camp rather than concentrating on the Roman centre. Unlike at Issus and Cynoscephalae, there was no great infantry battle in the centre. Livy did not provide a justification for the Roman victory, though he, like most modern commentators, had harsh words about the scythed chariots. Appian, however, in a section taken from Polybius, noted that Antiochus seems to have put his hope in his cavalry, whom he placed in numbers to his front. The compact (*puknēn*) phalanx was deployed in an inexperienced manner in a small space. He should have been very confident in it because of its training (*Syrian Wars* 32).

He added that Antiochus' friends 'blamed him for his final folly, making the strongest part of his army useless in a narrow space, and for placing his hope in the number of men tossed together and new to war' (*Syrian Wars* 37). All true, but it might be better to stress Eumenes' perfect execution of the counterattack and Antiochus' failure to keep control of his flank.

6.4 The Battle of Pydna, 168 BCE

Philip V died in 179 BCE and was succeeded by his son Perseus (*r.*179–168 BCE). Suspicious of Perseus' ambition, the Romans began a war in 172 BCE, fighting for three years in Illyricum and Thessaly before Lucius Aemilius Paullus was able to force a battle at Pydna in southern Macedonia in summer 168 BCE. Both commanders were experienced, with Paullus having fought in Spain and against the Ligurians and Perseus having had some success against the Romans earlier in the war. Many of the Roman troops were also very experienced, and Livy provided a nice speech for Spurius Ligustinus, a centurion who had already fought at Cynoscephalae, in Spain, and against Antiochus, claiming that 'I have been rewarded for my courage thirty-four times by my generals, I have received six civic crowns, I have served for twenty-two years in the army, and I am more than 50 years old' (42.34.11).

The preserved text of Livy, based on Polybius' lost account, has several significant gaps (Livy 44.36–42) which we can supplement from Plutarch's biography of *Aemilius Paullus* (16–23), also based on Polybius. Although Plutarch was critical of his account, Polybius had made great efforts to interview eyewitnesses; since he was in Rome where many Macedonians were taken as hostage afterwards, he could have talked to men who fought on both sides.

After the two armies contacted each other, Perseus camped on the plain south of Pydna and the Romans camped in the hills to the west. Both generals were reluctant to fight. Paullus wanted to avoid the plain as more suitable for the pike phalanx, while Perseus was reluctant to engage in the hills, so the armies stood opposite each other all day. Some small streams flowed near the two camps which were used by both sides for watering purposes. The next day, a clash at a stream escalated and both generals soon gave the order to engage.

There is a large gap in the text of Livy here, so we have lost his account of the deployments and the opening of the battle. When he detailed Roman troops for the campaign in 171 BCE, it was 28,000 infantry and 2,000 cavalry, including many veterans of the wars against Philip and Antiochus (42.31–32). Paullus also had some elephants; King Masannasa of Numidia had sent 22 (Livy 42.62.2). We do know that two Roman legions stood in the centre, flanked by allied regiments with the elephants on the right, supported by cavalry and light troops. For the larger Macedonian force, Plutarch gave 40,000 infantry and 4,000 cavalry at the start of the campaign, similar to Livy's description (42.51) of an army of 43,000 men made up of 3,000 Macedonian cavalry, about 21,000 pikemen, 2,000 *agēma* infantry, 3,000 light infantry, 12,000 Greek, Gallic, Paeonian, and Thracian infantry, and 1,000 cavalry and 1,000 infantry, Thracian allies led by King Cotys. At Pydna, Perseus deployed Thracians, mercenaries, and Paeonians on the left, then the *agēma* equipped as peltasts, and then 2 pike phalanxes about 20,000 strong, the *leukaspides* (White Shields) and *chalkaspides* (Bronze Shields), and more cavalry and light troops on the right. There was a cavalry: infantry ratio of 1:10 for the Macedonians, less for the Romans.

Figure 6.3: Roman Numidian cavalry, riding without saddle and bridle. This man has no shield, but some Numidians would have carried them, especially later in history. They weren't great at attacking disciplined troops but were more dangerous to less organized opponents. (© *Philip Sidnell*)

Plutarch described the opening of the battle in the afternoon, when the Macedonians met the Romans who were deployed about 2 stades (approx. 400m) from their camp. Paullus led his men in person, but Plutarch told stories about Perseus being both present and absent. Some Roman allied units met the enemy first.

> The Romans, when they attacked the phalanx, were unable to overpower it. Salvius, leader of the Paeligni, snatching the standard of those under him, threw it into the enemy. Then the Paeligni … rushed towards that place, and terrible acts and deeds happened on both sides in the fighting. For [the Paeligni] tried to push away the pikes with their swords and to take hold of their shields and grabbing with their hands to turn them away. But [the Macedonians] strengthening their front, with both hands on their weapons were even thrusting through those attacking, and neither the shield nor armour kept off the force of the *sarisa*. … When the front ranks [of the Paeligni] had been destroyed, those deployed behind them were pushed back; even though it was not a flight, it was a retreat (Plutarch, *Aemilius Paullus* 20.1–3).

As the text of Livy resumed, he described how: 'on the Roman right flank, close to the river, where the battle had begun, [Paullus] brought up the elephants and the <u>alae</u> of the allies, and from here was the first rout of the Macedonians' (44.41.3–4). In centre, in the process of defeating the Roman <u>principes</u>, the Macedonian formation had begun to lose its cohesion allowing the second Roman line of <u>hastati</u> to get into gaps in the pike phalanx and begin to push it back. The late-first-century CE compiler of stratagems, Frontinus (2.3.20) said that Paullus drew up in three lines of units, but then adds that they fought in column (<u>cuneis</u>). He also suggested that the Romans fell back deliberately to lure the phalanx on to rough ground which disordered it, an optimistic interpretation of the Macedonian success and perhaps showing that Frontinus drew on Livy. At this stage, Livy described the Roman First Legion deployed opposite a gap between the *agēma* and the *chalkaspides*, the Second Legion against the *leukaspides*.

> They were compelled to advance against the Romans running forwards in groups (<u>catervatim</u>), even though their line (<u>acie</u>) was broken in many places. And the Romans, wherever gaps appeared, began to push into their ranks. If [the Romans] had attacked frontally all along the line against a deployed phalanx, which happened to the Paeligni at the beginning of the battle as they recklessly met the <u>caetrati</u> [= peltasts],

they would have entangled themselves on the spears (<u>hastis</u>) and would not have withstood the compact line (Livy 44.41.8–9).

The battle was over within an hour, though the pike phalanxes held out for a long time. Roman casualties were small, 80 (according to Poseidonius) or 100 (according to Nasica), but some 20,000 Macedonians are said to have been killed in a vigorous Roman pursuit.

The Romans won the battle because, as at Cynoscephalae, they did not break following the initial Macedonian assault even though they were pushed back. This was one of the advantages of multiple lines, though it did require the second line to hold their nerve as the defeated men passed through their formation. It was also important that, as at Cynoscephalae, the Roman right led by the elephants was able to push back and then roll up the Macedonian flank. And finally, the Romans were able to take advantage of the disruption to the pike phalanx caused by the difficult terrain. Livy commented on this weakness of the phalanx after his description of the battle, reminiscent of the way in which Polybius discussed the pike phalanx after Cynoscephalae and probably drawn from his post-battle analysis.

6.5 Conclusion

After their defeats at the beginning of the Second Romano-Punic War, the Romans won a remarkable series of battles, winning at the Metaurus, Ilipa, Great Plains, Zama, Cynoscephalae, Magnesia, and Pydna. All of these battles were hard fought, and the Romans could have lost any of them. Their army was similar in all of these wars, so what changed between the initial encounters with Hannibal and the later Roman victories?

The most important factor was the resilience of the Roman heavy infantry which allowed elements of defeated armies to fight their way off the battlefield or else to die fighting uselessly. At Cynoscephalae, the Roman left was defeated, at Magnesia the Roman infantry could not defeat Antiochus' pike phalanx, and at Pydna the Romans were pushed back all along the line. Despite such setbacks, the Romans kept fighting. Important too were the elephants, the inspired action by an unknown tribune at Cynoscephalae, and Antiochus' inability to roll up the Roman line at Magnesia after breaking an allied legion, perhaps with his cataphracts. All of these outweighed any generic ability of legionaries to defeat pikemen. Philip's reluctance to fight in an area of walls and gardens before Cynoscephalae and the vulnerability of Perseus' phalanx on the hills confirm Polybius' concern for bad terrain and flanking attacks, although as we have seen, pike phalanxes attacked across watercourses at Issus and uphill at Sellasia, even if they suffered more from disorder than other heavy infantry formations on difficult terrain. Of far greater importance was managing the relationship between the flanks and the centre, something that Philip and Alexander were good at, and something that, for a few critical moments, eluded Philip V, Antiochus III, and Perseus.

As earlier, opportunities for regimental commanders were mostly on the flanks when leading light troops and cavalry. However, the structure of legions with many lower-level leaders and formed sub-units that could fight unsupported gave Roman heavy infantry leaders more opportunities to affect the flow of the battle, as with that unnamed tribune at Cynoscephalae.

Chapter 7

The Late Roman Republic

This chapter is concerned with battle in the Late Roman Republic, 150–31 BCE, a period which saw the continuation of the Roman wars of conquest and then a period of consolidation. These wars were numerous, including the Jugurthine War, the War against the Cimbri and the Teutones, several Mithridatic Wars, the War against Sertorius in Spain, Caesar's Conquest of Gaul, and the Wars of Crassus and of Antony against the Parthians. The wars of conquest were very different from fighting organized states like Carthage, Macedonia, and the Seleucid Empire, whose armies were based on cores of heavy infantry supported by cavalry, since the Romans now had to contend with the Parthians, who placed a much greater emphasis on cavalry, the tribes of Spain, Gaul, and Germany, and other states, including Mithridates' kingdom of Pontus and other Romans. At the end of this period there was a long series of Roman civil wars, in which Roman armies faced other Roman armies.

7.1 Sources

The most important writer for battle in this period is the Roman aristocrat Caesar. Gaius Julius Caesar (100–44 BCE) had an exceptionally busy life. His military experience was tremendous, though not unique; many Romans of his generation like Pompey or Lucullus also spent years on campaign. Caesar had fought in Asia and Spain before entering Gaul where in 58–56 BCE he conquered the region up to the Rhine, winning battles against the Helvetii and Suebi in 58 BCE, and against the Belgae in 57 BCE (below 7.4). From Gaul he crossed the Rhine in 55 and led expeditions to Britain in 55 and 54 BCE before facing a serious Gallic revolt in 53–51 BCE, being defeated at Gergovia in 52 BCE, but emerging victorious from a long siege at Alesia. The Gallic campaigns were described by Caesar himself in the seven books of the *Gallic War*, with an eighth book covering 51 BCE being written by one of his lieutenants, Aulus Hirtius. When civil war broke out in 49 BCE, Caesar rapidly drove Pompey out of Italy to Greece, and then defeated the Pompeian forces in Spain at Ilerda in that year. He was victorious over Pompey himself at Pharsalus in 48 BCE (below 7.6). After a brief visit to Egypt, he defeated Pharnaces at Zela in 47 BCE (below 7.7) before going on to fight at Thapsus in Africa in 46 and Munda in Spain in 45 BCE. These campaigns were described by Caesar in the *Civil War*, as far as Pharsalus, then by three continuators in the *Alexandrian Wars*, *African Wars,* and *Spanish Wars.*

Caesar's works were clearly written, and so traditionally one of the first Latin works read by students. They were also self-serving propaganda, intended to justify Caesar's actions to an audience in Rome. Caesar's prose was artfully constructed, and often made its points through omission and emphasis, a subtle approach reflecting both the man and the fact that many of his audience had their own memories of the events he was describing. However, Caesar was also the commander of the forces he wrote about so, unlike Livy or Tacitus, he described what he understood and practiced. Like Xenophon and Polybius, he was more concerned with leadership and logistics than most other writers, even if we accept that Caesar focussed on showing himself to best advantage.

We have other sources too. Sallust wrote a stylish history of the Jugurthine War that has a few useful details. In the early second century CE, Plutarch wrote a series of biographies of Romans of this period, although his interest in and understanding of warfare were not strong. In *Crassus* and *Antony* he made good use of well-informed accounts, but his reading of Sulla's memoirs used for *Marius* and *Sulla* and was not critical. Although Livy's work, which would have been detailed, is lost for this period, it was the basis of the more general histories of Cassius Dio and Appian that do survive.

7.2 Roman Equipment and Organization

Following the defeats of Carthage, Macedonia, and the Seleucid Empire, Roman control spread over the whole of the Mediterranean and deep into Europe. Equipment changed little, but the organization of Roman armies changed greatly. As earlier, legions were raised for particular campaigns and were then disbanded, though the continuous wars meant that many legions continued to exist for a long time. Legions were still identified only by numbers until the end of the first century BCE, after which they began to acquire names too. Under the Middle Republic, the heavy infantry of a legion had been organized into 30 maniples with 6 tribunes and 60 centurions, but no overall commander. Sometimes a cohort was formed out of a maniple each of hastati, principes, and triarii. By the early first century BCE, the 30 maniples were permanently combined into 10 cohorts of 480 men each. Each cohort had 6 centurions, with the senior centurion commanding the unit as well as his century. The 1,200 light troops (velites) in Middle Republican legions were

Figure 7.1: Late Republican Legionary from the end of the first century BCE. This soldier is modelled on the Vachères warrior, wearing a mail shirt, a Montefortino helmet with a large, slightly oval-shaped shield. This man has just thrown his *pilum* and is now steeling himself to receive an attack of the enemy. (© *Philip Sidnell*)

eliminated. These changes kept the new legions at a similar strength, but they were easier to manage with ten sub-units all equipped in the same way. Caesar often assigned commanders to legions, but they still did not have a formal commanding officer. Actual strengths were often lower than 4,800, so that in the Pharsalus campaign Caesar's 7 legions totalled 20,000, i.e. about 3,000 men each.

There were no significant differences between legionary equipment in the third and first centuries BCE, but with the elimination of the <u>triarii</u> and <u>velites</u> all Roman heavy infantry were equipped in the same way, with a large shield, helmet, mail shirt, heavy javelin (<u>pilum</u>), and short sword. The <u>pilum</u> was a heavy javelin weighing about 1.5kg with a range of around 30m. Plutarch's *Marius* (25.1–2) described a modification of the <u>pilum</u> so that it would bend more often when caught in an enemy's shield, a good example of the fixation of some ancient sources with technical details and with little archaeological support.

Heavy infantry legions were supported by various units known as auxiliaries. These units were raised in Italy and the provinces for campaigns, were often named after their commanders who included local leaders and Roman centurions and prefects. They varied in size between 200 and 800, though about 500 men was most common, and included light and heavy infantry, and various types of cavalry. Light infantry were mostly javelinmen, archers, or slingers. Cavalry were either heavy cavalry with shields, body armour and spears, or else lighter cavalry with javelins, and perhaps no armour or shields, including the Numidians famous for riding without bridles. Very few of the cavalry came from Italy. The proportion of cavalry to infantry was rarely above 1:10, and when Caesar fought at Pharsalus it was 1:22.

Figure 7.2: Gallic cavalryman. Most of the cavalry in Gaul was provided by mounted nobles, whether fighting for or against Rome. They might also fight dismounted. This man is wearing very fashionable trousers and a decorated shield, but also has a mail shirt and helmet. He might throw or stab with his spear, and has a sword for backup. (© *Philip Sidnell*)

7.3 Organization and Equipment of Rome's Enemies

The Romans fought against many tribal societies in northern Italy, Spain, and Gaul. Our sources frequently displayed prejudicial attitudes, often describing their enemies in stereotypical terms as 'barbarians'. These societies had few urban centres, very limited use of writing, and very weak logistical systems, aspects which changed little throughout antiquity, though continued exposure to warfare brought about an improvement in practice.

Gallic and German armies were dominated by unarmoured warriors armed with shields and spears, supported by small numbers of cavalry and javelinmen. Polybius' descriptions of earlier Celts were still relevant in the first century BCE. At Telamon in 225 BCE, he described the Insubres and the Boii from the Po Valley wearing trousers and cloaks, but did not mention armour, and then added that the Gaesatai fought naked (2.28.7–8). He also noted that the shield used by the Iberians and Celts [= Gauls] was about the same, but their swords had a different style. [With the Iberians,] the point was no less able than the cut to cause harm, but the Gallic sword had one use, the cut, and this from a distance (3.114.2–3).

Aristocrats had better equipment, mail body armour, swords, and helmets. Light infantry and archers were only rarely used. The cavalry of the Cimbri at Vercellae in 101 BCE wore helmets, metal body armour, and shields, and fought with javelins and swords. Caesar thought German cavalry, who did not use saddles, better than Gauls. British armies used light chariots for skirmishing. There was no organization or formal leadership, though we might expect aristocrats to fight in the front ranks and for tribal leaders to command their own contingents.

Parthian armies were dominated by aristocratic cavalry, usually with metal body armour and helmets, armed with lances, and sometimes riding armoured horses. These were supported by light cavalry armed with bows, and by some infantry. The accounts of Carrhae, Antony's campaign in 36 BCE, and the battle against Ventidius focus on the cavalry but give no details of Parthian organization.

Pontic armies from eastern Anatolia clashed with the Romans unsuccessfully at Chaeronea in 86 BCE, Orchomenus in 85 BCE, the Lycus in 66 BCE, and Zela in 47 BCE (below 7.7), but they were victorious at the River Amnias in 88 BCE, an unnamed battle against Murena in 82 BCE, Zela in 67 BCE (where 24 tribunes and 150 centurions fell), and Nicopolis in 48 BCE. Mithridates of Pontus' early armies were built around a pike phalanx, with Plutarch mentioning a unit of

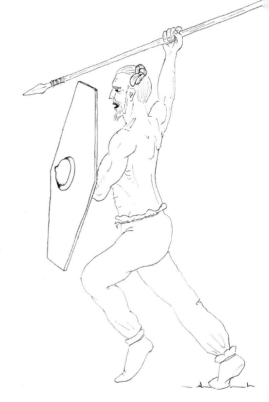

Figure 7.3: German heavy infantry, a tall man charging rapidly in the hope of terrifying the Roman legionary that he's about to attack. He doesn't have any armour though, just a simple shield and a spear that lacks a butt-spike. (© *Philip Sidnell*)

Figure 7.4: Parthian cataphract, inspired by the Dura graffito. He's got full body armour, a combination of metal plates and mail, as well as a helmet, while his horse wears full barding made of scales. He sits in deep saddle and has a lance, but all the weight means that probably he doesn't move as quickly as many cavalry. (© *Philip Sidnell*)

Figure 7.5: Parthian light infantryman, based on a relief from Haštrūd with a broad-headed javelin especially suitable for unarmoured targets. He doesn't have any armour but carries a large shield that would have been useful for skirmishing. (© *Philip Sidnell*)

chalkaspides (*Sulla* 16), but later forces were organized 'Italian fashion' (Appian, *Mithridatic Wars* 87) and included cataphracts (*Lucullus* 26). They also made good use of scythed chariots (below 7.8). As with Rome's other enemies, our limited evidence is almost entirely from Roman sources, but the Hellenistic roots of the kingdom and its successes suggest organized and well-led armies.

7.4 The Battle of the River Sabis, 57 BCE

The Battle of the River Sabis (often identified as the River Sambre though this is not certain) took place in northern Gaul as part of Julius Caesar's campaign against four tribes of the confederation of the Belgae: the Nervii, Atrebates, Viromandui, and Aduatuci. We have only Caesar's account (*Gallic War* 2.16–28). His army was made up of eight legions of heavy infantry supported by a non-Roman advanced guard of Balearic slingers, Cretan archers, and Numidian and Gallic Treveri cavalry. Caesar had sent scouts and centurions ahead of his army to find a place to camp. They located a good site on a hill overlooking the Sabis. They were aware that the Nervii, Atrebates, and Viromandui, all led by Boduognatus, were across the river. No numbers were given for the Belgae at the battle, but Caesar at the start of the campaign claimed that the Nervii could field 50,000 warriors, the Atrebates 15,000, and the Viromandui 10,000 (*Gallic War* 2.4).

The Roman advanced guard of light troops and cavalry crossed the river and engaged with some of the enemy's cavalry while the main force of six legions was beginning to set up camp on the hill and the baggage train arrived. At this point, the Belgae attacked at great speed, running downhill out of the woods to the river (Caesar mentioned the distance as being 200 paces, around 120m), then crossing the river (which was about 1m deep, but very wide), and then charging uphill against the Roman line. Caesar commented that 'with incredible speed they rushed to the river so that at almost the same time the enemy seemed to be in the woods, and in the river, and in hand-to-hand combat with us' (*Gallic War* 2.19). The Romans were caught by surprise, so that troops fought with their shield covers still on and not in their assigned ranks but wherever they found themselves, though still organized by legions.

Fierce fighting followed. On the Roman left flank Legio IX and Legio X quickly defeated the Atrebates and in the centre Legio VIII and Legio XI pushed back the Viromandui. However, as the Roman left and centre advanced, this allowed the Nervii on the Roman right flank to penetrate a gap which had developed between the Roman centre and right flank. Exploiting this, some of Nervii entered the Roman camp, while others threatened to encircle Legio

VII and Legio XII on the right flank. At this point, most of the Roman light troops, including the allied cavalry from the Treveri, fled and

> all the centurions of the fourth cohort [of Legio XII] had been killed, the standard-bearer was dead, the standard lost; of the other cohorts almost all the centurions were either wounded or dead (*Gallic War* 2.25).

The loss of many Roman junior leaders suggests the fierceness of the fighting. In this situation, Caesar saw that 'the rest were less energetic and that some, deserted by the rear ranks, left the battle and escaped the weapons' (*Gallic War* 2.25).

Seeing that the Nervii were in a position to roll up the Roman line, Caesar moved from the centre to the right flank, deploying the last two legions which had just reached the battlefield. He was assisted by Titus Labienus who sent Legio X across the battlefield from the left flank. These two actions restored the Roman line.

This battle is a good example of how the Roman army fought in the late Republic. This was not a set-piece like Magnesia, Mons Graupius, or Strasbourg, but a battle that evolved rapidly, like Cynoscephalae and Pydna. For the Belgae, the setting up of the Roman camp offered the opportunity to catch the Romans by surprise, an opportunity they exploited skilfully. Caesar's account highlighted the importance of experienced troops as well as his leadership and that of Labienus, but when such leadership was lacking, as may have been the case in the earlier battles against the Cimbri and the Teutones, Roman armies were often defeated by barbarian enemies. The confident tone of Caesar's account contrasts with the failure of his scouts to detect the enemy main body, leading to a series of crises on the battlefield. For the Romans all ended well, but Caesar gives the impression of a disaster saved by his leadership. The final literary touch is his omitting mention in the conclusion of any Roman casualties while claiming that the Nervii were almost destroyed as a military force.

7.5 The Battle of Carrhae, 53 BCE

Caesar's campaigns in Gaul brought him great wealth and a reputation. His political rivals needed similar victories to compete, leading Marcus Licinius Crassus, governor of Syria in 55 BCE, to attack the Parthian Empire in Mesopotamia. Following some preliminary campaigning in 54 BCE, he led a larger expedition in 53 BCE which was defeated at Carrhae. Our source material for the battle is the biography by Plutarch (17–27) and the history of Cassius

Dio (40.21–25), both based on Livy who used an account by the survivor Cassius. However, the emphasis of both Plutarch's biographical account and of Cassius' memoir lay not in explaining the battle but in making the defeat the responsibility of Crassus.

Crassus' army, of 7 legions (less 7,000 men detached as garrisons), 4,000 light infantry and 4,000 cavalry, probably 25–30,000 in total, faced a Parthian force of 10,000 cavalry led by the Suren (head of an aristocratic family of that name). The Roman force was close to the typical ration of 1:10 cavalry to infantry, though Crassus had rejected an offer of additional cavalry from allied Armenians.

More importantly than being outnumbered in cavalry, Crassus was outfought. His initial deployment was in a long but shallow line, but after he became concerned about being outflanked he formed a large square, each face consisting of 12 cohorts. Plutarch then described this force as moving forward and having flanks commanded by Cassius and by Crassus' son, Publius. As the Romans began to be harassed by the Parthian horse archers they adopted the testudo formation.

> So as long as they hoped that after pouring forth their arrows [the Parthians] would hold off from battle or fight hand-to-hand, they endured; but when they saw that many camels were present, loaded with arrows, from whom the first of those harassing them took more, then Crassus, seeing no end, began to lose heart and ordered them to look out, sending messengers to his son to force a close engagement with the enemy (Plutarch, *Crassus* 25.1).

Publius led out 1,300 cavalry, 500 archers and 8 cohorts of heavy infantry (around 4,000 men if at full strength). When he advanced too far he was surrounded and destroyed. With the loss of this force and the death of his son, Crassus lost control over the battle. The Romans stood in position and were harassed by the Parthian archers, now resupplied with arrows, until nightfall. At the end of a long day, Cassius led the Romans off the battlefield. The Romans suffered terribly, but despite the long-lasting storm of arrow shot, the Parthians were never able to break their formation. The next day, Crassus was killed in the course of negotiating with the Suren. We have no figures for battle losses, but in the campaign the Romans lost 30,000 men; 10,000 taken prisoner, the rest missing, injured, or killed.

In subsequent Roman campaigns against the Parthians, Ventidius was able to win several victories in 38 BCE and despite the failure of Antony's expedition in 36 BCE, the Romans did not suffer another defeat like Carrhae. Ventidius and Antony led armies similar to that of Crassus, but they made better use of cavalry and light infantry, especially slingers, to keep the Parthian archers at bay. Nonetheless, fighting the Parthians continued to be difficult. As Antony was retreating from Phraaspa in 36 BCE, Flavius Gallus, in command of his rearguard, was cut off from the main body and before he could be rescued lost 3,000 men and died of his wounds (Plutarch, *Antony* 42–43). Roman defeat at Carrhae is best explained as the result of Crassus' poor generalship and the strength of the Suren's leadership, rather than the result of Parthian cataphracts and archery. The only other ancient battle where archery was important was Taginae (below 9.8) and there is no battle where it was decisive. Ventidius and Antony were more successful than Crassus, but a lesser general than Antony might have lost his whole command in the retreat from Phraaspa.

7.6 The Battle of Pharsalus, 48 BCE

In 48 BCE, the two Roman generals Caesar and Pompey met at Pharsalus in Greece in the first great battle of this Roman civil war. Pharsalus lay in southern Thessaly, close to Cynoscephalae (above 6.1). Caesar's account was written soon after the battle with reconciliation in mind, so that Pompey and his senior leadership were made responsible, not his troops who were usually described as 'Pompeians', rather than 'enemies'. This account rapidly became the standard version, so was used by Appian (*Civil Wars* 2.70–82) and by Plutarch in his lives of Pompey and of Caesar, though they both also used the lost history of Asinus Pollio, who fought in the battle for Caesar. Appian also made use of Lucan's Pharsalia written in the mid-first century BCE, an epic poem which devoted only one book to the battle and though exciting to read in Latin cannot be used to write military history.

After leaving Italy at the start of the Civil War in 49 BCE, Pompey began levying troops from various allies and collecting forces assigned to Roman magistrates across the eastern Mediterranean. The result was a patchwork army of 11 legions, with some veterans, but many new recruits, totalling 45,000 men; a particular strength was his cavalry, some 7,000 strong. Caesar had only 1,000 cavalry and 22,000 infantry, but his army was far more cohesive, with a core which had been fighting together for a decade in Gaul.

> He had the very experienced legions of remarkable courage, VII, VIII, and IX, and the highest hopes of the picked young men of XI, who were now in their eighth year of service, although in comparison with the rest had not got the same reputation for experience or courage (Caesar, *Gallic War* 8.8).

Both armies deployed their infantry in the traditional three lines of cohorts. Pompey's right flank was against the River Enipeus, so he deployed his legions up to it according to Caesar, though Appian claimed that Pompey had cavalry on both flanks. The two centres were similar in length, so the larger number of Pompey's infantry meant that his lines were deeper than those of Caesar. Pompey placed all of his cavalry on his left flank, supported by slingers and archers. Against this, Caesar placed his own cavalry, with light infantry intermingled, and also detached six cohorts from his third line to make a fourth line opposing the Pompeian cavalry. Caesar was on the right flank, opposite Pompey.

In the centre, Caesar's troops advanced, but the Pompeians sacrificed the initiative and, instead of charging, stood to receive the Caesarians. Pompey had hoped that gaps would open up in the advancing Caesarian formation which he could exploit. When the experienced Caesarian cohorts saw that the Pompeians were standing, they slowed their advance. This allowed them to reform closer to the Pompeians before attacking. Although Caesar criticized Pompey for this manoeuvre, as being against the troops' natural instinct to want to get the battle started, he understood the logic. Against less experienced troops, this might have been successful; it anticipated later Roman practice when troops regularly stood to receive enemy attacks.

While the infantry clash took place, Caesar's cavalry were pushed back by the Pompeian cavalry, but he then committed his fourth line of infantry. Instead of counhtercharging the infantry, Pompey's cavalry fled. This failure allowed Caesar's fourth line to reach the edge of the heavy infantry clash and fall on the rear of the Pompeian left flank. Caesar then committed his third line of cohorts to the infantry battle and with his left flank crumbling Pompey withdrew. The battle was over.

Caesar admitted to losing 200 soldiers and 30 centurions, though Appian knew of another account which gave 1,200 casualties. Among the Pompeians, Caesar said 15,000 fell, although Appian quoted Asinus Pollio's figure of 6,000.

Unlike Crassus at Carrhae, Caesar managed his situation of being heavily outnumbered in cavalry. Caesar's account highlighted Caesar's genius in forming a fourth line, sending it against the cavalry, and then outflanking the main body. As at Cannae, infantry engaged to their front were very vulnerable when hit in the flank and rear, but unlike Cynoscephalae, this was a planned manoeuvre by the general, not an inspired act of leadership by a regimental commander. And as at Cannae, Caesar relied on his heavily outnumbered but experienced troops in the centre to resist the enemy for long enough for his flanking attack to be successful. The loss of thirty centurions shows the fierceness of the fighting that did take place. As might be expected from his own description, Caesar comes off well, but he did win the battle despite being heavily outnumbered in infantry and, especially importantly, in cavalry.

7.7 The Battle of Zela, 47 BCE

After Pharsalus, Caesar went to Egypt and then to Pontus in central Anatolia. Here, Pharnaces, son of Mithridates VI of Pontus, had taken advantage of the disruption after Pharsalus to occupy Armenia Minor. Domitius Calvinus, the Roman governor of Asia, fought against Pharnaces at Nicopolis in 48 BCE, but his force of four legions was defeated and the king occupied Pontus. The following year, Caesar arrived to restore the situation. The Anatolian campaign lasted less than three months, prompting Caesar's famous 'I came, I saw, I conquered'. The battle is described in the *Alexandrian War* (72–77), a continuation of Caesar's *Civil War*. Its authorship is disputed, but it was probably written by Aulus Hirtius, who also wrote Book 8 of the *Gallic War* and another work covering events after Pharsalus. The author was not at the battle, but did receive information from Caesar himself.

Caesar's army was only four legions: the veteran Legio VI from Alexandria, experienced but now under 1,000 strong, a legion belonging to King Deiotarus of Galatia that was equipped and trained in the Roman style, Legio XXXVI, and one recently raised in Pontus. Legio XXXVI and the Pontic legion had been part of Calvinus' force when it was defeated at Nicopolis Deiotarus also sent some cavalry, but we have no details of any Roman light troops. Pharnaces' army is not described, so that we can only say that it was confident, and experienced, used scythed chariots, and the cavalry outnumbered the Roman cavalry at Nicopolis.

On 2 August, Caesar left his baggage in a camp 5 miles from Zela and advanced towards the city and Pharnaces' forces. He selected a new camp site about a mile from the king's camp, the two being separated by a valley, and some material, probably stakes, was pre-collected to speed the process of building the new camp. When Pharnaces saw the Romans, he deployed his army, but Caesar placed only a forward line of troops and continued to entrench his camp. Pharnaces now advanced and though initially Caesar thought this was foolhardy, and indeed is described as laughing, he quickly realized that he would have to fight, so recalled the men building the fortification and formed a line of battle. We have no sense of the times and distances involved, but the Romans were not fully formed for battle when Pharnaces' army contacted them.

The lead elements of Pharnaces' force were some scythed chariots. Their presence suggests that the valley between the two armies was gentle and open, and that our account exaggerated the difficulty of the terrain. The scythed chariots were defeated by Roman missiles, presumably pila thrown by the legionaries. The two bodies of infantry then clashed in fierce fighting. The Romans were successful at first on their right where Legio VI stood, and then more slowly in the centre and on their left. The Pontic forces fell back and were then unable to reform on the other side of the valley.

Caesar, 'as he remembered the sudden danger, the easy victory made him very happy, as it had come from very difficult circumstances' (*Alexandrian War* 77). And yet, the difficulties from which Caesar emerged were of his own making: misjudging the ground, Pharnaces' intentions, and his speed of advance. It was remarkably like the River Sabis. With no details of the numbers of men on either side or whether there were cavalry on the flanks this is not a battle where we learn much about how regiments fought. However, it shows the importance of experience with Legio VI being successful first, despite its small numbers, as well as the honesty of the *Alexandrian War* which allows us to see Caesar at fault, even though he was in the end victorious. The battle is also of interest because of the scythed chariots, a weapon system which, like elephants, is often misunderstood.

7.8 Scythed Chariots

Chariot warfare, involving a mobile fighting platform drawn by horses, had disappeared rapidly once riding became widespread, so that in the period covered by this book we rarely hear of chariots, most famously in Britain in the first century BCE. Scythed chariots were very different. They were used between the fifth and first centuries BCE, not as fighting platforms, but to disrupt enemy forces before the main clash. They were used by the Achaemenid Persians at Cunaxa and at Gaugamela and later by the Seleucids. Near Apollonia in 220 BCE, the Seleucid rebel Molon deployed his scythed chariots in front of his centre in the hope of disordering Antiochus III's pike phalanx (Polybius 5.53.10). Having defeated them at Apollonia, Antiochus did not use scythed chariots against the Ptolemies at Raphia in 217 or Panium in 200 BCE, but he then chose to use them against the Romans at Magnesia (above 6.2). Scythed chariots were also used by Pontic armies, successfully at the River Amnias in 88 BCE, unsuccessfully at Chaeronea in 86 BCE and, as we have seen, at Zela in 47 BCE.

Their function was to disorder the enemy so they were always placed in advance of their own troops. They could be neutralized by opening up gaps in a formation, as happened at Cunaxa, Gaugamela, and Chaeronea, or by light troops or cavalry armed with missiles, as at Gaugamela and Magnesia. As Zela showed, Roman javelins would also work. Against well-led and organized troops they were rarely effective, but not many armies were more vulnerable.

Since experienced generals like Antiochus III and Archelaus chose to use scythed chariots, we should be reluctant to follow the dismissive comments of Livy, who had no military experience, regarding Magnesia. Instead, we should see them as an inexpensive tool that might disrupt the enemy if things worked out well. Like elephants, scythed chariots were effective against poorly trained troops who might be unnerved by the spectacle of the scythed chariots driving towards them, apparently out of control.

7.9 Battle in the Late Roman Republican Period

Roman battle in this period was characterized by fighting against a great variety of enemies on many different terrains across the Mediterranean. The Romans won many battles but lost many too.

7.9.1 Who was a regimental commander?

The Romans were involved in nearly continuous wars from the end of the second century BCE onwards. Although the requirement of ten years' military experience before entering the Senate had ended in the early first century BCE, many Roman centurions and tribunes had very long service records. A centurion in Africa claimed thirty-six years of service (*African War* 45). Even at the beginning of a career, inexperienced men had veteran colleagues who could advise them. Regimental commanders were literate, many of them in Greek as well as in Latin. Individual initiative seems not to have been as encouraged as in the Middle Republic, with Caesar noting that the 'duties of a legate and of a general are different. One should do everything as ordered, the other should freely plan for the most important matters' (*Civil War* 3.51.4–5). Among the enemies of the Romans, many Gauls and Germans were experienced warriors, but had little practice in manoeuvring large armies. In the East, Pontic officers had acquired much experience during the wars of Mithridates and Pharnaces so were probably little different from their Roman counterparts. Finally, Parthian regimental commanders were hereditary aristocrats, with a culture encouraging personal leadership, but varying levels of experience in battle. By the time of the war against Antony in the 30s BCE, many of these men might be quite experienced.

7.9.2 Training and discipline

Roman armies continued to train before campaigns, for example Marius before the campaigns against the Cimbri and Teutones and Caesar in

46 BCE in Africa before Ruspina and Thapsus. This training was especially necessary for rapidly raised troops in the civil wars. Although still raised for the occasion, many legions remained in the field for a long time and began to build permanent identities, like Caesar's Legio X, raised in 61 BCE and serving continually until the fifth century CE. Continuous regiments were reinforced by experienced centurions. The earlier animal standards for Roman legions were supplemented from the early-first century BCE by eagle standards, attributed to Marius by Pliny the Elder and shown on coins from the 80s BCE, while cohorts also had their own standards. Regular pay, medical care, and rewards for bravery in battle all helped build cohesion. Discipline continued to be fierce, with execution by comrades still occurring and mutinies being common. Roman equipment and organization were easy to imitate, but practice was harder. In the mid-first century BCE, King Deiotarus of Galatia raised two legions in Roman style. One of these was broken at Nicopolis, but Caesar was still happy to use it at Zela the following year (*Alexandrian War*, 34, 37, 68).

Gallic and German armies were not paid, provided their own food, and did not train, even if men practised individual skills. Nor was there any formal organization. They often had their families with them, as at Vercellae in 101 BCE and Vesontio in 58 BCE; Roman writers claimed that they stood behind the battleline to encourage their warriors (Plutarch, *Marius* 27.2; Caesar, *Gallic War* 1.51). Parthian armies with their feudal nature were similarly weaker in formal training, though we can say nothing about how they were fed. Pontic armies had some training, but we can say little about them.

7.9.3 Infantry and cavalry spacing

We have no evidence for infantry spacing in this period, so are forced to assume that heavy infantry fought as in previous periods, so spaced at 2m per man. Though Gauls are sometimes described as having slashing swords that might need more space than a Roman with a shorter, thrusting sword, no source suggests that they were spread out more widely than the Romans. Cavalry and light-troop spacing was presumably also the same as earlier.

7.9.4 Deployment for battle

Legions were the primary unit of Roman battles, but contemporary sources often talk about numbers of cohorts. In planned battles, Roman armies typically deployed in one long formation made up of three lines of cohorts (triplex acies) in a chequerboard formation, with cavalry and light troops on the flanks. Unlike the middle Republic, the front was no longer regularly screened by light infantry although light troops did deploy in front of the main line at Ruspina in 46 BCE and were placed in unit intervals by Metellus in Numidia in 109 BCE (Sallust, *Jugurthine War* 49.6). The best troops were often placed on the right flank, where Caesar placed Legio X at Pharsalus and Legio VI at Zela. Variations on this were usually in response to inferiority in cavalry, so that Crassus deployed in a square at Carrhae, at Pharsalus Caesar formed a fourth infantry line on his right flank by detaching some cohorts from his third line, doing the same at Thapsus on both flanks, and at Ruspina he faced some cohorts backwards when encircled. It was possible to lengthen the formation by using only two lines of cohorts *Gallic War* 3.24). There were occasional cases of outflanking manoeuvres before the start of battle, as Caesar did against the Helvetii in 58 BCE (*Gallic War* 1.21–22), Occasionally, the Romans waited to receive an enemy attack, if possible standing on a hill, as at Zela, as by Gnaeus Pompeius at Munda, and by Ventidius at Gindarus. This gave a slight advantage, but uphill attacks by Romans were successful at Ilerda and Munda.

Germanic armies were arranged by tribes (*Gallic War* 1.51), with cavalry and light troops on the flanks. We can say little about most other enemies of Rome, though their deployments were probably similar.

7.9.5 *Manoeuvre during battle*
The standard Roman heavy infantry formation was a line six ranks deep. The formations described earlier by Cato in his military manual (cuneus, forceps, globus, and saw) are only rarely attested. The use of a cuneus as an attack formation to break through the enemy was suggested by some surrounded troops in Gaul (Caesar, *Gallic War* 6.40). Caesar described another of Cato's formations, the globus, in a civil war clash between his troops and those led by the Pompeian general Afranius at Ilerda in Spain in 49 BCE.

This was the style of fighting of those soldiers, to run forward with great speed at first, to take a position boldly, not to put much effort into keeping their ranks, to fight scattered and dispersed. If they were heavily pressured, they did not think it shameful to retire and to give up that position, being used to this style of fighting among the Lusitanians and other barbarians.... This manner disturbed our men then, not being used to this style of fighting. For they thought that they would be surrounded from their open flank by those running forward individually. They themselves, however, thought it necessary to keep their ranks and neither leave the standards nor, without good reason, give up a position which they had taken (*Civil War* 1.44).

Once battle had begun, Romans only moved troops around the battlefield in the case of difficulties, as at the Sabis River or Munda, where Gnaeus Pompeius moved a legion from his right flank to reinforce his left, which was being pushed back (*Spanish War* 31). Against Germans in 58 BCE, Publius Crassus, assigned to command Caesar's cavalry, ordered the third line of troops to support the Roman right flank (*Gallic War* 1.52) and Labienus also took action at the Sabis River and at Alesia (7.87). These sorts of actions were usually taken by generals, and only rarely by legionary commanders.

Rome's enemies usually fought in a linear fashion too, though Caesar thought his army was not well-suited to fighting the British tribes who, like the Lusitani, preferred skirmishing to close order formations.

> They never fought densely but in a scattered fashion, and at great intervals; they had skirmishers and main bodies and one in succession relieved another, and the uninjured and fresh succeeded the tired (*Gallic War* 5.16).

All cultures could close up and cover themselves with their shields to form what the Romans called a <u>testudo</u>, strengthening their defence against missiles but making movement slow (Caesar, *Gallic War* 2.6, 7.25).

Roman light troops were usually relegated to the flanks, though occasionally were used as a screen in the centre or to support cavalry, as at Pharsalus. Celtic, German, and Numidian armies also used light infantry to support their cavalry (Caesar, *Gallic War* 1.48, 7.80; Sallust, *Jugurthine War* 59.3). The Roman use of artillery was usually confined to sieges.

7.9.6 Morale and the will to engage

Getting troops to advance into combat was difficult on some occasions, hard to stop on others. At Thapsus, Caesar's army was composed of a mixture of veterans and new recruits. Before the battle started, men were getting jittery.

> when suddenly on the right flank, without orders from Caesar, a trumpeter compelled by the soldiers began to sound the charge. After this, all the cohorts began to advance their standards against the enemy, although the centurions, standing in the way, began to resist and by force restrain the soldiers from attacking without the general's order. But they could not accomplish this (*African War* 82).

The lack of control here was the result of the men's inexperience, but a much more experienced army at Gergovia was also hard to control and was defeated by the Gauls. Similarly, in Judaea in 38 BCE during Antigonus' revolt, the whole Roman force was destroyed because they were newly-recruited cohorts from Syria, and so-called veteran soldiers were not mixed in with them to help the ability of men inexperienced in war (Josephus, *Jewish War* 1.324).

The performance of Caesar's veterans at Pharsalus was very different.

The presence of six centurions in every cohort provided a core of junior leaders who were expected to lead from the front, like the tribunes in a legion. Caesar often named courageous centurions, like Crastinus, who led the attack at Pharsalus (*Civil War* 3.91), and in fighting at the Pontic camp after Orchomenus in 85 BCE, Appian tells us 'No one dared until the military tribune, Basillus, jumped over first and killed the man in front of him. Then the whole army rushed in with him' (Appian, *Mithridatic Wars* 50). They often took heavy casualties, especially in defeats. At the poorly recorded battle of Zela in 67 BCE, a remarkable 24 tribunes and 150 centurions fell in one of Mithridates' great victories; we have no such figures for Carrhae. With centurions and tribunes carrying out such leadership roles, there was less need for a general to be involved in fighting himself.

The Celts and Germans were often described as being frightening because of their size. Polybius noted that the Romans 'had seen in previous fighting that the spirit of their first attack, as long as they were fresh, was most to be feared from all the Gallic peoples' (2.33.2) and Plutarch described attacks of the Cimbri and Teutones as being 'with the speed and force of fire' (Plutarch, *Marius* 11.8). The Parthians are described as using drums to make noise before the battle (Plutarch, *Crassus* 23.7, 26.3), while Gallic armies often had trumpets.

7.9.7 Infantry combat

The expected mode of attack for Romans was for their infantry line to advance to javelin range, throw their <u>pila</u>, and then charge to fight with swords. Sometimes it happened as planned, or even faster, as at a battle against the Suebi in Gaul in 58 BCE:

Thus our men, when the signal had been given, fiercely made an attack against the enemy and the enemy in the same way suddenly and swiftly ran forward so that there was no time to throw <u>pila</u> at the enemy. With the <u>pila</u> discarded, the fighting was hand-to-hand with swords (*Gallic War* 1.52).

At other times, there was a series of confrontations with missiles being thrown but less fighting. After five hours of fighting at Ilerda, Caesar's troops had exhausted all their missile weapons (*Civil War* 1.46). Appian described fighting at Forum Gallorum in Italy in 43 BCE thus: 'when they were tired, as if exercising, they separated from each other for a short breather, and then engaged again' (*Civil Wars* 3.68). And at other moments, the enemy did not stand. In 54 in Gaul, 'Caesar, having made a sortie from all the gates and having sent out the cavalry, swiftly put the enemy to flight, so that no one at all stood to fight' (*Gallic War* 5.51) and a year later against the Pictones:

> suddenly the legions in close order came into sight of the enemy. When they saw them, the squadrons (turmae) of barbarians were shocked and the enemy line of battle terrified, with the column of baggage disturbed, with a great shout and scattered everywhere they turned to flight (*Gallic War* 8.29).

7.9.8 Cavalry combat

Cavalry were unable to defeat formed heavy infantry, though at Gindarus in 38 BCE, a Parthian army led by Pacorus attacked a Roman camp on a hill, perhaps emboldened by their victory at Carrhae.

> But in a sudden sortie, they were pushed downhill with no difficulty, since they were cavalry. And then bravely defending themselves, since most of them were cataphracts, they were disturbed by the surprise and by each other and suffered from the hoplites and especially from the slingers, being reached from a distance with their powerful throws which were very hard to bear. And in this fighting Pacorus falling hurt them the most, for as soon as they saw that their leader had been killed, although a few men struggled fiercely for his body they were killed and all the rest yielded (Cassius Dio 49.20.2–3).

As with Cyrus at Cunaxa and Cleombrotus at Leuctra, the death of the general was decisive.

The main use of cavalry was in harassment operations, using missile weapons to attack the enemy and perhaps creating an opportunity. When infantry were harassed by cavalry, the best response was to keep them at a distance with infantry armed with missile-weapons or to use short, controlled attacks by cavalry. When executing these controlled attacks it was often difficult to distinguish between the enemy breaking, or simply giving up ground in a feigned flight. Over-pursuing could lead to detachments being cut off, as happened to Publius Crassus at Carrhae and to Flavius Gallus in 36 BCE during Antony's campaign.

Battles between the Romans and the Parthians usually involved the Romans taking a defensive position because of their small numbers of cavalry. The Parthian cavalry tried to wear down their enemies with archery, then use their cataphracts to attack any weak points in the line. As long as the Parthians could resupply with arrows, battles lasted for a long time, with Carrhae only coming to an end at nightfall.

7.9.9 Pursuit

The small numbers of cavalry in Roman armies of this period limited the opportunities for effective pursuit. In 57 BCE, as Caesar's troops pursued some defeated Belgae, 'without any danger, our men killed as great a number as there was time in the day; at sunset they stopped the pursuit' (Caesar, *Gallic War* 2.11). After many civil war battles there was less of a pursuit, with most campaigns decided after a single large battle.

7.10 Conclusion

For the Romans, this period was characterized by large forces of well-armoured heavy infantry that overwhelmed their enemies in battle. The use of cohorts as manoeuvre units was potentially more flexible than the army of the Middle Republic, though the command structure of legions was still focussed on linear operations and we are not clear on how cohorts were commanded. Though generals did manoeuvre troops, there is little evidence for independent action by tribunes and centurions. They did, however, provided combat leadership, often at a great cost, a very different role from their generals who rarely fought in person. The Romans usually had only a few cavalry and light troops, especially in the West, but the domination of Roman armies by heavy infantry allowed fewer opportunities for these men to influence the flow of battle.

Chapter 8

The Early Roman Empire

This chapter is concerned with battle in the Early Roman Empire, roughly 31 BCE–250 CE; henceforth all dates are CE unless otherwise specified. The end of the Roman civil wars of the late Republic saw further wars of conquest which extended Roman territory in Europe to the Rhine and Danube Rivers, followed by a long period of stability.

8.1 Sources

The most important writers for battle in this period are Josephus, Tacitus, and Arrian. Josephus was born c.37 CE to an aristocratic family in Jerusalem. When the Jewish Revolt of 66–73 CE broke out he led a group of Jewish rebels in Galilee. After the war Josephus became a Roman citizen and spent the rest of his career in Rome where he wrote the *Jewish War*, a history of the revolt, in Greek. Josephus commanded the defences in the siege of Jotapata in 67 CE and after his capture was with Titus at the siege of Jerusalem, so had seen much war. Josephus' style was simple but clear, though he made little use of technical vocabulary, often calling troops 'hoplites' and using the vague term *tagma* (unit) for a Roman legion. Like Polybius, he included a digression on the Roman army (*Jewish War* 3.70–109) intended to show its workings for an unfamiliar audience.

Publius Cornelius Tacitus was a Roman senatorial aristocrat of the late first and early second century. As part of his senatorial career, he commanded an auxiliary regiment and served as military tribune in a legion, though we have no details. His early works included the *Germania*, a description of Germanic culture, and the *Agricola*, a biography of his father-in-law Gaius Julius Agricola, governor of the province of Britannia, who fought at Mons Graupius (below 8.5). He also wrote two larger works, the *Annals*, covering the Julio-Claudian dynasty (14–68 CE) after Augustus and the *Histories*, covering the Flavian dynasty (69–96 CE). Neither of these has survived in their entirety, but we have the first five books of the *Histories* which covered the Roman Civil War of 69 CE and the beginning of the Batavian Revolt. For both, Tacitus used written sources, though for later events, mostly in the books we don't have, could rely on his own memories and talk to participants. Tacitus wrote a highly literary Latin full of stylish epigrams and compressed language, very different from Caesar, and though equally enjoyable to read, is not always as clear. With the exception of the account of Mons Graupius, his battle descriptions are highly compressed and his explanations of why battles were won are often simplistic and moral, perhaps because, like Livy, he had no personal experience of battle. When he described the fighting at First Cremona in 69 CE, his words are generic and stylish:

> from near and far they were charging in bands and wedges. … They fought hand to hand, struggling with bodies and shield bosses; there was no throwing of pila, but with swords and axes, they shattered helmets and breastplates (*Histories* 2.42).

In Latin it is compact and powerful, the first clause consisting of only six words (comminus eminus, catervis et cuneis concurrebant) clearly carefully chosen for clashing consonants, and not a statement about the formations used.

The third author for this period is Arrian whom we have already met as a historian of Alexander (above 4.1). He also wrote a short work in Greek about a battle against the Alans when he was governor of Cappadocia under Hadrian (117–138 CE). This is a detailed description of how a Roman army fought in the second century CE, showing how it had begun to evolve into the army of the Late Roman Empire. This work was quite different from his tactical manual, the *Taktikē Technē*, which, like those of Aelian and Asclepiodotus, was based on Polybius' lost tactical work via Poseidonius. It was a very theoretical work, so the description of infantry formations envisaged an ideal phalanx of 16,384 men, half pikemen, half light infantry, deployed at various depths between 8 and 32 ranks. There are a few comments alluding to contemporary practice and a useful section on contemporary cavalry exercises.

We have a few other useful sources. The first-century CE writer Onasander wrote a short handbook in Greek which gave good advice on how a general should behave, but is less useful on how to fight a battle. He tried to avoid technical vocabulary and detailed examples, and though often describing the Hellenistic world, also referred to Roman practices, including the placing of light infantry in front of the main line of battle rather than behind or mixed in with the more heavily armed men (Onasander 17), leaving an interval between formations for light troops to retire through (Onasander 19); the use of a testudo (described but not named) when faced by light troops without your own (Onasander 20); use of a reserve force (Onasander 22); and making noise when attacking and running (Onasander 29). Other evidence is non-literary. Some regimental rosters on papyrus give information about unit organization, while numerous career and funerary inscriptions for soldiers illustrate equipment, or add details about army composition and organization, for example showing that centuries were typically named after their centurions. An interesting series of inscriptions from Lambaesis in North Africa documents a speech made by Emperor Hadrian after reviewing exercises conducted by Legio III Augusta and their attached auxiliary regiments. We also have pseudo-Hyginus' work on laying out camps, helpful for unit organization.

8.2 Roman Equipment and Organization

With the end of the civil wars at Actium in 31 BCE, many of the troops raised for these wars were paid off. A series of reforms followed which began to create the standing army of the Empire, though with continuing evolution throughout the first and second centuries. As in the late Republic, units were legions and auxiliaries. Legions remained formations of heavy infantry identified by number and now usually a name. Many had been formed under the late Republic, like Legio X Gemina, Caesar's favoured Tenth Legion, but others like Legio I Adiutrix were new creations. They were still divided into 10 cohorts of 480 men each, though by the late first century CE the first cohort of each legion had become 800 strong. There were a few attached horsemen, messengers and scouts rather than cavalry, and some stone-throwing and bolt-shooting artillery. In practice, legions were often much weaker than establishment; the four legions that Germanicus led across the Rhine in 14 totalled 12,000 men (Tacitus, *Annals* 1.49). A legion was now assigned a legate as a permanent commanding officer, assisted by six tribunes, five of whom had already commanded an auxiliary cohort, the other being a young senator. As in the late Republic, the role of these tribunes in battle is unclear. There were no structures between the ten cohorts and the legion itself, leaving the cohort as the typical manoeuvre unit, probably commanded by its lead centurion. Legions were well-suited for battle against other linear formations of infantry such as Gauls and Germans. Detachments (vexillationes) were often used to supplement forces on other frontiers, commanded by legates or tribunes. These varied in size and composition and could be drawn from both legions and auxiliary units, typically organized as drafts of men, rather than complete cohorts.

Legions were supported by various auxiliary regiments, with similarly mixed origins, so that Ala I Gallorum Atectorgiana was recruited from Gaul and originally led by Atectorix, while after the annexation of the kingdom of Nabataea in 106 CE six regiments were made out of the royal army as Cohors

I-VI Ulpia Petraeorum. Auxiliary regiments were numbered and named, sometimes after their first commander, more often after regions or tribes. Infantry cohorts normally consisted of six centuries of eighty men, while cavalry alae normally had sixteen turmae of thirty-two men. Larger units, with milliaria added to their title, began to be used from the late first century CE, and consisted of eight centuries of infantry and twenty-four turmae of cavalry respectively. Finally, there were cohortes equitatae, mixed formations of cavalry and infantry, with establishments often suggested of four turmae of cavalry and six centuries of infantry and for milliary units eight turmae and ten centuries. These mixed units were well-suited for frontier patrolling, but in battle the cavalry were pulled out and formed into composite regiments. Infantry cohorts were usually commanded by a prefect, while by mid-first century CE cavalry alae were led by a more senior prefect who had already served as a legionary tribune. During the early-first century CE commanders were often of the same ethnicity as their men, like the Cheruscan Arminius and the Batavian Civilis, both from tribes on the northern Rhine. This practice became less common from the later first century, but even during these revolts members of their families remained loyal to Rome. Some auxiliary regiments were heavy infantry, but many were archers, slingers, and various types of cavalry.

There were no formal structures above regiment level, though auxiliaries were attached to legions in a loose fashion; for example, in 69 CE Tacitus mentioned eight cohorts of Batavians as being attached to Legio XIV (*Histories* 1.59). Titus in Judaea in 70 CE had a force of four legions, with vexillationes from two more, twenty cohorts of infantry and eight alae of cavalry, as well as troops from the allied kingdoms of Commagene and Nabataea, perhaps 40,000 men (Tacitus, *Histories* 5.1), with a cavalry to infantry ratio of about 1:10. This use of allied troops was typical of operations in the East in the first century CE though also found on a smaller scale in the West. Overall, early imperial Roman forces were better supported by light troops and cavalry than those of the late Republic.

Legionary infantry were still equipped with a large shield, metal body armour (usually mail), and a metal helmet, and armed with a short sword and one or two heavy javelins (pilum). Roman mail was similar to that used in earlier periods. At the start of the first century CE mail was supplemented by a new type of banded metal armour known to modern scholars as lorica segmentata; we don't know what the Romans called it. Its weight, at about 5–6kg, was similar to mail. This was widely used for about two centuries, after which mail was the dominant form again. The continued use of mail during and after the period of lorica segmentata suggests this armour had both advantages and disadvantages, with cost and ease of maintenance being important factors to consider as well

Figure 8.1: An early imperial Roman legionary from the period of the Civil Wars of 69 CE, equipped with a newer-style rectangular shield. He's wearing *lorica segmentata*, though other contemporaries would have worn mail. Once he's thrown his *pilum*, he'll engage with his short sword. (© *Philip Sidnell*)

Figure 8.2: Early imperial Roman auxiliary infantry, from the end of the second century, running towards the enemy. He's equipped with a long *spatha* rather than a shorter *gladius* as backup for his spear. He's well armoured, with a mail shirt, oval shield, and helmet. (© *Philip Sidnell*)

as protection. Helmets were open-faced, usually with cheekpieces, with some styles used more often by legionaries having protruding neck defences. Roman shields of what are traditionally called the legionary type were large and semi-cylindrical, about 1m in height and 0.6m across the chord, made of plywood, weighing around 5kg and with a metal boss and horizontal handle. There were also large oval shields, traditionally described as auxiliary shields, that were similar in size, made of edge-jointed boards, and slightly convex. Latin has several words for shields (clipeus, scutum, parma, caetra), but these cannot be assigned with any confidence to any particular design.

A short sword, called a gladius by modern scholars, was typically used by legionary troops. This had two edges and could be used for cutting, though it was better suited for thrusting. Blade lengths for surviving examples range between 0.40 and 0.75m. There was also a longer sword, around 1m in length, carried by cavalry and many auxiliary infantry, and called a spatha by modern scholars. Spears of about 2–2.5m were used one-handed by auxiliary infantry and by cavalry. Horse archers were used occasionally, and from the early-second century CE there were some units of cavalry described as cataphracts, equipped with heavier body armour, a two-handed lance (contus), and perhaps

Figure 8.3: Early imperial Roman auxiliary cavalryman. This man is equipped with throwing javelins kept in an under-leg quiver, though others might have used a vertical quiver behind the saddle. He's got lots of other equipment to juggle too, a shield and sword, and then he's impeded by his helmet and mail shirt. The metal horse ornaments add to the noise he'd make as he rode into action. (© *Philip Sidnell*)

horse armour. Most cavalry wore armour and used shields, though the north African cavalry depicted on Trajan's Column do not have them.

As in the late Republic, the heavy javelin (<u>pilum</u>) weighing about 1.5kg was used by legionary infantry, while lighter javelins were used by cavalry and auxiliary infantry. The bows used by Roman archers were recurved composite bows, with finds of bone ear laths being common in forts. Finally, bolt-shooting and stone-throwing artillery could be used on the battlefield. Some of the engines were small enough to be carried by one or two men, others were placed on small carts.

By the middle of the second century CE, further changes were taking place to infantry equipment so that distinctions between legionary and auxiliary equipment began to disappear. The oval shield became the most common type, <u>lorica segmentata</u> fell out of use, and there was a drift away from the combination of <u>pilum</u> and short sword in favour of spear and long sword.

8.3 British, Germanic and Sarmatian Equipment and Organization

The European enemies of the Roman Empire differed little from the Gauls and Germans whom Caesar had fought in the 50s BCE. In Britain, Celtic society was similar to the Gallic communities in the first century BCE, organized by tribes under kings with fortified proto-urban centres and using coins with written legends. Across the Rhine and Danube, Germanic tribes were less technologically developed without proto-urban centres, coinage, or writing. On the central Danube the Romans faced the Sarmatians, tribes based on the plains with a greater emphasis on cavalry.

Tacitus described Germanic equipment at several points in his historical works. Although his *Germania* often idealized the Germans, treating them as 'noble savages' in counterpoint to the corrupt Romans, the less ideologically driven *Annals* and *Histories* presented a similar perspective. In a speech before Idistaviso in 16 CE, the Roman general Germanicus said:

> It was not only plains that were good for a Roman soldier for battle, but if he thought about it, woods and clearings. For the huge shields of the barbarians and their great spears could not be wielded among the trunks of the trees and the bushes springing from the ground like the pilum, gladius, and tight-fitting body-armour. Let the Romans pile on the blows, let them seek out the face with their sword points. There was no German armour (lorica), no helmet, no shields strengthened with iron or sinew, but a weaving of wicker or thin planks, painted with colour. Although their first line had spears, the rest had weapons that were fire-hardened or too short (Tacitus, *Annals* 2.14).

This speech is consistent with other descriptions which emphasize the lack of armour and the use of spears and javelins and with burials in which body armour and helmets are rare and most weapon were spears; swords or archery equipment are only found occasionally. The better equipment and any body armour belonged to aristocrats and their retinues. There were only a few cavalry equipped with shields who fought by skirmishing with javelins.

Tacitus' description of Sarmatian cavalry is very literary, has them equipped with horse armour, body armour but no shield, and lances (*Histories* 1.79) which is consistent with the imagery on Trajan's Column, and Arrian's description of armoured horsemen with lances (*kontoi*) in the *Ektaxis kata Alanos* (17). The focus of our sources on the cavalry means that we can say little about other troops or about force mixes, though Arrian mentioned unarmoured cavalry in the force that he faced.

8.4 The Battle of Idistaviso, 16 CE

The Battle of Idistaviso took place in 16 CE in northern Germany between a Roman army commanded by Germanicus and a Germanic alliance headed by Arminius. This was the final battle in the Roman attempts to regain control of territory across the Rhine following the disastrous ambush at the Teutoburger Wald in 9 CE, when three legions had been destroyed. The only source is Tacitus' *Annals* (2.16–18), based on Pliny the Elder's lost *German Wars* and perhaps a despatch by Germanicus to Rome.

The Roman force, which had campaigned together for the past three years, consisted of the armies of Upper and Lower Germany, each of four legions and auxiliaries, including units of horse and foot archers, and two cohorts of Praetorians. Four full-strength legions would have been 20,000, but two years earlier, Germanicus led the army of Lower Germany across the Rhine: 4 legions totalling 12,000 men; 26 cohorts of auxiliary infantry; and 8 alae of cavalry. If the auxiliaries were similarly understrength this would give a cavalry to infantry ratio of about 1:10. There are no details of the German army other than the presence of the Cherusci and Chauci.

The battle occurred on the plain of Idistaviso, an unknown site east of the River Weser. The Germans deployed on the plain with a forest behind them, the Cherusci being placed on a hill on one flank. Tacitus described the Roman marching order, but not their deployment. The battle opened with an advance of the Cherusci and an attack on them by some Roman cavalry, while other cavalry regiments were sent on an outflanking march. As fighting started in the centre, the Romans pushed the enemy back. Tacitus used his sources selectively, describing one unspecified flank as having some archers and auxiliary cohorts of Raetians, Vindelicians, and Gauls, but saying nothing about the other. Instead, he placed literary effects above detailed description, emphasizing the providential vision of eight eagles which matched the number of legions, and enjoying the contrast between the Romans in the centre pushing the advancing Germans into the forest from the plain at the same time as the outflanking Roman cavalry was pushing other retreating Germans out of the woods onto the plain. The battle lasted from late morning to dark. In the pursuit the Romans cut down many Germans, some of whom were slaughtered crossing the Weser, but no casualty figures were given.

In previous Roman operations against Arminius in 14 and 15 CE, there were numerous surprise Roman attacks on German settlements and fighting in swamps. Here, Germanicus forced a field battle against Arminius on his terms, but we don't know how he did this, or how or why the Romans won this battle. Tacitus was more interested in the heroism of Arminius than in detailed description.

8.5 The Battle of Mons Graupius, 84 CE

Following the end of Roman attempts to conquer Germania, the island of Britain was conquered, there was fighting against the Parthians in Armenia, and major revolts in Britain and Armenia. In 69 CE a renewed civil war resulted in much fighting in Italy, including two battles at Cremona, and an associated revolt by Civilis on the Rhineland. Towards the end of the first century, Domitian (81–96 CE) fought against the Chatti in Germania. It was during this period that the Battle of Mons Graupius was fought in northern Britain in late summer, conventionally dated to 84 CE, though it could be 83 CE. The only source we have is three sections (35–37) of Tacitus' *Agricola*, a biography of his father-in-law. He was well informed, but like Polybius on Scipio, probably portrayed Agricola's accomplishments in the best light. The location of the battle is unknown, though the subject of much study.

Agricola was campaigning in the southern Highlands of modern Scotland. He had sent some troops to Germany to support Emperor Domitian's war against the Chatti, so not all of his units were at full strength. Agricola had elements of three legions (II Augusta, IX Hispana, XX Valeria Victrix), 8,000 auxiliary infantry including two Tungrian and three Batavian cohorts, and 3,000 cavalry. The Romans were outnumbered by the Britons whom Tacitus said exceeded 30,000. The Britons had some cavalry and chariots, with Tacitus alluding to Caesar's descriptions of British chariots in the first century BCE. Before the battle began dramatic tension was created by a pair of speeches delivered by the opposing commanders, the British general Calgacus being allowed to deliver one of the best criticisms of the Roman Empire written by a Roman historian: 'they made a desert and called it peace.'

As the Romans left their camp, they saw the Britons standing at the foot of a hill, their rear ranks spreading upwards behind. Agricola deployed his infantry in two lines of units, auxiliary infantry in front, legionary infantry at the back, with cavalry on the flanks. Tacitus praised 'the great glory of a victory won without Roman blood' (35), as if the auxiliaries were of less worth because they were not Roman citizens. His explanation implied great confidence in a Roman victory, though it ignored the common practice of using auxiliaries to fight in difficult terrain. The numbers of Britons led to a discussion about whether the Romans risked being outflanked, but having consulted his officers, Agricola decided not to bring the legions into the battle line, but to extend it by thinning its depth.

The speeches completed, the battle opened with skirmishing, both sides using missile weapons, and the Britons their cavalry and chariots. Agricola then sent six cohorts towards the enemy centre. Although these were successful, the

Roman cavalry on the flanks were being pushed back and the Romans began to be outflanked by the enemy descending from the hill. At this point Agricola committed four <u>alae</u> of cavalry that he had kept as a reserve. They hit the enemy in the flank and rear. Being attacked in the flank while engaged to the front broke the enemy rapidly, similar to Cynoscephalae and Pharsalus. As some of the fleeing Britons entered the woods they rallied and ambushed some of the pursuing Romans, leading Agricola to call off the pursuit. Total casualties were 360 Romans, including Aulus Atticus, commander of an auxiliary infantry cohort, and around 10,000 Britons.

As at Idistaviso, Tacitus' interests lay in the dramatic, not the technical. Agricola's victory at the end of seven year's campaigning evoked Caesar's success at Alesia in the seventh year of his Gallic campaigns, while Tacitus claimed in a later section that Domitian was reluctant to give Agricola credit for the victory. He did, however, show how Agricola deployed his army in a carefully thought-out fashion, discussed whether to change deployment with his staff, executed this changed deployment, kept a reserve which was committed at the correct time in the battle, and called off a dangerous pursuit. All of this matches Tacitus' likely source for the battle, Agricola himself, and thus a focus on the general's battle.

8.6 Arrian, *Ektaxis kata Alanos*, 135 CE

There were two poorly known campaigns in Dacia under Trajan (98–117 CE), commemorated by Trajan's Column in Rome and a monument erected by the army at Adamklissi in modern Romania. Then under Hadrian (117–138 CE), Cappadocia in eastern Anatolia was raided by some nomads from the Caucasus, probably in 135 CE. Arrian was governor of Cappadocia during this war. He wrote a work traditionally known as *The Order of Battle against the Alans* (*Ektaxis kata Alanos*) which described the march order, deployment, and tactics for the army he led against the raiders. Although written by an informed contemporary about his own experiences, there are numerous questions about the document as we have it. It was written in Greek, though the language of command in the Roman army was Latin, so was not Arrian's actual orders. The Greek text was not a literal translation of a Latin original, but imitated the style of Xenophon, with numerous literary usages, for example using 'phalanx' to refer to a legion. And it is unlikely that the first section on the marching order before the battle, the second on deployment, and the third on how to fight the battle were written at one time in one document, so our Greek text was derived from at least two Latin documents. We can identify most of the regiments in Arrian's force, but he often used informal names, such as Keltoi for Cohors I Germanorum Milliaria Equitata. He was very concerned to name the commanders of the formations and to delineate who was in command of which part of the battlefield. The text was set in the future, with a series of third person imperatives, i.e. 'let this happen', 'let them do this', which is one way to write military orders, but shows a description of intent, not a record of events.

Arrian's force was composed of two legions, XII Fulminata and XV Apollinaris, four cavalry alae, five regular and four milliary cohortes equitatae, an infantry cohort, some local militia, and some Armenian allies. At full strength, this would have been about 17,000 men with a cavalry to infantry ratio of 1:4. He said little about the enemy whom he called Scythians (the title of the work is a modern convention), other than expecting them to be cavalry, some armoured, who would either charge the infantry line or attempt to outflank it.

The first two sections detailed the marching order and the deployed army, but nothing was said of how units were to deploy, suggesting that this was not handled by the army commander (unless this was in a part that has not survived). Arrian imagined fighting on a plain, but gave no sense of what to do if the actual plain was too wide or too narrow for his force. On his right flank he intended to put some infantry archers on higher ground behind an infantry cohort, doing the same with light infantry javelinmen behind more infantry on the left. In the centre, the legions were deployed eight deep, with Arrian wanting the men to stand close together (*pyknē*). Here, despite the clarity of his description, we face considerable confusion because of his vocabulary. The first four ranks were equipped differently from the back four ranks, the front group being armed with *kontoi*, the rear with *longchai*. From Arrian's description of the *kontoi* having iron points which bent from their softness and his ordering them to be thrown, these must be pila, even though *kontos* usually means a long spear held in two hands. He also envisaged the *longchai* being thrown over the heads of the front four ranks, suggesting this was his translation of the Latin word lancea, even though a *longchē* was typically a spear held in one hand. Behind the main infantry line Arrian placed the infantry archers of four cohortes equitatae in a single rank, and artillery on both flanks and behind the main line. Two alae of cavalry were on the flanks, behind the screening infantry, and the rest behind the centre with the horse archers meant to shoot over the heads of the infantry.

The third section covered Arrian's plan for fighting the battle, with his troops waiting silently until the enemy came in range before raising a shout and shooting at them. No differentiation was made between the types of missiles, though the effective ranges of artillery, bows, and javelins were all different and most shooters would have been unable to see their targets. If the enemy were repelled, Arrian wanted only half of his cavalry in the centre to pursue, with the other half ready to assist if the enemy turned to fight again. He also issued instructions for what to do if the enemy tried to encircle the Roman line, ordering the infantry on the flanks to extend their formation into higher ground. After this, the text breaks off as Arrian was explaining that these flanking cavalry were unarmoured, unlike those in the centre.

If this was an actual description of preparation for a battle it would be invaluable, but we need to acknowledge the likely differences between Arrian's notes and discussions with his officers and the written document that we have. Arrian's plan was defensive, i.e. waiting to receive the attack of an enemy expected to be entirely of cavalry, similar to Vegetius' standard deployment (3.14) and to Narses' actions at Taginae (below 9.8). His unit commanders were told how to fight the battle, but not how to control their men, though they were warned about the possibility of a feigned flight. His vision was similar to Agricola at Mons Graupius, that is of the army commander managing a collection of regiments, but made more use of cavalry and archers than earlier Roman armies. We don't know if this deployment was Arrian's own response to the Alans or a general evolution, though later Roman armies did place a similar emphasis on standing to receive the enemy with missile weapons. There is little other contemporary evidence for deploying a Roman army eight deep, though it aligns well with the eight men in a tent-unit (contubernium).

8.7 Battle in the Early Roman Empire

What do these case studies tell us about the mechanics of battle in the early Roman Empire? Despite our great knowledge of the Roman army as an organization, we know less about battle at this period or about how Rome's enemies fought than in some periods and are often dependent on one source requiring interpretation.

8.7.1 Who was a regimental commander?
Most officers followed a career track of commanding an auxiliary cohort, then serving as tribune in a legion, and then commanding a cavalry ala. Commanders of individual Roman legions were appointed by the emperor directly, and though not necessarily experienced, had seasoned tribunes and centurions to advise them. Armies of multiple legions were usually commanded by an experienced general. All regimental commanders were supported by long-service centurions as well as military handbooks, but the well-practiced troops of the late Republic were replaced from Augustus' reign with a newer

generation of less experienced men. At some periods, especially the reigns of Domitian and Trajan, there was a lot of conflict, which would have increased skill levels on the battlefield.

The leaders of Rome's enemies were similar to those in the previous period, experienced as warriors, but not at manoeuvring large armies, though the frequent fighting in the Rhineland in the early first century CE and in Dacia in the late first and early second centuries CE gave some leaders a lot of experience. Most would be aristocrats with a strong martial tradition, but dependent on their own experience and unable to read or write.

8.7.2 Training and discipline

Roman soldiers under the Empire enlisted for long terms, twenty-five years by the mid-first century CE. Recruits who satisfied the physical criteria, which included a height qualification and having good eyesight, began physical and weapon training. Once they joined their units, individual training continued, with Josephus claiming it occurred daily. There were regular exercises at unit level, well-illustrated by the Lambaesis inscriptions in North Africa that record Hadrian's comments to Legio III Augusta and several attached regiments of auxiliaries. Mock battles, that is army level training, were recommended by Onasander (10) and Josephus famously claimed 'their exercises are battles without blood, their battles are exercises with blood' (*Jewish War* 3.75–76).

Long terms of service spent living together in camps, gave Roman regiments strong small-unit cohesion. Loyalty to the emperor was encouraged by an annual oath and his image on one of the unit's standards, as well as by regular pay, food, and medical care. Loyalty to units was strong, encouraged by regimental shield designs, standards, and long histories. Fierce rivalries between units were common, while the civil wars of 69 and 193 CE show competition between the army groups of the Rhine, Danube, and the East. Tacitus even claimed that after the commander of Legio II Augusta Poenius Postumus had kept his unit out of the Battle of St Albans, he killed himself 'having heard of the successes of the Fourteenth and Twentieth, since he had cheated his legion of equal glory by his refusal' (*Annals* 14.37). Successful soldiers and officers were awarded with decorations for bravery. Although often compared to a modern army, Roman armies were also characterized by frequent mutinies, fierce standards of physical discipline sometimes involving execution by comrades, and theft from and abuse of civilians. When Civilis had won a victory over some Romans in 69 CE

the defeated, as had then become their fashion, did not blame their laziness, but the perfidy of their general. Dragging him from his tent, his clothing ripped, his body beaten, they ordered him to tell for what price, with which accomplices he had betrayed the army (Tacitus, *Histories* 4.27).

Germanic, British, and Sarmatian warriors had different expectations. Martial prowess was important to individuals, but there was little solidarity beyond one's family or tribe, marked by standards of some sort (Tacitus, *Histories* 4.22). Armies often had their families with them, with Tacitus describing how they stood behind the battleline to encourage their warriors (*Annals* 14.34; *Histories* 4.18). Men provided their own food and equipment, were not paid, did not train, and were subject only to informal discipline. We should expect these armies to have low levels of resilience.

8.7.3 Infantry and cavalry spacing
Despite the abundant evidence for organization in this period, we can say little about spacing, so can only assume it was similar to earlier periods with heavy infantry taking up 2m. When faced with a cavalry attack, Arrian ordered his men to stand close together, perhaps at 1m. We have no sense that Roman spacings were any different from those of their enemies. Josephus reported troops in Judaea as fighting three deep on two occasions, and Vegetius imagined troops three or six deep, deriving this from his earlier sources. These lines were shallower than those of the Classical Greek period, the result of better trained and led troops.

8.7.4 Deployment for battle
The normal Roman deployment was still the <u>triplex acies</u>, three lines of cohorts of heavy infantry, flanked by cavalry and light troops. Two lines were used by Cerialis against some Germans in 70 CE with auxiliaries before the legions (Tacitus, *Histories* 5.16), similar to Agricola at Mons Graupius, and Arrian used only a single line against the Alani. The third line of cohorts could function as reserves, though units were sometimes set aside for this purpose (Tacitus, *Histories* 2.24). Although Roman legionaries and auxiliaries could have similar sets of equipment, their intended battlefield roles were different. Legions were organized as groups of cohorts used to fighting in three lines, so were better at hand-to-hand combat in flat terrain. Auxiliary cohorts, however, were smaller, always had the same commander, and were more used to working alone, so were often used in difficult terrain like the forests at Idistaviso or the hills of Mons Graupius. Flanking marches were often ordered by generals, either at an operational level to come up on the rear of the enemy or on the battlefield to outflank one end of the enemy line as at Idistaviso. These marches were usually performed by cohorts or <u>alae</u>, not by entire legions. Thus Apronius in

28 sent a mixed force of infantry and cavalry round the flank of some Frisians in Germany (Tacitus, *Annals* 4.73) and in 70 CE Cerialis sent two <u>alae</u> round the flank of a German army (Tacitus, *Histories* 5.18).

German and British armies typically deployed in a line, with the few cavalry on the flanks and sometimes with light troops ahead of the main body. Occasionally they made use of difficult terrain like forests and marshes which would have caused difficulties for both sides, but gave good opportunities for ambushes. Armies of Sarmatians and other nomadic peoples were dominated by mounted troops so fought by skirmishing, charges, feigned withdrawals, and working their way round the enemy flanks.

8.7.5 *Manoeuvre during battle*

Roman infantry formations were similar to those of the late Republic, so that they usually fought in a line. There were a few mentions of columns when attacking, described as 'like a wedge' (<u>velut cuneo</u>) (Tacitus, *Annals* 14.37) or used by a legion assaulting a camp outside Cremona 'advancing in columns' (<u>cuneis</u>) (*Histories* 3.29). During Civilis' revolt, Herennius Gallus, commanding Legio I Germanica and some newly raised auxiliaries from the Belgae, sortied from camp

> to surround the Batavians who were less in number. But they, veteran soldiers, joined into columns (<u>cuneis</u>), closely ordered everywhere, secure to the front, back, and flanks. Thus they broke through the thin line of our men (Tacitus, *Histories* 4.20).

The <u>testudo</u> could be used when under prolonged missile attack, but the other formations described by Cato (<u>forceps</u>, <u>globus</u>, and saw), are not attested.

There was occasional use of artillery on the battlefield, as described by Tacitus at Second Cremona (*Histories* 3.23), illustrated on Trajan's Column, and planned by Arrian in his *Ektaxis*. The small bolt-shooters were light enough to be moved by one man, though they needed a crew to handle ammunition, but larger stone throwers were used at Second Cremona.

For Germanic infantry, the most common unit formation was a line and, with their leaders usually fighting in the front ranks, opportunities for manoeuvre were limited (Tacitus, *Germania* 7.1). Although Tacitus often described Germans as fighting in <u>cunei</u>, there is little sense of these being triangular wedges. Instead, this was the appropriate word for groups of Germans like those whom Civilis deployed in 70 CE, 'not spread out in column, but in cuneis' (*Histories* 5.16) or a <u>cuneus</u> of Bructeri swimming the Rhine (*Histories* 5.18).

8.7.6 *Morale and the will to engage*

One important part of Roman success was the large number of centurions, usually six in a cohort. They had a long tradition of leadership and were expected to drive their units forwards, though this often came at a cost. When Tacitus reported on the performance of Legio VII Galbiana at Second Cremona, he mentioned the deaths of six centurions including the legion's lead centurion Atilius Verus (Tacitus, *Histories* 3.22). Similarly, Josephus mentioned the centurion Julianus at the siege of Jerusalem in 70 CE, 'seeing the Romans were already giving way and defending themselves poorly, he sprang forward and prevailing straightaway turned the Jews to flight, alone'. Then he slipped, was killed trying to get up, and the Romans broke (*Jewish War* 6.82).

Despite the presence of their centurions, Roman soldiers were often ready to rush into battle. At Second Cremona, the Vitellianist soldiers forced a battle in the evening, although they had marched all day. We occasionally find a failure for both sides to meet because one group retired or broke when attacked. Tacitus described a skirmish in 69 CE at The Castors:

> Then the Othonian infantry burst forth. With their line of battle destroyed, [the Vitellians] turned to flight, as did some reinforcements, for Caecina indeed had not summoned his cohorts at the same time, but individually, which increased the confusion in the battle when the panic of those fleeing affected scattered men, not being strong at any place. And a mutiny broke out in the camp because they were not all led forth (*Histories* 2.26).

Germanic armies usually attacked with a swift charge, perhaps a symptom of their desire to get the battle over with (Tacitus, *Annals* 1.51, 4.47). These assaults were often noisy (Tacitus, *Germania* 3). In other battles, like Idistaviso or Mons Graupius, the enemy stood to receive a Roman attack, sometimes making use of hills.

8.7.7 *Infantry combat*

Roman army infantry tactics were unchanged from the late Republic, i.e. advance to <u>pilum</u> range (approx. 30m), throw <u>pila</u>, then raise a shout and follow the centurions forward. Tacitus described Cerialis' men fighting some Germans in 70 CE as exchanging missiles followed by hand-to-hand fighting (*Histories* 5.17–18). The enemy might not stand, but if they did then there was a period of backwards-and-forward combat, depending on the resilience of the troops. At First Cremona, Legio I Adiutrix fought against XXI Rapax.

The First having scattered the front ranks of the Twenty-first carried off
their eagle. This legion, fired up by this loss, drove back the First after its
legate Orfidius Benignus was killed, and captured many standards and
vexilla (Tacitus, *Histories* 2.43).

A few months later at Second Cremona

Antonius reinforced his slipping line by calling the praetorians who,
when they entered battle drove back the enemy, then were themselves
driven back (Tacitus, *Histories* 3.23).

Though Tacitus' descriptions are vague, they are similar to accounts from other
periods. In this phase of battle, Roman resilience, a product of training, armour,
and leadership, meant they took longer to break than most of their enemies.

8.7.8 Cavalry combat

Cavalry fighting other cavalry usually used loose formations with much
backwards and forwards movement, lulls in fighting, and shooting missiles.
When describing a battle in the Caucasus, Tacitus noted that 'in the manner
of a cavalry battle, there were interchanges of front and back' (*Annals* 6.35).
The feigned flight, that is the withdrawal and then the return of a cavalry
regiment, was often used. At the Castors, 'the cavalry were ordered to advance
further and, after provoking a battle, voluntarily to retreat, and draw on the
enemy into hasty pursuit, until the ambushes could be sprung' (Tacitus,
Histories 2.24). Arrian's *Taktikē Technē* described exercises including a circular
formation known as the Cantabrian for throwing javelins, consistent with
Josephus' descriptions of skirmishes at Ascalon and Bethennabris (*Jewish War*
3.12–21, 4.423–427).

Cavalry were sometimes ordered to fight on foot as when Vespasian used
them to lead an assault on Jotapata in 67 CE (Josephus, *Jewish War* 3.254–255).
Cavalry had difficulties against formed infantry, and at Asciburgium in 70 CE
Civilis' troops, either Roman rebels or Germans, were attacked by Vocula.
'The cavalry burst forth, but being received by the ordered ranks of the enemy,
fled back to their own men' (Tacitus, *Histories* 4.33). However, when facing
loosely ordered or poorly disciplined men it was very different, and Josephus
described the slaughter meted out by an ala of cavalry to a group of rebels
outside Jerusalem in 66 CE.

For overtaking those fleeing they turned them back, and having crowded
them together from their flight, they burst into them and killed so

many, one after another wherever they turned, and encircling them and harassing them they threw javelins at them easily (*Jewish War* 3.17).
Even legions were vulnerable when disordered, and in fighting before Second Cremona, the line of I Italica and XXI Rapax was attacked by some supporters of Vespasian:

> The victorious cavalry charged the wavering line and the tribune Vipstanus Messala followed with the Moesian auxiliaries, whom many of the legionaries were keeping up with although they were led forth rapidly. Thus, the mixed infantry and cavalry broke the line of the legions (Tacitus, *Histories* 3.18).

8.7.9 Pursuit
A vigorous pursuit was usually part of a battle, with the pursuit after Idistaviso covering 10 miles. Tacitus judged Vocula harshly for failure to pursue after a victory against Civilis (*Histories* 4.34). If there were uncommitted cavalry reserves these made pursuits even more effective. Arrian's *Ektaxis* shows an awareness that enemy who fell back might sometimes return to the fight, so he issued orders that only half the cavalry should pursue and the others should follow up more slowly, ready to intervene if there was a feigned flight. The ambush of some pursuing Romans at Mons Graupius shows other dangers in pursuing too eagerly.

8.8 Conclusion

This army of the early Roman Empire was for the most part a garrison army, with many duties that took it away from focusing on the battlefield. Military experience was retained through long service soldiers and centurions, though not always relevant to large battles. It was thus very different from the armies of the middle and late Republic which were campaigning armies raised for a purpose, and often, like the army of Alexander the Great, acquiring a great amount of combat experience. Like the Roman army of earlier periods, it continued to evolve in how it behaved on the battlefield. Roman successes were the result of leadership by centurions and tribunes working with armoured heavy infantry rewarded for bravery and fearful of punishment. Such forces could be beaten in the first attack, but in longer battles were unlikely to be defeated. Unit commanders in legions had little to do in these situations, with most significant decisions being made by the general. Commanders of auxiliary regiments often had more chances to make their own decisions. This was especially true of cavalry regiments who were usually only commanded by men who had already some experience of leading infantry.

Chapter 9

The Late Roman Empire

This chapter is concerned with battle in the Late Roman Empire between the fourth and sixth centuries CE. At the beginning of this period, the Romans controlled the Mediterranean, with a northern frontier on the Rhine and Danube Rivers in Europe, where their enemies were the confederations of the Franks, Alamanni, Sarmatians, and Goths, and an eastern frontier in Mesopotamia and Armenia where the Sasanians had replaced the Parthians as the major enemy in the third century CE. During the fifth century CE the Romans lost control of the West, though the lack of source material means we have difficulty in tracing these developments or discussing the wars against the Huns. In the sixth century CE Justinian brought Africa and Italy back under Roman control.

Roman armies of this period used to be thought of as being less effective than those of the early Roman Empire, with manpower shortages resulting in large numbers of non-Roman recruits and reduction of unit sizes. More recent research has challenged these theories and sees the late Roman army as highly effective. This effectiveness was not enough, however, to counteract the political changes which led to the collapse of the Western Empire by the mid-fifth century CE.

9.1 Sources

The two major historical sources for this period are Ammianus Marcellinus and Procopius. Ammianus Marcellinus was a Roman army officer in the mid-fourth century CE who wrote a history covering 96–378 CE, though only the books covering 353–378 CE survive. He appeared as a character in his own history when he was besieged at Amida on the eastern frontier in 359 CE and in Julian's invasion of Persia in 363 CE, but never described a field battle in which he was personally involved. With the rank of protector, Ammianus was a staff officer, not a combat commander, so was more interested in the larger framework of managing armies than the details of what happened in battle. As well as his own experiences, he had numerous high-ranking contacts, made use of official records, and was an assiduous reader of Roman history. Although he came from the Greek-speaking eastern part of the Empire, Ammianus wrote in Latin. He was a great stylist, consciously writing in the tradition of Livy and Tacitus, and frequently alluding to their work. His dense, adjective-filled prose is exciting to read in the original, but his use of the grand style produced impressionistic and formulaic battle descriptions. As a military historian, Ammianus was prepared to use technical language and often named commanders of regiments, but also used antiquated terms to provide literary variety, e.g. using maniple or turma to describe regiments.

Procopius wrote in the mid-sixth century CE, focussing on the emperor Justinian's wars in Persia, Africa, Italy, and the Balkans. He came from Caesarea in the province of Palestina Prima. Although not a soldier, he was a secretary to Justinian's great general Belisarius, accompanying him on campaigns in Mesopotamia, Africa, and Italy, so was often around soldiers and was well-informed, though he usually described Belisarius in a positive light. Procopius wrote in a classicizing style in a very clear but literary Greek. Like Ammianus, he was very fond of allusions to earlier historians, especially Thucydides and Xenophon. Procopius provided significant details of numbers, deployments, and movements, but the comparison at the very beginning of the *Wars* of the bow-armed cavalry of his own day to Homer's depiction of archers is unusual.

Numerous other writers provide minor details, especially Agathias who wrote a continuation of Procopius which had a good description of Casilinum in 554 CE. There are occasional useful inscriptions, though fewer than for the early Empire, papyri, and a complete list of regiments at the end of the fourth century CE in the *Notitia Dignitatum*. Finally, we have two military manuals by Vegetius and Mauricius. Vegetius wrote *On Military Matters* during the late-fourth century CE (or the mid-fifth century; the dating is difficult). This was a literary work in relatively ornate Latin, containing recommendations for restoring Roman infantry to their former glory, and saying less about contemporary cavalry, which he saw as effective. Although Vegetius based his work on earlier manuals from as far back as the second century BCE, he added numerous comments on contemporary practice, so that it is often unclear whether he was describing the past or the present. None of his writing suggested that Vegetius had any military experience, in which it is very different from the *Strategikon*, usually accepted as being written by Emperor Mauricius (582–602 CE), before coming to the throne. This was a very practical work, deliberately written in a clear and simple Greek by an experienced soldier, offering advice about organization, equipment, and battlefield management. At the same time, it was aware of older manuals and occasionally reworked material from Aelian, especially in Chapter 12.B focusing on infantry.

9.2 Late Roman Equipment and Organization

During the late-third and early-fourth centuries the Roman army of the early Empire had evolved into a system of field armies (<u>comitatenses</u>), which did most of the fighting, and border troops (<u>limitanei</u>), responsible for frontier policing. The older auxiliary and legionary regiments were usually on the borders while new regiments made up most of the field armies. Field army infantry regiments ranged from 500 to 2,000 in strength, commanded by a tribune or prefect. Like the auxiliary regiments of the early Empire, they were easier to manage than the earlier 5,000-man heavy infantry legions of ten cohorts. Cavalry regiments were around 600 at full strength, also commanded by a tribune or prefect. Armies contained significantly more cavalry than in the early Empire. At Strasbourg, there were 3,000 cavalry and 10,000 infantry, while an army sent against some Goths in 478 had 8,000 cavalry and 30,000 infantry, both giving cavalry to infantry ratios of around 1:3.5.

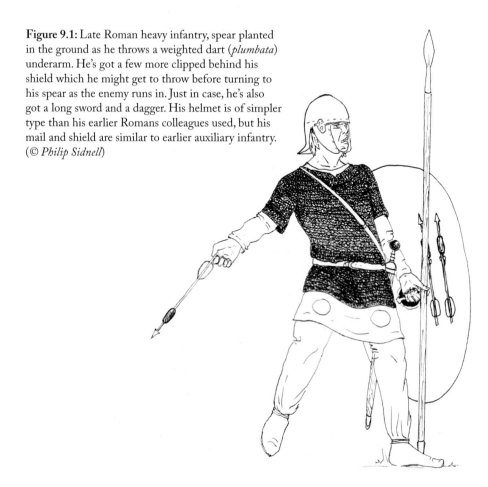

Figure 9.1: Late Roman heavy infantry, spear planted in the ground as he throws a weighted dart (*plumbata*) underarm. He's got a few more clipped behind his shield which he might get to throw before turning to his spear as the enemy runs in. Just in case, he's also got a long sword and a dagger. His helmet is of simpler type than his earlier Romans colleagues used, but his mail and shield are similar to earlier auxiliary infantry. (© *Philip Sidnell*)

All Roman heavy infantry were equipped with state-provided body armour, helmets, and shields. Armour was usually mail (though scale was used), worn over a padded garment, and weighing 5–10kg. Some front-rank men were also equipped with greaves. Shields were oval, made of edge-jointed wooden planks with metal bosses, around 1.05m in height, 0.9m in width, slightly concave towards the bearer, and weighing around 5kg. They were usually painted with a regimental design, shown in the *Notitia Dignitatum* for field army infantry and western cavalry regiments. Offensive equipment was a spear, 2–2.5m long with an iron head and butt-spike, supplemented by a longsword, a slashing

Figure 9.2: A late Roman horse archer, unarmoured, wearing a *pileus* felt cap popular with soldiers off the battlefield. He's using a steppe saddle, though he might also have a horned saddle. His quiver is steppic style with arrows stored points up, though others might use a tubular quiver with flights up. (© *Philip Sidnell*)

Figure 9.3: A late Roman cataphract, wearing a shirt of scale armour similar to men on the Arch of Galerius and the Arch of Constantine, as well as a large shield and a helmet. He's got a spear that he's using one-handed and a long sword if needed. His horse is well-protected, with scale armour and metal chamfron. (© *Philip Sidnell*)

weapon 0.7–0.9m long and 40–60mm wide, known to scholars as a <u>spatha</u>. A significant change from the early Empire was a greater emphasis on missile weapons. Most infantry had several javelins of various weights (<u>veruta</u>, <u>spicula</u>, <u>pila</u>) and sometimes weighted darts (<u>plumbatae</u>) which had a range of 80m. There were also regiments of light infantry, variously equipped with javelins, bows, and slings.

Heavy cavalry were intended to fight hand to hand and were equipped with spears and swords, body armour, helmets, and shields. By the sixth century CE many were also equipped with bows, the result of contact with the Huns. Mauricius, however, was aware that not all men could handle both bow and lance and adds that archers in the middle of units should not have shields. A sub-category of heavy cavalry were cataphracts (sometimes called <u>clibanarii</u>; meaningful distinctions between the two words are difficult to make with the evidence we have), contact cavalry equipped with armoured horses. Mauricius does not mention them by name though he did recommend horse armour for the front ranks. There were also light cavalry units, either javelin-armed skirmishers or horse archers, often recruited from local populations in the eastern Empire. Some generals had large cavalry bodyguards, known as <u>bucellarii</u>, which could function as combat units on the battlefield. In the later sixth century CE the stirrup was beginning to appear in Europe though it had no impact on cavalry tactics. In contemporary Greek it was known as a *skala*, meaning a ladder, suggesting it was a mounting aid.

Many soldiers were recruited from outside the Empire. As long as the army was able to train men, these recruits were given Roman citizenship, integrated into their regiments, used Roman equipment, and were no different than ethnic Romans from all parts of Europe, the Near East, and North Africa. Many were fully integrated into Roman society like the anonymous Vandal cavalry officer who had a Roman wife and raised his son Stilicho in a Roman environment. Others, however, kept in touch with their homeland, like the anonymous Alamann

> serving among the emperor's Armigeri who returned home because of pressing business. As he was rather loose in his speech, to the many who asked what was happening in the palace, he said that Gratian, summoned by his uncle Valens, would soon march towards the East (Ammianus 31.10.3).

This recruiting of individuals was different from the use of allies, fighting under Roman command with their own equipment and organization, a practice which became very common in the fifth-century West. Theodosius I's army at the Frigidus in 394 CE included a Gothic contingent which had tribal leaders like Alaric, but was commanded by the Roman officers Bacurius and Gainas (himself a Goth). Allies were often hired for specific periods; Narses dismissed 5,500 Lombards after his victory at Taginae in Italy in 552 CE (Procopius, *Wars* 8.33.2).

9.3 Germanic, Hun, and Avar Organization and Equipment

During the first century CE, there were numerous tribes opposing the Romans along the Rhine and Danube, like the Chatti, Chamavi, and Cherusci of the northern Rhineland. From the late-third century CE, the Romans began to use umbrella terms like Franks to describe these tribes, though there was no king of all the Franks and the Chatti, Chamavi, and Cherusci continued to exist. It was similar with Alamannic tribes in the southern Rhineland, Sarmatian tribes in the central Danube, and Goths and later Huns on the lower Danube. Sometimes, however, capable leaders were able to unite several tribes into a temporary confederation that could field larger armies, as with the Alamanni at Strasbourg (below 9.5) and the Huns under Attila. In the fourth century CE, societies across the Rhine and Danube were still less developed than the Celtic or Spanish tribes of the first century BCE, still not being urbanized or monetized, and with only a limited ability to use writing, so that logistical structures were weak. However, continued warfare with the Romans had led to improvements in military practice so that the tribes who faced Rome on the Rhine in the fourth century were better soldiers than those who had fought at Idistaviso in the first century CE (above 8.4). This experience was, however, matched by the Romans, also better soldiers in the fourth century and with greater resources.

Individual Germans provided their own equipment. We have a good understanding of what was available from both literary sources and well-preserved ritual deposits of military equipment dating from the third to the fifth centuries CE, from Illerup and Nydam in Denmark for example. We also have some burials with weapons, a frequent custom outside the empire and increasingly common inside. Although we know much about what was available, we can say little about the scale of issue, other than that these societies had much less wealth than the Roman state.

Body armour was mostly mail but occasionally scale, or lamellar armour made of horn plates. Roman literature suggests that most infantry were unarmoured, perhaps wearing heavy tunics, but aristocrats had metal armour and helmets. Ammianus described the Alamannic king, Chnodomarius, at Strasbourg:

> a red crest fitted to his head, riding in front of the left flank … majestic on his frothing horse, standing tall with a spear of formidable size and standing out from the rest by the gleam of his armour (16.12.24).

Circular and oval shields were close to 1m in diameter, made of wooden boards glued together with a metal boss and a horizontal handle. They were covered with leather which was sometimes painted, perhaps in patterns like Roman shields.

The dominant offensive weapon was the spear, similar to Roman spears, 2.0–2.5m in length. The small numbers of swords deposited in the Danish bog finds and in burials, much smaller than the number of spears, suggests their rarity; this was very different to the Roman army where almost every soldier had one. Some men carried heavy javelins for throwing similar to Roman <u>pila</u>, like the <u>angones</u> described by Agathias for the Franks (2.5) and known from archaeology, and Vegetius suggested that two or three were carried (1.20). Other throwing weapons included heavy knives (saxes), and axes (<u>franciscae</u>). Bows rarely occur in the archaeological record of western Europe, though there were some bow parts and arrows preserved at Nydam and we sometimes hear of infantry archers. Cavalry were few in number, but equipped similarly to their elite heavy infantry with helmet, mail, shield, spear and sword. Some men carried bows and rode horses, but we have no accounts of units of horse archers among the Goths or Franks.

The armies of the Huns and Avars on the lower Danube, and of the Turks in the Caucasus, were very different from these infantry-based armies. These societies were in transition from pastoral nomadism to agriculture and though heavily focused on cavalry their armies always included large number of allies whose infantry were equipped like Germans. Heavy cavalry were similar to elite Roman cavalry, equipped with lance and bow, body armour, shield, and sword; a few elites might have horse armour. These heavy cavalry were supported by large numbers of more-lightly equipped horse archers.

9.4 Sasanian Equipment and Organization

The Sasanian Persian Empire was a strongly structured state centred on the Iranian plateau and southern Mesopotamia, reaching the Caucasus in the north and India in the east. Kings had access to enormous military resources, so that Persian armies could be as large as 50–60,000 men. The ability to feed these armies and to undertake sieges of several months shows a strong logistical system. The Sasanians defeated Roman field armies on several occasions, including Barbalissus in 252 CE, and captured Emperor Valerian between Carrhae and Edessa in 260 CE. The Sasanians did not have a standing army, though there was a permanent royal cavalry regiment, but expected their aristocracy to provide most troops. The noble families of the Karens and Surens can be traced back to the Parthian Empire; a Suren led the Parthian army at Carrhae (above 7.5).

The most prominent troops in our Roman accounts are the cataphracts, heavily armoured men, with mail, scale, or lamellar armour, often riding armoured horses. Sasanian sculpture shows men equipped with lances used in two hands, but also equipped with spears and shields. Ammianus was with the Roman army outside Ctesiphon in 363.

The Persians deployed trained regiments (<u>turmae</u>) of cataphract cavalry so dense that the thin plates continuously closely-fitted to the curves of their bodies with their brightness dazzled our eyes as they advanced, while the whole host of the horses were protected by leather coverings. In support were placed units (<u>manipuli</u>) of infantry, carrying for protection oblong and curved shields which were covered with wicker and rough hide, were moving in very close order. Behind these were elephants with the appearance of walking hills (24.6.8).

However, most troops in Sasanian armies were heavy infantry equipped with body armour, shields, and spears. Light infantry were often provided by Daylami from the south Caucasus. Persian light cavalry, many equipped with bows, were supplemented with allies or mercenaries, often Huns or Turks from the empire's northern frontier. Indian elephants were used,

Figure 9.4: A Sasanian heavy infantryman with an oval shield, mail shirt, and helmet, equipped with a spear and long sword. The elements of his equipment were similar to Roman infantry, but he looks very different with a Persian shield decoration, beard, and trousers tucked into his boots. (© *Philip Sidnell*)

some with archers on their backs, at Maranga and Sumere in 363 CE, at Phasis in 556 CE, and at Blarathon in 591 CE. In Mesopotamia, both Romans and Sasanians had alliances with Arab tribes whose strength tended to be in scouting and raiding, not in battle.

9.5 The Battle of Strasbourg, 357 CE

The Battle of Strasbourg took place in Gaul (modern France) beside the Rhine when the Roman Emperor Julian defeated an army of Alamanni. The major source is the contemporary Ammianus Marcellinus (16.12), though a shorter account was written by another contemporary, Libanius (*Oration* 18.53–68).

Figure 9.5: A Sasanian cataphract, modelled on the image of Khusrau II from Taq-I Bustan. He doesn't have a shield so can use his lance in both hands. He's got some colourful decoration in the form of tufts on the horse armour, loosely flowing clothing, and a ribbon streaming from his helmet. He's also got a bow that he might shoot at the enemy before charging or if he dismounted. (© *Philip Sidnell*)

His account is similar to that of Ammianus, both being based on Julian's own description, although both writers could have talked to participants.

King Chnodomarius crossed the Rhine into Roman territory in late 357 CE leading 30–35,000 men from a confederation of seven Alamannic tribes. Julian led 13,000 men from the field army of Gaul against them. For the Romans, it was often difficult to force Germanic armies to fight and when the Alamanni were located, the Roman troops clamoured to engage immediately, despite having marched all morning. Although Julian was concerned that the men were tired and had not eaten, he decided to fight anyway.

At the start of the battle, the Alamannic right flank rested on a canal where they concealed some troops in the reeds and in ditches. Their centre was made up of infantry, and their left flank, under Chnodomarius, had most of their cavalry, interspersed with light troops. The Romans deployed their infantry in multiple lines, with most of their cavalry, including cataphracts and horse archers, and their elite troops on the right with Julian. Their left flank, under the command of the magister militum, Severus, was refused to avoid being ambushed from the broken ground by the canal. Ammianus described the

Alamanni as being in <u>cunei</u> which he contrasted with the Roman line which was like 'an indestructible wall' (16.12.20).

The first phase of the battle involved the throwing of missiles, quickly followed by an Alamannic charge against the Roman cavalry. The cavalry broke following the wounding of their commander but were then rallied by Julian behind the Roman infantry. On their left the Romans were now advancing, but in the centre the Alamannic charge was unable to break the Roman line and steady hand-to-hand fighting followed. At this point a group of Alamannic nobles attacked in a <u>globus</u> formation, bursting through the first Roman line before being repulsed. The rest of the first Roman line remained intact and the breakthrough was repulsed by the regiment of the <u>Primani</u> from the Roman second line. With the failure of this attack, the Alamanni routed and were pursued by the Romans as far as the Rhine. Casualties were reported by Ammianus as 6,000 Alamanni to 247 Romans, including four tribunes.

The episodic nature of the fighting is suggested by the attack by a <u>globus</u> of elite Alamanni in the course of the main infantry engagement. Although Julian was often later impetuous, in his first battle he was very cautious with a passive battle plan, like Arrian against the Alani (above 8.6). In this respect it was like the plan adopted by Pompey at Pharsalus which, as we have seen, was criticized by Caesar (above 7.6). Standing to fight maximized the Roman use of missile weapons, but also suggested great confidence in their ability to hold off an attack. Roman resilience in not breaking from either the first or second attack of Alamanni was critical, while the continued use of multiple lines meant that the army continued to fight well even as the Roman first line was penetrated. This battle was a great success for the Romans, with an outnumbered force under an inexperienced commander performing well. Battle remained an uncertain prospect, however, as our next case study shows.

9.6 The Battle of Adrianople, 378 CE

In 376 CE the eastern Roman emperor, Valens (364–378 CE), received an appeal from some Goths north of the Danube who wished to escape the attacks of various Hunnic groups. These Goths were admitted peacefully to Thrace, but as plans to settle them in Roman territory collapsed, war began. Our major source is Ammianus Marcellinus (31.12–13) who had by now retired from the army but, as at Strasbourg, his account may go back to a contemporary report, as well as talking to survivors.

In spring of 378 CE, Valens arrived in Thrace in June while the western emperor, Gratian (375–383 CE), was on his way from Gaul with another army. The scattered Goths began to concentrate in August, and then Valens' scouts located a group of 10,000 near Adrianople (modern Edirne in European Turkey). Ammianus reported a debate over whether to wait for Gratian. Valens hoped to defeat in detail what he thought was an isolated group of Goths, but was opposed by Victor, magister equitum, and others. Ammianus added to the dramatic tension by describing Victor as the delayer (cunctator), alluding to Fabius Maximus' strategy of avoiding contact with Hannibal. Valens decided to fight and, as Victor's advice was ignored, an inevitable disaster similar to Cannae followed the emperor.

Valens left his baggage under guard at Adrianople and marched towards the Goths on 9 August; the weather was hot. As the Roman army marched, scouts reported that the Gothic force was encamped within a circle of wagons containing their families. The Romans began to deploy for battle in the early afternoon with their right flank cavalry in position ahead of the main infantry line, but the left flank cavalry still coming off the line of march. At the same time, the Goths opened negotiations.

However, at this point, the battle began in an unplanned fashion, similar to Marathon, Cunaxa, and Pydna, with an attack by two Roman regiments, the Scutarii (led by the tribune Bacurius, Iberian royalty before serving Rome) and the Sagittarii (under the tribune Cassio), drawn into combat as skirmishing escalated. As these two regiments engaged and then were pushed back, other Roman units were drawn into contact along the main battle line, with the infantry on the Roman left flank advancing as far as the Gothic wagons. Even at this point, though the battle had started prematurely, Valens had no cause for concern.

Suddenly it became apparent that the Roman scouting had missed some of the Goth cavalry, commanded by Alatheus and Saphrax, who arrived on the Roman left, striking the Roman battle line, already engaged to its front, in the flank. There was a confused period of heavy fighting, described by Ammianus in terms deliberately reminiscent of Livy on Cannae, followed by a Roman withdrawal in serious disorder. Although the Roman line was broken, it did not shatter and we hear of Valens taking refuge with the Lanciarii and Mattiarii, legiones palatinae. Victor went to bring the reserve unit of the Batavi to assist the emperor but in the confusion, they could not be found. Valens was injured by an arrow and took refuge in a farmhouse which was then burned by the Goths. Although one of the emperor's bodyguards escaped, Valens' body was never recovered. Fighting continued, and the battle and pursuit was only brought to a conclusion by nightfall.

The Romans had been severely defeated in a battle that had been fought from early afternoon to dark, more than six hours in the summer. Ammianus claimed that two-thirds of the army was lost, though he does not say how many

Romans were on the battlefield, and describes it as the worst Roman disaster since Cannae. He also recorded the officer casualties, probably using an official casualty report, including thirty-five tribunes and two senior generals, Trajan, magister militum, and Sebastianus, magister peditum.

Ammianus' account focussed on Valens' decision to engage the Goths, rather than waiting for Gratian. By doing so, he avoided blaming soldiers or officers, but allowed for the role of chance in the premature starting of the battle. Once Valens had decided to engage, the events on the battlefield were determined by the Gothic cavalry attacking the Roman left when it was already engaged to its front. Ancient armies often suffered badly in these sorts of situations, as at Issus or Cynoscephalae. This attack was possible because the Gothic cavalry had not been detected, but also because they arrived at the right time and place. Had they come earlier, they might not have contacted the Roman infantry while they were fighting, later and the battle might have been over. Unlike at Cannae or Zama, the Romans were not encircled and many escaped. As at Cannae, Roman responses to the battle did not suggest that they had concerns about the army itself, with there being no changes in organization, equipment, or the way the army fought.

9.7 The Battle of Callinicum, 531 CE

The lack of literary sources for the fifth century CE means we can say little about Roman wars with the Vandals or Huns, but in the sixth century CE the survival of Procopius' work allows us to analyse the Roman wars fought under Emperor Justinian (527–565 CE). The Battle of Callinicum (modern Raqqah in Syria) took place in Mesopotamia between the Romans and the Sasanians on 18 April 531 CE. Unusually, it was described in detail not only by Procopius (*Wars* 1.18.24–56), who may have been present himself, but also by another sixth-century writer, Malalas (18.60–61), and we have a third brief account in pseudo-Zachariah's sixth-century ecclesiastical history (*HE* 9.6). The Romans lost the battle. When the news reached Constantinople, Emperor Justinian ordered Constantiolus, the dux Moesiae Secundae, to investigate. He visited the region and talked to survivors before reporting back, after which the Roman commander Belisarius was replaced. Although this report has not survived, it is suggestive of a structure that allowed Roman generals to learn from defeat. We have no way of deciding between Procopius' pro-Belisarius version and the hostility to him in Malalas' account, possibly influenced by Constantiolus' report.

The battle occurred when Belisarius, leading Roman forces totalling 20,000 as well as his own Arab allies, caught up with a Persian force of 15,000, led by Azarethes, opposite Callinicum on the River Euphrates. No mention is made of Persian infantry in the battle and the Persians may have been entirely mounted. There were also some Arab allies among the Persians. As at Strasbourg in 357 CE, the Roman troops were eager to fight. Although Belisarius was concerned that many of the troops had been fasting for Easter, he chose to fight; as Cunaxa, Pydna, and Adrianople showed, battles often started without the general's approval.

Belisarius placed his left flank, composed of his infantry, which Procopius described as a phalanx, against the Euphrates. The Roman centre was made up of cavalry, and the right flank, where the ground was rougher, was occupied by their allied Arab cavalry led by Arethas. Procopius' description of where the soldiers stood is clear but gives us no idea of the numbers of Roman cavalry and infantry. The Persian commander, Azarethes, 'stationed the phalanx opposite the enemy' (Procopius 1.18.30) with his Persian troops opposite the Romans and his allied Arab cavalry guarding his left flank and facing the Roman Arabs.

The battle began with skirmishing, mostly by archers, in which Procopius noted that the Persians shot more rapidly than the Romans. Sixth-century Roman concern for rate of shot in battle is seen in Mauricius' recommendation that Roman infantry be trained to shoot rapidly and attack swiftly 'for with a delay in closing more missiles from the continuous archery of the enemy fall on the soldiers and horses' (*Strategikon* 11.1.59–63).

Inconclusive skirmishing continued until late in the day. Then the Persians launched an assault against the Roman right flank which pushed back the Arab cavalry, allowing the Persians to get into the rear of the Roman cavalry. Many of the Roman troops fled at this point and a newly recruited regiment of Isaurian infantry suffered severely, according to Procopius not daring to resist the enemy. However, some of the infantry by the river continued to fight, forming a *foulkon*, the contemporary term for what earlier Romans had called a testudo, to which other Romans, including Belisarius, retreated.

> Joined closely to one another all the time in a small space, making the strongest wall with their shields, they were shooting more easily at the Persians than they were shot at by them. Often after withdrawing, the barbarians would advance against them to disorder and break up the line, but unsuccessful, they were driven back again from there because their horses, disturbed by the clatter of shields, were rearing up and fell into disorder along with their riders (Procopius, *Wars* 1.18.46–48).

The Persians continued to attack until nightfall but were unable to break the Roman formation.

Malalas' account added details of the Roman infantry deployment, placing regiments of limitanei towards the river and field army regiments of Isaurians with the Arabs. It also specified that it was a regiment of Phrygians who fled, not Isaurians. His statements that Belisarius fled by boat and the commanders of the limitanei, Sounikas and Simmas, led the successful infantry battle cannot be reconciled with Procopius' account, but otherwise the two accounts fit together well.

The battle shows the ability of well-led and well-trained infantry to resist cavalry, as well as the way in which cavalry attacked infantry by riding towards them in the hope that their formation would waver. The newly recruited regiment of Isaurians (or Phrygians), however, were unable to resist the enemy. Belisarius' deployment with cavalry in the centre was unusual, a response to facing an all-cavalry Persian force; he was also able to make good use of the terrain by anchoring one flank on the Euphrates. However, in the late-sixth century CE Mauricius suggested deployments for mixed infantry and cavalry forces and for pure cavalry forces, and it may be that Callinicum is simply the first place that we hear of this arrangement.

9.8 The Battle of Taginae, 552 CE

A few years after Callinicum, in 535 CE, Justinian's troops invaded Ostrogothic Italy in what developed into a long war dominated by skirmishes and sieges. The Roman commander in 552 CE was Narses who launched a new attack on the city of Rome by marching south from Ravenna. The Gothic king, Totila (541–552 CE), met him at Taginae (Gualdo Tadino) in the Apennines. The battle is recorded only by Procopius (*Wars* 8.29–32), at this point reliant on official records and accounts provided by others rather than his own experiences.

After some skirmishing, the armies deployed for battle. Totila, in the speech to his men presented by Procopius, stressed the diverse nature of Narses' army, which included contingents of Heruls, Lombards, and Huns. No totals are given for either side, but the Roman left flank was commanded by Narses, the right by Valerian, both with large contingents of infantry archers forming a crescent. In the refused centre were the allied cavalry of the Heruli and Lombards, fighting on foot. He also placed 1,000 cavalry behind his left flank, ready for an outflanking manoeuvre and kept another 500 cavalry as a reserve. The Goths formed up in two lines, cavalry ahead of infantry. Totila had seen the Roman archers and, according to Procopius, being aware that his troops would suffer heavily if they engaged in prolonged missile combat, ordered them not to use their bows, but only their spears, similar to orders given by the Vandal king, Gelimer, at Tricamarum in Africa in 533 CE.

As the battle began, the Gothic cavalry advanced between the horns of the Roman crescent and were exposed to the Roman arrow storm.

> Therefore, the Goths threw away many men and many horses in this business, not yet contacting the enemy. After many heavy losses, coming to the attack after a long time and with difficulty, they arrived at the line of the enemy (Procopius, *Wars* 8.32.10).

Although the Gothic cavalry did come into contact, they began to be pushed back onto their infantry. The Goths soon broke, with some 6,000 falling and many being taken prisoner. Totila was wounded in the retreat and died soon afterwards.

Narses' victory was a triumph for the Roman system, trusting his infantry to repel the Gothic charge in the same way as Julian at Strasbourg and Belisarius at Callinicum. Indeed, most Roman generals thought infantry were effective on the defensive and a generation later, Mauricius advised commanders not to 'commit many cavalry in infantry battles' (12.B.23.14–18). Totila's main hope of success in his first major field battle was similar to that of many armies, the fierceness of this charge; when it failed, Roman resilience carried the day.

9.9 Battle in the Late Roman Empire

The Roman army of the fourth century CE onwards was a formidable opponent. Troops were well-trained and equipped, with tactics well-suited to their enemies both in Europe and on the eastern frontier. The enemies of Rome were similarly aware of their own strengths and weaknesses, with Germanic armies focussing on the shock of their initial attack, Huns and Avars interested in wearing down and outflanking their enemies, and Sasanians focusing on heavy cavalry in combined-arms formations.

9.9.1 Who was a regimental commander?
Some Roman regimental commanders were promoted after long service, like Abinnaeus in Egypt, who had already been in the army for thirty-three years. These men had administrative experience but were not necessarily experienced in combat. Others were younger men like Ammianus Marcellinus (and sometimes foreign royalty like Bacurius) spending several years attached to a senior officer's staff before being appointed to command a regiment; many of these men had extensive experience in battle. All were literate and

assisted by staffs of professional soldiers. Regimental commanders rode horses, even in infantry regiments. Sasanian officers were aristocrats, often with good knowledge of their own men, though perhaps less experienced on average than their Roman counterparts. Germanic leaders would be tribal aristocrats, forced to be brave by position and culture, with varying amounts of military experience; many of them fought on foot. The Persian officers would be able to read and write, but few Germans could.

9.9.2 Training and discipline

Both Vegetius and Mauricius discussed various types of training, from individual physical training and proficiency in weapons (with Mauricius emphasizing the need to shoot rapidly with bows), to exercising as units, and as an army.

> After the individual training of each *tagma* has been successfully accomplished in the aforesaid manner, it is necessary to draw up the whole army and in every way as though for a pitched battle to deploy in formation, the heavy infantry and light infantry and cavalry and wagons, and the rest of the baggage train (*Strategikon* 12.B.17).

Each regiment had a training officer, the campidoctor, and some weapon instructors are known. Vegetius described the military step, learnt 'so that all soldiers may keep ranks as they move' (1.9). Most of this training was in how to use weapons and how to deploy, with commands still in Latin in the sixth century CE, rather than more complex exercises, but it was still far in advance of non-Roman armies at any period. In the West there was less training as the fifth century continued.

This training helped create group loyalty that was reinforced by long terms of service, pay, food, medical treatment, decorations for bravery, individual shield patterns for regiments, regimental standards, and even short haircuts. Roman discipline continued to be fierce, with disobedience to orders or mutiny potentially being punished by death. Despite this discipline, Roman troops were often poorly behaved, being ready to abuse emperors and officers and prone to attack without orders. Officers who performed poorly might be relieved of their positions.

Only the standing troops among the Persians were trained, so unit skills were not strong, though many individuals had good riding and weapon skills. At Blarathon in 591 CE, Theophylact noted that the Persian troops were noisy in the attack, whereas the Romans were silent (5.9.6). Germanic and steppe armies were described by the Romans as being poorly disciplined. Individuals practiced weapon and riding skills, but there was no unit training. None of these armies had any professional soldiers, though many of the warriors had substantial experience. Organization was by social groups of various sizes, with the better equipped and bolder tending to fight at the front.

9.9.3 Infantry and cavalry spacing

Both Vegetius (3.14) and Mauricius (12.B.16) suggested 3ft [approx. 1m] per heavy infantryman, described both in terms of distance, but also as 'no light between them' and 'shields touching each other at the edges'. This would be a tighter formation than earlier Roman armies, the result of an emphasis on receiving enemy attacks with missile shot and spear. Between each rank Vegetius suggested 6ft [approx. 2m]. Vegetius imagined men fighting three and six ranks deep, whereas Mauricius suggested either eight ranks of heavy foot with two ranks of light troops behind, or four ranks of heavy and one light (12.B.7), based on a file (*akia*) of sixteen men, similar to the deployment used by Arrian against the Alani (above 8.6). Light infantry spacing was looser in both breadth and depth. We have no information about typical spacing for other cultures.

Mauricius recommended heavy cavalry regiments deploy eight or ten deep (2.6), which feels very deep, perhaps because of the large number of archers in these formations; he also noted that traditional earlier practice was four deep. In close order, cavalry fought 3ft [approx. 1m] apart though on the march used a more open order with room to turn each horse (3.2). Although Mauricius gave specific suggestions for how to fight various enemies, there is no sense that cavalry spacing among other cultures was different.

9.9.4 Deployment for battle

Late Roman infantry tactics tended to be defensive, waiting for the enemy to attack them at Strasbourg, Taginae, and Casilinum. A dependable infantry core allowed Roman commanders to make good use of archers, either in the rear ranks of the main line of battle, or as separate units on the flanks. Although armies normally deployed with infantry in the centre and cavalry on the flanks, heavier cavalry closest to the infantry, there were frequent variations. Vegetius provided a list of seven deployments taken from Cato's second-century BCE manual (3.20). In addition to the standard deployment, he suggested an advanced left or right with an outflanking attack on the opposite side, a refused centre with and without skirmishers in front, extending a refused left flank once engaged, and anchoring one flank on a terrain feature so that the light troops and cavalry could be deployed on the other flank. Mauricius' list of possible deployments was shorter, consisting of a standard deployment, variations for when the enemy line was longer and shorter, and an envelopment. Vegetius and Mauricius both recommended keeping a small reserve force (Vegetius 3.17; *Strategikon* 12.B.8), as seen at Adrianople and Taginae.

Vegetius suggested that infantry legions should deploy in two lines of cohorts (3.14), similar to Julian's deployment at Strasbourg, while three lines were used at Ctesiphon. Mauricius recommended two or three lines for cavalry, though his details of the risks of a single line suggests this was common (2.1–2.2). His recommended spacing between the lines was four bowshots [approx. 1,200m] (2.13). In large armies, the centre regiments were in close order, with their flanks in open order (3.7) and with gaps of a bowshot [approx. 300m] between units.

Although Vegetius mentioned Roman light troops screening the main line of battle (2.17), we have no evidence for this as a regular practice, perhaps because of the large amount of missile power available, and this is probably an artefact of Cato's manual. Bolt-shooting artillery was described by both Vegetius and Mauricius, and often appeared at sieges but is not recorded in battle.

Germanic deployments typically involved forming up in a single long line, described by Mauricius as 'by tribes and by their kinship and attachment to each other' (11.3.4). Lack of training and practice means that forming this line was slow. Any light troops were deployed in front of the main line and some preliminary skirmishing usually took place before the main body of the enemy was engaged. Cavalry were deployed on the flanks. Though these tactics were simple, they suited Germanic command systems. They were most successful in surprise attacks or when fighting in mountains, forests, or marshes which limited Roman use of cavalry and missile weapons and often turned battle into a series of ambushes. This is what Chnodomarius hoped for at Strasbourg. Cavalry-only armies of the steppe peoples deployed either in large clouds of cavalry that fought by skirmishing or in multiple lines while Sasanian deployment emphasized the use of their cataphracts, often in a single line of units.

9.9.5 Manoeuvre during battle

The typical Roman infantry formation was a line several ranks deep, though Vegetius drew on the work of Cato the Elder to describe several other formations, the cuneus, forceps, globus, and saw (Vegetius 3.18–19). The cuneus, also known to the troops as the 'pig's head' (Ammianus 17.13.9), was an attack column, narrower in front and broader behind, intended to break the enemy line with a concentration of missiles. It was used only by infantry and was not mentioned as a Roman formation by Procopius or Mauricius.

The <u>forceps</u> was intended to counter the <u>cuneus</u>. The <u>globus</u>, also known from the fourth century CE as the *drungus*, was a non-linear formation, useful for skirmishing and on the wings. The saw formation involved rotating groups of attackers in order to buy time to repair the line, i.e. a temporary raising of the intensity of battle. There was also the <u>testudo</u> or *foulkon* was intended to resist archery and cavalry, with men standing closely together and covering themselves with shields. Cavalry were usually deployed in lines or a <u>globus</u> but could also form Cantabrian circles for javelins and larger looping formations for horse archers (Procopius, *Wars* 5.27.19). They were sometimes supported by light infantry (Vegetius 3.16; Procopius, *Wars* 6.1.2).

The most common manoeuvre on the battlefield was an attempt to turn the enemy flank, with Mauricius recommending all armies have flanking units to attempt this and to defend against similar attempts by the enemy. Defending against an outflanking attempt could be done by reserve forces or by angling a flank back (Vegetius 3.19). Terrain was sometimes used to hide ambushes on the battlefield; for example, at Satala in 530 CE, 1,000 cavalry were hidden behind a hill (Procopius, *Wars* 1.15.9–17). At Casilinum in 554 CE the Frankish main body penetrated the Roman line, but the Romans did not break and, as fighting continued in the centre, the Roman cavalry lapped round the flanks of the Frankish column (Agathias 2.7–10).

Germanic armies made use of lines and the <u>globus</u>, as described by Ammianus at Strasbourg. As earlier, descriptions of wedges were either attack columns or conventional descriptions. Sometimes light troops were used to support cavalry (Ammianus 16.12.21). Some armies were composed of people on the move, not just soldiers and sometimes formed wagon laagers on the battlefield as at Adrianople.

Steppe peoples usually fought in loose formations, with Ammianus describing Huns as 'entering battle in wedges (<u>cuneatim</u>) ... suddenly with great energy after scattering they attack' (31.2.8), and Mauricius noted that rather than an unbroken line, they used 'formations in wedges (*kounois*)', that is to say, scattered (11.2). When used to describe Rome's enemies, <u>cuneus</u> now meant an unordered group.

The strength of the Sasanians lay in their mounted archers, so Mauricius recommended Roman generals fight in open terrain and attack rapidly, whereas the Sasanians preferred broken ground enabling them to wear down the enemy with archery.

9.9.6 Morale and the will to engage

Roman troops were encouraged by their leaders. Centurions are rarely mentioned at this period, but individual soldiers were often brave; Ammianus noted the courage of two soldiers, Salvius and Lupicinus who led a charge at Solicinium in 368 (27.10.12). More often though, regimental commanders led attacks, with both Ammianus and Procopius recording the names and often the deaths of numerous officers, like Principius and Tarmutus who held up a Gothic attack outside Rome in 537 CE so their men could escape.

> Principius, his whole body mangled, fell there, and around him forty-two [Gothic] infantry, but Tarmutus, holding two Isaurian javelins, one in each hand, kept on stabbing at those coming up as he turned from side to side until, wounded in his body, he was exhausted (Procopius 5.29.41–42).

Such leadership was not always necessary, however, given the eagerness with which many Roman troops approached battle. Both Vegetius and Mauricius were concerned that troops had eaten and were rested before fighting, and even when this was not the case, as at Strasbourg, Adrianople, and Callinicum, the troops were eager to fight. Some of this was the result of confidence, but often of nervousness.

Among non-Roman armies, this pre-battle stress meant that troops did not always stand to fight when engaged. At a battle between some Lombards and Gepids c.550 CE,

> So already they were both very close, but the armies could not yet see each other. Then the fears known as panic suddenly fell on them both, the men fleeing for no reason, and they carried everyone backwards, with only the leaders being left there with a few men. And though trying to pull them back and restrain them, they could not accomplish this whether begging pitiably or threatening fearfully (Procopius, *Wars* 8.18.4–6).

9.9.7 Infantry combat

During the early phases of battle, Roman light troops skirmished with the enemy. In earlier periods, such skirmishing was followed by a Roman infantry assault, but in the late Empire, Roman infantry frequently stood to receive enemy attacks, maximizing the effectiveness of their large number of missile weapons. Ammianus described a small action against some Alamanni at Cabillona in 365 CE.

> when they saw the barbarians at a distance, the Romans began to attack with arrows and other light missiles, and they with the same weapons vigorously shot back. But when the forces came to close quarters and fought with drawn swords, the line of our men, broken by the very fierce

charge of the enemy, found no opportunity to resist or act bravely, and all were driven by fear into flight when they saw Severianus thrown from his horse and pierced by a missile weapon. Finally, Charietto himself, while he fearlessly held back those retreating by standing in their way and by the reproachful sound of his voice, tried to wash away the shameful dishonour by his boldness in standing firm for a long time, but died struck down by a fatal weapon. After his death the <u>vexillum</u> of the Eruli and Batavi was snatched away, which as an insult the capering barbarians frequently raising it up high showed it off, until after hard struggles it was recovered (Ammianus 27.1.3–6).

Hand-to-hand combat was still often described in impressionistic terms with Ammianus' writing about Strasbourg being reminiscent of Homer or one of his imitators:

There were manifold movements, our men now resisting, now retreating, and by the pressure of their knees (<u>obnixi genibus</u>) some of the most experienced barbarian warriors were working to push back the enemy. Indeed, with the greatest resolution hands were engaged with hands and shield-boss pushed against shield-boss, and the sky re-echoed with the loud cries of those boasting and falling (16.12.37).

Most Germanic armies engaged quickly all along the line. Waiting would be hard on their nerves, particularly as these armies were not trained, and there was a distinct urge 'to get it over with'. Attacking rapidly also minimized the period of exposure to Roman missiles. As they rushed to contact, the line lost any cohesion that it may have had. At Casilinum in 554 CE the Franks attacked the Romans, shouting as they came forward. 'not quiet and in order, but they were in tumult and haste', suggesting that their triangular wedge formation (*embolon*) was more accidental than deliberate (Agathias 2.8.7–9). The first shock could lead to victory but if not, Roman armies usually prevailed because of their superior training and protection. Other armies of Persians, Huns, Avars, and Turks, were slower to commit to battle because of their larger numbers of archers, often forcing the Romans to attack them.

9.9.8 Cavalry combat
When fighting other cavalry, most combat was like that between Romans and Goths in 537 CE.

For a long time, however, the battle was not hand-to-hand, but they kept on advancing and retreating at each other and each making sudden pursuits, as if they wished to spend the rest of the day at this (Procopius, *Wars* 6.2.11).

As cavalry came to close quarters, Mauricius recommended charging in close order 'not too fast, but at a canter' (3.5), being concerned about loss of formation in the attack, though charging in loose order at a gallop was a possibility. The feigned flight was described by Mauricius as a typical tactic of the 'Scythians', i.e. Huns and Turks (4.2).

Cavalry found it very difficult to attack well-formed heavy infantry, though Vegetius suggested that cataphracts could be used in front of or in the line with heavy infantry where in hand-to-hand fighting 'they often break the line of the enemy' (3.23). They could also be placed on the flanks of the infantry line, as was done by Julian at Strasbourg. The dense formations favoured by Roman heavy infantry made them especially resilient to cavalry charges, as at Callinicum and Taginae, but they were also well-suited to defence against nomads. German infantry could adopt similar formations, as some Franks did when faced at Ariminum in 554 CE, until the Roman general Narses used a feigned flight to draw them out of formation (Agathias 1.21–22), a tactic suggested by Mauricius (11.3). If the cavalry could contact enemy infantry while they were already engaged in the front or flank, as happened at Adrianople, then disaster usually followed. And as in other periods, light infantry in the open were very vulnerable to cavalry.

9.9.9 Pursuit

For Romans, the end of the battle was seen as a chance to turn a victory into a massacre with Mauricius stating 'it is necessary to keep going until the complete destruction of the enemy' (7.B.12). Pursuit was particularly effective at Strasbourg as the Alamanni were forced to enter the Rhine to escape, though Ammianus praised Julian for not allowing his men to pursue into the river. At Adrianople, the fighting continued until nightfall which limited the Gothic pursuit of the Romans. Pursuits against nomads were especially dangerous because of the difficulty of distinguishing between a genuine rout and a feigned flight, so that Mauricius recommended that Romans stay close to their supporting troops.

9.10 Conclusion

In the battles of this period, Roman infantry were now used more passively than in earlier periods, standing to receive the enemy attack and supported by large amounts of missiles. This made good use of their high levels of resilience, the result of training, good pay, and heavy armour, but required close control by regimental commanders. Successfully repelling an assault by the enemy was rarely visible in our sources, but failure could be conspicuous. Cavalry were present in much larger numbers than earlier, and by the fifth century CE there were numerous flexible bow-and-lance-armed regiments. All troops could be hard to control, but they were led by officers who often took great risks on the battlefield, wanting their courage to be seen by their generals. Such opportunities were much greater for the commanders of cavalry regiments.

Chapter 10

Conclusion

My focus on the regimental commander's battle in antiquity has allowed for a prolonged examination of the model of ancient combat as suggested by Sabin and others. Rather than focus on a single period, I have chosen to look at all periods of Greek and Roman warfare where we have detailed ancient descriptions of how men fought. This wide-ranging approach allows for several general conclusions about ancient battle.

The first is that primary sources vary enormously in their value. The writing of history in antiquity was a much more literary endeavour than the writing of history is now, and we must be constantly aware of this, thinking about the style, use of technical language, and the interrelationship between our textual sources. In this book I've focused very much on the words of authors who had contemporary military experience, especially Xenophon, Polybius, Caesar, and Mauricius, though the small number of such authors means that other writers often have to be used. As I hope to have shown, describing ancient battle is not easy, and we need to be cautious about how we use writers who do not show that they understand battle, especially Herodotus and Plutarch. Furthermore, the value of many ancient writers varied depending on who they used as sources, so that some parts of the work of Livy, Plutarch, Appian, or Diodorus are very useful and other parts are not.

Despite the significant challenges posed by the literary sources, they are consistent in showing the mechanics of ancient battle. The stresses in getting men to engage in hand-to-hand combat, and the behaviour patterns involving attacks, skirmishing, cavalry combat, pursuit, and casualties are repeated across antiquity in many accounts that provide plausible detail. Some of this similarity may be the result of the literary influence of earlier works, and ancient writers were very well-versed in their predecessors. Nonetheless, this model is preferable to believing that men engaged in hand-to-hand combat without hesitating. Although such readiness to engage is implicit or ignored in many ancient and modern writers, as an explanation it fails to account for both the frequent eagerness or reluctance to enter battle and the presence of the same phenomenon in later periods of history. I prefer to believe that humans in all periods were similarly reluctant to engage in hand-to-hand combat than that ancient soldiers were braver than later soldiers. Good generals were aware of this balance and after his defeat at Gergovia, Caesar observed that 'he wished as much moderation and restraint from his soldiers as courage and greatness of spirit' (*Gallic War* 7.52.4).

Battle in antiquity tended to be a simple matter. Most generals found it difficult enough to line up their troops in order to move forward towards the enemy. Even doing this well was difficult, with uncontrolled advances common as soldiers were overwhelmed by the urge to get on with fighting as at Marathon, Cunaxa, and Adrianople. And in the same way, an understandable fear of combat often caused men to break and run rather than fight, as at Cunaxa and the Tearless Battle. In this sort of world, Hannibal's planning of the envelopment of the Romans at Cannae was an extraordinary achievement, while Polybius' description of Scipio's manoeuvring at Ilipa is unusual both as a piece of literature and as military history.

Over the period studied there was great change in levels of professionalism. In the described world of Greek and Roman cultures, the amateur armies of Classical Greece, with the exception of the Spartans, stand out. From the later fourth century BCE onwards, Hellenistic and Roman armies were usually composed of paid and trained professionals fighting in regiments with officers, logistical systems, and medical services. Despite our ignorance of Persian, Carthaginian, Parthian, and Sasanian practices, their effectiveness as armies suggests that their armies had many similarities to those of Mediterranean states. Tribal societies were less professionally organized, though still often dangerous. From prolonged wars such societies had often developed effective practices, particularly avoiding pitched battle and concentrating instead on low-intensity warfare. For all cultures, increasing professionalism resulted in an increasing use of multiple lines of units in battle, combined with greater resilience and more effective use of supporting arms. Over time, generals were more often found leading from the rear than from the front. There was also an increasing use of cavalry, though this was not a constant development. A common ratio of cavalry to infantry was 1:10, suggestive of the expense of maintaining horsemen. When armies had much greater numbers of cavalry than the enemy they were often very effective, and the armies of Alexander and Hannibal both had large numbers of well-led horsemen. Roman armies before the late imperial period had small numbers of cavalry, often falling below the ratio of 1:10, though Zama was an exception. It was not just numbers that made cavalry effective, and like other weapon systems they need to be considered as part of an army, not in isolation. In this respect, I have argued that the shortcomings of pike phalanxes, elephants, and scythed chariots were not as great as often assumed, but also that there is no convincing evidence for the use of triangular wedges by ancient cavalry or for archery as a major factor in ancient battles.

Finally, what could regimental commanders do? Their greatest opportunities to have an impact on the battle were in command of contingents of light troops and cavalry. The closeness of engagement ranges and the short time to cross them, especially with cavalry, meant that there were many fine decisions to be made on both sides. When the decision-making was good on one side and poor on another, heavy infantry or pursuing cavalry could be handled roughly or the light troops could have little effect. For officers of heavy infantry their leadership was more important in keeping troops fighting than in changing the flow by acts of initiative, so acts like those of the anonymous Roman tribune at Cynoscephalae need to be recognized as the rare moments when regimental commanders did win battles in antiquity.

Further Reading

In recent years the internet, digital publishing, and open access have transformed the world of scholarly publishing that underlies all work on ancient battle. Material that was often restricted to university libraries at the end of the twentieth century is now much more easily available to those interested. Nonetheless, it remains difficult to interpret. I've chosen to keep this section short and focused on work that I have found most useful or provocative in preference to an exhaustive list of books and articles.

Primary Sources

Translations of all the authors referred to can easily be found on the internet, though many of these versions are quite dated and the more recent Penguin Classics, the Landmark series, or the Oxford World's Classics are better. Perseus (https://www.perseus.tufts.edu/) gives easy access to older translations and to Greek and Latin texts of many authors. For most ancient authors there are recent companions, edited collections of essays usually written with undergraduates in mind and more accessible than some scholarly articles.

Chlup, J. and Whately, C. (eds), *Greek and Roman military manuals: genre and history* (Abingdon, 2020).

Lendon, J.E., 'Battle description in the ancient historians, part I: structure, array, and fighting', *Greece and Rome* 64.1 (2017), pp 39–64 and 'Battle description in the ancient historians, part II: speeches, results, and sea battles', *Greece and Rome* 64.2 (2017), pp 145–167.

Rance, P. and Sekunda, N. (eds), *Greek Taktika: Ancient Military Writing and its Heritage* (Gdańsk, 2017).

Battle in General in All Periods

Beyerchen, A., 'Clausewitz, Non-Linearity, and the Unpredictability of War', *International Security* 17.3 (1992–1993), pp 59–90.

Black, J., *Rethinking Military History* (London, 2004).

DeVries, K., 'Catapults Are Not Atomic Bombs: Towards a Redefinition of "Effectiveness" in Premodern Military Technology', *War in History* 4 (1997), pp 454–470.

Dupuy, T.N., *Numbers, Prediction and War* (Indianapolis, 1979).

Keegan, J., *The Face of Battle* (London, 1976).

Millett, A.R. and Murray, W. (eds), *Military Effectiveness* (London, 1988).

Tactical Surveys in Other Periods

Craighill, W.P., *The 1862 Army Officer's Pocket Companion* (New York, 1862).

Griffith, P., *Forward into Battle* (Chichester, 1981).

Griffith, P., *Battle Tactics of the Western Front: the British Army's art of attack, 1916–18* (New Haven, 1994).

Muir, R., *Tactics and the Experience of Battle in the Age of Napoleon* (New Haven, 1998).

Nolan, L.E., *Cavalry: Its History and Tactics* (London, 1853).

Nosworthy, B., *The Anatomy of Victory* (New York, 1990).
Nosworthy, B., *The Bloody Crucible of Courage* (New York, 2003).

Ancient Battle
Culham, P., 'Chance, command, and chaos in ancient military engagements', *World Futures* 27.2 (1989), pp 191–205.
Ardant Du Picq, C., *Battle Studies* (New York, 1920).
Konijnendijk, R., 'Risk, Chance and Danger in Classical Greek Writing on Battle', *Journal of Ancient History* 8.2 (2020), pp 175–186.
Sabin, P., 'The Face of Roman Battle', *Journal of Roman Studies* 90 (2000), pp 1–17.
Sabin, P., *Lost Battles* (London, 2007).
Sidebottom, H., *A Very Short Introduction to Ancient Warfare* (Oxford, 2004).
Whatley, N., 'On the Possibility of Reconstructing Marathon and Other Ancient Battles', *Journal of Hellenic Studies* 84 (1964), pp 119–139.
Wheeler, E.L., 'Firepower: missile weapons and the "Face of Battle"', *Electrum* 5 (2001), pp 169–184.

Surveys of Ancient Warfare
Campbell, B. and Tritle, L.A. (eds), *The Oxford Handbook of Warfare in the Classical World* (Oxford, 2013).
Erdkamp, P. (ed), *A Companion to the Roman Army* (Oxford, 2007).
Lendon, J.E., *Soldiers and Ghosts* (New Haven, 2005).
Sabin, P., van Wees, H., and Whitby, Michael (eds), *Cambridge History of Greek and Roman Warfare* (Cambridge, 2007).
Sidnell, P., *Warhorse* (London, 2006).

Equipment
There is a great deal of useful information about equipment in the well-illustrated Osprey volumes.

Coulston, J.N.C. and Bishop, M.C., *Roman Military Equipment* (London, 2006).
Curta, F., 'The earliest Avar-age stirrups, or the "stirrup controversy" revisited', in Curta, F. and Kovalev, R. (eds), *The Other Europe in the Middle Ages: Avars, Bulgars, Khazars, and Cumans* (Leiden, 2008), pp 297–326.
Head, D., *Armies of the Macedonian and Punic Wars* (2016).
James, S., *Excavations at Dura-Europos, Final Report VII: the Arms and Armour and Other Military Equipment* (London, 2004).
Jørgensen, L. *et al.* (eds), *The Spoils of Victory: the North in the Shadow of the Roman Empire* (Copenhagen, 2003).

Classical and Hellenistic Greek
Bar-Kochva, B., *The Seleucid Army* (Cambridge, 1976).
Bardunias, P. and Ray, F., *Hoplites at War* (Jefferson, NC, 2016).
Echeverría Rey, F., '*Taktikè technè*: the neglected element in Classical "hoplite" battles', *Ancient Society* 41 (2011), pp 45–82.
Hanson, V.D., *The Western Way of War* (New York, 1989).
Hanson, V. (ed), *Hoplites* (London, 1991).
Kagan, D. and Viggiano, G. (eds), *Men of Bronze* (Princeton, 2013).
Konijnendijk, R., *Classical Greek Tactics: A Cultural History* (Leiden, 2017).

Krentz, P., *The Battle of Marathon* (New Haven, 2010).

Matthew, C., *Storm of Spears* (London, 2012).

Matthew, C., *An Invincible Beast: Understanding the Hellenistic Pike Phalanx in Action* (London, 2015).

Schwartz, A., *Reinstating the Hoplite: Arms, Armour and Phalanx Fighting in Archaic and Classical Greece* (Wiesbaden, 2009).

Spence, I.G., *The Cavalry of Classical Greece* (Oxford, 1993).

Taylor, R., *The Greek Hoplite Phalanx* (London, 2021).

van Wees, H., *Greek Warfare: Myths and Realities* (London 2004).

Wheeler, E. (ed), *The Armies of Classical Greece* (London, 2016.

Middle Roman Republic

Cornell, T., Rankov, B., and Sabin, P. (eds), *The Second Punic War: A Reappraisal* (London, 1996).

Daly, G., *Cannae: The Experience of Battle in the Second Punic War* (London, 2002).

Erdkamp, P., 'Late-Annalistic Battle Scenes in Livy (Books 21–44)', *Mnemosyne* 59.4 (2006), pp 525–563.

Hoyos, D. (ed), *A Companion to the Punic Wars* (Oxford, 2011).

Lazenby, J., *Hannibal's War* (Warminster, 1978) (new preface, Norman OK, 1998).

Levene, D.S., *Livy on the Hannibalic War* (Oxford, 2010).

Quesada Sanz, F., 'Not so different: individual fighting techniques and small unit tactics of Roman and Iberian armies within the framework of warfare in the Hellenistic Age', *Pallas* 70 (2006), pp 245–263.

Slavik, J.F., 'Pilum and Telum: The Roman Infantryman's Style of Combat in the Middle Republic', *Classical Journal* 113.2 (2018), pp 151–171.

Taylor, M.J., 'Roman Infantry Tactics in the Mid-Republic: a reassessment', *Historia* 63.3 (2014), pp 301–322.

Zhmodikov, A., 'Roman republican heavy infantrymen in battle', *Historia* 49 (2000), pp 67–78.

Late Roman Republic and Early Roman Empire

Anders, A., 'The "Face of Roman Skirmishing"', *Historia* 64.3 (2015), pp 263–300.

Cagniart, P.F., 'Studies on Caesar's Use of Cavalry during the Gallic War', *Ancient World* 23.2 (1992), pp 71–85.

Campbell, D., *Deploying a Roman Army* (Glasgow, 2022).

Campbell, J.B., *The Roman Army 31 BC–AD 337: A Sourcebook* (London, 1994).

Charles, M., 'Mons Graupius revisited: Tacitus, Agricola and auxiliary infantry', *Athenaeum* 92.1 (2004), pp 127–138.

Goldsworthy, A., *The Roman Army at War: 100 BC–AD 200* (Oxford, 1996).

Kagan, K., *The Eye of Command* (Michigan, 2006).

Late Roman Empire

Elton, H., *Warfare in Roman Europe: AD 350–425* (Oxford, 1996).

Haldon, J.F., *Warfare, State and Society in the Byzantine World, 565–1204* (London, 1999).

Halsall, G., *Warfare and Society in the Barbarian West, 450–900* (London, 2003).

Lee, A.D., *Warfare in the Roman World* (Cambridge, 2020).

Nicasie, M., *Twilight of Empire* (Amsterdam, 1998).

Sarantis, A. and Christie, N. (eds), *War and Warfare in Late Antiquity: Current Perspectives* (Leiden 2013).